COURTS AND JUDGES

Books in this Series

22.50

Volume 15. **Sage** Criminal Justice System Annuals

COURTS
AND JUDGES

JAMES A. CRAMER
Editor

SAGE PUBLICATIONS   Beverly Hills   London

For information address:

SAGE Publications, Inc.
275 South Beverly Drive
Beverly Hills, California 90212

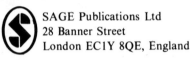

SAGE Publications Ltd
28 Banner Street
London EC1Y 8QE, England

Printed in the United States of America

Library of Congress Cataloging in Publication Data

Main entry under title:
Courts and judges.

   (Sage criminal justice system annuals; 15)
   Bibliography: p.
   1. Courts—United States—Addresses, essays, lectures. 2. Judges—United States—Addresses, essays, lectures. I. Cramer, James A. II. Series

KF8719.A2C68	347.73'1	81-5611
ISBN 0-8039-1640-X	347.3071	AACR2
ISBN 0-8039-1641-8 (pbk.)		

CONTENTS

Dedicated to my wife, Mary Jane

PREFACE

This volume is designed to offer the reader a sourcebook of recent empirical research and thought on several of the major issues relating to the organization of the courts and functions of the judiciary. Hopefully, it will be of interest to researchers, practitioners and policy makers alike. The articles selected represent years of research by authors drawn from the disciplines of criminology, law, political science, and sociology. The authors have employed a variety of conceptualizations and methodologies in compiling the body of works presented here. And, while it was not possible to address all of the major issues pertaining to the organization and tasks of the judiciary, an attempt was made to focus on some of the more critical aspects which are in need of greater understanding.

The reader will note that in some instances, for example the socialization of judges, differences surface between the respective contributing authors. These differences reflect both the perspectives of the authors and the current state of knowledge in the field. There does not exist a seamless webb of knowledge on matters concerning the judiciary. Furthermore, as with most areas of social inquiry, no single theory or approach will likely be sufficient for understanding and explaining the complex organization of the courts and decision making of the judiciary. Those who cast about in search of a single theory are apt to be dogged by frustration, disappointment, and, ultimately, defeat.

I would like to express my appreciation to the contributing authors for their cooperation in assembling this volume of essays. The role of the National Institute of Justice in furthering knowledge about the criminal justice system should also be recognized. Most of the chapters in the present work are the direct result of research funded by the Institute. This support is gratefully acknowledged.

Chapter 1

INTRODUCTION

JAMES A. CRAMER

Criminal Justice, The Courts, and Organizational Theory

In the past two decades the courts, and criminal justice system generally, have undergone a reconceptualization in the minds of many legal practitioners and researchers. Previously the justice system was viewed as being a unique amalgamation of agencies, loosely bound together by a body of law and a set of overlapping functions. It was argued that the system and its specific agencies were unlike other kinds of organizations, particularly in terms of the functions fulfilled and the nature of the relationship between the components within the overall organization.

Now, however, there is a growing body of literature that suggests that the criminal justice system and its agencies share many characteristics with other types of complex organizations (Eisenstein and Jacob, 1977; Stott et al., 1977; Sarri, 1976; Feely, 1973). Thus, it is increasingly common to see criminal justice agencies being cast into the existing body of organizational literature. The fact that this was relatively uncommon before the 1960s had the effect of fostering the belief that the criminal justice sytem was somehow different than other forms of organizations that were commonly the focus of social research. This implied, although it was usually never stated, that a different body of theory would be needed to understand and explain how the system worked. This attitude, coupled with problems of access to certain criminal justice agencies by social scientists, had the effect of dampening the interest of researchers whose concerns were not confined solely to an analysis of the justice system.

In no criminal justice agency has the impact of organizational analysis had greater impact than in the courts. There are several factors that may account for this. These include, among others, the structure of the courts, the division of labor among court personnel, and access by researchers to the court system.

First, the court system as a unit is probably the most structured of all criminal justice agencies. There is a readily identifiable organizational structure. The span of control of each of the divisions of the court is clearly delineated and a formal hierarchy of court personnel can be observed. Although some researchers, notably Eisenstein and Jacob (1977), have reported that they have failed to ascertain a recognizable hierarchy in the courtroom workgroup, this should not be confused with the hierarchy within the court structure itself. Whether the unit of analysis is a specific court, the body of courts in a particular jurisdiction, or the complete court system on the state or federal level, a logically consistent and integrated organizational structure and hierarchy exists.

Second, the division of labor in the courts is more clearly prescribed than in other criminal justice agencies. The functions are not, for example, as blurred as those within the police organization, whose frequently overlapping functions between patrolmen and investigators or between departments such as traffic and patrol are characteristic of that organization. Thus, the *formal* division of labor in the courts is much more likely to be paralleled by the *actual* division of labor in the day-to-day operations than that which occurs within the police organization. This is not to suggest that there are not considerable differences in how work gets done or between "law on the books and the law in action." There is ample evidence to suggest that is indeed the case. What can be said, however, is that even when judges differ markedly in their practices in matters such as plea negotiation and sentencing, their *functions* are remarkably constant.

A third factor which may account for the focus of organizational theory and research on the courts is the general accessibility for conducting research. Two factors seem relevant here. First, the physical arrangement of the court system(s) in any given jurisdiction is appealing. The activities of the judges are generally confined to the courthouse, their chambers, or the courtroom. Second, most judicial activities occur in a public setting. Arraignments, bail hearings, preliminary hearings, guilty pleas, and trials are open proceedings. And while other activities, such as preplea discussions and certain pretrial hearings, are sometimes held in chambers, it is usually possible to obtain permission from the presiding judge to gain entrance for purposes of observation. By way of contrast, many of the activities of the police (investigation, interviewing, report writing) and the prosecutor (case preparation, screening) occur in the privacy of their offices, hidden from public view.

Organization of the Book

This volume is divided into two basic components: the courts and the judiciary. By the courts I refer to the agencies which have the authority and jurisdiction to conduct legal proceedings of a civil and criminal nature for the purpose of resolving disputes of fact and law. Courts may be either trial or appellate. The former conduct pretrial hearings, guilty pleas, trials, and sentencing hearings. Appellate courts serve primarily to resolve issues of law as it applies to particular cases.

The term *court organization* as it is conventionally used may encompass not only the activities of judges but also additional staff personnel including the clerk, bailiffs, recorders and secretaries, and personnel outside the court staff including prosecutors, defense attorneys, and the police. Some research has focused, for example, on the courtroom workgroup (Eisenstein and Jacob, 1977; Lipetz, 1980). Others have examined the decision-making process in the courts (Mather, 1979; Wilkins et al., 1976; Walker, 1972) and yet others, on the roles of the actors (Cramer et al., 1980; Wice, 1978; Jacoby, 1977; Alschuler, 1975, 1968; Frankel, 1972). Thus, the term *courts* has been used to suggest a varying range of activities including a range of actors and decision points. In this volume the courts will be limited primarily to the organization of judicial activity at both the trial and appellate levels. The participation and decision making by actors outside the court organizational hierarchy, such as prosecutors and defense attorneys, will not be addressed.

The second part of this volume is focused on the judiciary. By this I mean the occupation of the judiciary as a professional group. Here again we will, for the most part, exclude other court personnel from our discussions. Thus the book will address the issues of court organization and judicial behavior as two interrelated but analytically distinct phenomena. By combining these two sets of essays, we are afforded the opportunity to focus on both the structure and organization of the court system and the judicial decision-making processes which take place within that framework.

REFERENCES

ALSCHULER, A. (1975) "The defense attorney's role in plea bargaining." Yale Law Review, 84.

——(1968) "The prosecutor's role in plea bargaining." University of Chicago Law Review, 36.

CRAMER, J., McDONALD, W.F., and ROSSMAN, H. (1980) "Judicial participation in plea bargaining," in W.F. McDonald and J.A. Cramer (eds.) Plea Bargaining. Lexington, MA: Lexington Books.

EISENSTEIN, J. and JACOB, H. (1977) Felony Justice. Boston: Little, Brown.

FEELY, M. (1973) "Two models of the criminal justice system: An organizational analysis." Law and Society Review, 7.

FRANKEL, M. (1972) Criminal Sentences. New York: Hill and Wang.

JACOBY, J. (1977) The Prosecutor's Charging: A Policy Perspective. Washington, DC: Department of Justice.

LIPETZ, M. (1980) "Routine and deviations: The strength of the courtroom workgroup in a misdemeanor court." International Journal of Sociology of Law, 8.

MATHER, L. (1979) Plea Bargaining or Trial. Lexington, MA: Lexington Books.

SARRI, D. (1976) "Modern court management: Trends in court organization concepts—1976." Justice System Journal, 2 (Spring).

STOTT, E., Jr., FETTER, T.J., and CITES, L. (1977) Rural Courts: The Effect of Space and Distance on the Administration of Justice. Williamsburg, VA: National Center for State Courts.

WALKER, T. (1972) "A note concerning partisan influence on trial judge decision making." Law and Society Review, 6.

WICE, P. (1978) Criminal Lawyers. Beverly Hills, CA: Sage.

WILKINS, L., KRESS, J., GOTTFREDSON, D., CALPIN, J. and GELMAN, A. (1976) Sentencing Guidelines: Structuring Judicial Discretion. Albany, NY: Criminal Justice Research Center, Inc.

Part I

COURT ORGANIZATION

Chapter 2

ORGANIZATIONAL DESIGN
FOR COURTS

THOMAS A. HENDERSON
RANDALL GUYNES
CARL BAAR

He only says, "Goodfences make good neighbours."
Spring is the mischief in me, and I wonder
If I could put a notion in his head:
"*Why* do they make good neighbours? Isn't it
Where there are cows? But here there are no cows.
Before I built a wall I'd ask to know
What I was walling in or walling out,
And to whom I was like to give offense."

(*Mending Wall* by Robert Frost)

This essay examines the judiciary from the perspective of organization theory in order to understand and assess efforts to improve court performance through changes in manage-

Authors' Note: *Preparation of this article was supported by Research Grants 79-NI-AX-0075 and 80-IJ-CX-0095 from the National Institute of Justice. The opinions expressed are those of the authors and do not necessarily represent the funding agency.*

ment structure. Characterizing the courts in formal organization terms leads to an identification of those things which must be taken into account when designing a court structure. To illustrate the concepts, the discussion focuses upon what has become the dominant approach to reform in the states—unification. The reforms promoted under this rubric represent an explicit attempt to design a formal organization through the manipulation of such structural components as trial court jurisdictions, financing, budgeting control, administrative responsibility, and rule-making authority (Berkson and Carbon, 1978).

Management of the courts has become an increasingly important issue at federal, state, and local levels of government. In addition to unification, courts have experimented with such things as case flow management techniques, automated recordkeeping systems, various administrative positions within the court, and alternative calendaring systems (Sipes et al., 1980; Skumpsy et al., 1980; Flanders et al., 1977; Institute for Law and Social Research, 1976). All of these reform efforts rest on a common set of assumptions about the court, namely, that the courts are formal organizations and, as such, can be affected through structural manipulation. Rarely is this assumption examined systematically to test its implication for court organization.[1] It is presumed that because such activities as recordkeeping, budgeting, financing, and personnel issues are common administrative problems, the procedures and practices found in nonjudicial settings are appropriate for the court. However, given the unique characteristics of the judiciary, the effectiveness of these reforms may depend as much upon the validity of the assumptions underlying the changes as upon the care with which they are implemented. An inappropriate concept of the court as a formal organization is likely to lead to inappropriate solutions to management problems in the judiciary.

In keeping with these critiques, the purpose of this essay is two-fold: first, to develop a general theory of court organization which takes account of the unique qualities of the judiciary while placing it in the context of other formal organizations and, second, given this theory, to identify basic precepts from the appropriate organization theory literature which can be used to assess the effects of proposed structural reforms. The essay begins with a general review of organization theory as it relates to the courts and the assumption on which it rests. It then turns to two key concepts drawn from the writings of Thompson (1968): core technology— that is, the basic production process of an organization—and institutional issues—that is, the place of an organization in its environment. These concepts are applied to the courts in a form which lays the foundation for the final section of the chapter, which examines the criteria for the design of judicial management structures.

COURTS AS FORMAL ORGANIZATIONS

A formal organization is distinct from other social organizations in that they are deliberately created for a certain purpose or set of purposes and operate under an explicit set of rules and procedures. Blau and Scott make this important distinction: "The goals to be achieved, the rules the members of the organizations are expected to follow, and the status structure that defines the relations between them (the organizational chart) have not spontaneously emerged in the course of social interactions but have been consciously designed a priori to anticipate and guide interaction and activities" (1962: 5; also see Etzioni, 1964: 3; Simon, 1957: 4; Thompson, 1967). The function of the formal structure is to reduce the uncertainties associated with collective action so that the purposes of the organization will be realized. If the explicit design is incomplete, or inappropriate, informal arrangements will emerge among organization members or between members and nonmembers to complement or even overwhelm the intentions of the formal structure. Because of the complexity of most organizations, no formal structure can eliminate all of the uncertainties with which its members must deal. However, the fact that an explicit set of expectations exists leads to a set of dynamics which are less likely when the interactions are governed by informal arrangements alone.

The distinction between organizations of purposive design from those based on other foundations is critical to the current endeavor. Court unification is predicated on the assumption that manipulation of the formal structure of the judiciary will lead to changes in court performance. The reforms are, in effect, an attempt to design an organization through an explicit definition of the interactions and activities of court personnel. By way of contrast, interactions and activities of the participants in the trial process which are examined by Eisenstein and Jacob (1977) are the product of informal arrangements among the participants based on mutual adjustment. The participants are drawn from a variety of organizations—prosecutor's office, public defenders' office, law firms, sheriff, police, corrections— rather than a single source. Because their individual goals and objectives overlap at times, accommodations can be developed to govern their continuing interaction. But there is no overarching purpose to which they must all subscribe and which justifies the organization. Nor is there an explicit structure which defines their respective roles, binds them together in a common purpose, and is subject to change through a formal redefinition.

This is not to deny the significance of the work group as described by Eisenstein and Jacob. On the contrary, as they make clear, the informal arrangements which develop among the judge, prosecuting attorney, and defense counsel in the criminal court are inevitable in many settings. But these arrangements must be treated as a contingency which must be taken into account in the design of the formal organization rather than as an alternative approach to structuring the judiciary.

The building blocks of formal organizations are (1) the differentiated tasks required to accomplish their goals and objectives and (2) the mechanisms for coordinating these tasks so that they are mutually reinforcing and supportive rather than in conflict. Mintzberg begins his effort to develop a comprehensive theory of formal organization with these twin concepts. "The structure of an organization can be defined simply as the sum total of the ways in which it divides its labor into distinct tasks and then achieves coordination among them" (1979: 2). The complexity of an organization is reflected in the extent of its task differentiation and specialization and the nature of the coordinating mechanisms necessary. At one extreme are simple organizations which combine all roles and skills in a few people. Coordination can be achieved through either direct supervision or through mutual adjustments among equals or near equals. At the other extreme are the complex structures associated with large organizations with highly differentiated tasks and many specializations. Coordination can only be achieved through formal rules and procedures as physical distance, infrequent contact, and disparate skills impede the development of informal arrangements among actors.

Courts vary widely in their degree of complexity. The traditional structure of the trial courts in most states has been more akin to that of a simple organization than complex. In a single-member court, for example, there is little or no task differentiation or specialization. The same person determines points at law, holds hearings, schedules meetings, and hires personnel. Support services are provided by a small staff—for example, secretary, recorder, or judicial clerk—or by an external organization—for example, county clerk, county recorder, or sheriff. The operations of the courts are likely to be a function of the personality of the judge and the informal arrangements which have evolved among the key actors with whom the judge works—lawyers, clerks, bailiffs, and county commissioners—as much as formal rules and regulations.

Several courts, especially large, urban courts of general jurisdiction, have taken on many of the attributes of a complex organization. The presence of such diverse skills as probation officers, family counselors, budget personnel, evaluation staff, fiscal officers, and data processors, to name a few, as well as several judges suggest a differentiated task structure and a set of coordinating mechanisms based on established rules and procedures. Informal arrangements are likely to be an inadequate foundation for integrating the various activities into a common purpose.

The design of the tasks and coordination mechanisms cannot occur in a vacuum. If the formal structure is to be a major influence on performance, it must take into account the kinds of problems the organization will address. These problems can be divided into three distinct levels of activity and control: technical, institutional, and managerial (Thompson, 1967: 10-11; also see Mintzberg, 1979: Part III; Down, 1967). Technical refers to the activities associated with the basic production process of an organization, for example, the assembly line of an auto plant or the operating room of a hospital. Institutional level activities are those necessary to maintain the organization within its environment. Included here are the efforts to define the boundaries between members and nonmembers and to insure that the organization has access to the resources it needs from external sources. Finally, the managerial level contains the activities and techniques used to provide services to and deal with the uncertainties which arise out of other levels of an organization. The activities associated with this level include coordination of the tasks in the technological core, control over input and output of the organization, and internal allocation of resources (Downs, 1967: 44-47; Mintzberg, 1979: 267-287).

Although each level of activity in the organization has unique problems associated with it, it is the interaction among the three which defines the criteria for organizational design.

COURT UNIFICATION
AND ORGANIZATIONAL DESIGN

There is little consensus on the exact reforms which are to be included in the concept of court unification. In a review of the literature, Berkson and Carbon (1978) list 22 specific reforms which have been promoted under this rubric including such things as state financing of courts, use of parajudges, requirements for statistical recordkeeping, and a simplified court structure. They distill these various components into five categories: consolidation and simplification of court structure; centralized management; centralized rule making; centralized budgeting; and state financing. Although observers may quarrel with individual items which Berkson and Carbon include or exclude from their definition, their conclusion is based on an implied consensus on the components derived from a thorough review of the literature beginning with Pound in 1906 and ending with the American Bar Association standards published in 1974 (Berkson and Carbon, 1978: 3). Since our purpose is to use court unification reforms for illustrative purposes rather than as the object of the critique, their summary provides a useful overview of one approach to organizational design for the courts.

Structuring the activities of the managerial level of an organization is the most common focus of organizational design and it raises questions concerning control, centralization, departmentalization and staff-line relations. Most of the court unification reforms identified by Berkson and Carbon are concerned with the appropriate structure for this level of court activities. Financing, budgeting, personnel administration, recordkeeping, and uniform rules and procedures are management level questions. They deal with how the activities of the court should be coordinated, where the support services should be located in the judiciary, and how the exchanges between the courts and other actors are to be carried out. Whether the changes advocated are appropriate for the courts depends upon two sets of contingencies: the core technology and the environment (Gallas, 1976).

The formal design of the managerial level of an organization must reflect the needs of the core technology. The ultimate justification of a particular configuration of management activities must be the services it provides to the core. If the formal structure is inappropriate, informal arrangements will emerge to compensate for the inadequacies of the formal. Thus, a centralized management structure for a state judiciary must be considered from the perspective of the activities it is expected to serve, that is, the various trial courts and/or appellate courts in a system.

Although the management structure must be directly linked to the requirements of the core technology, the problems it must resolve to meet those needs will vary depending upon the environment. Calendar management in a rural setting, for example, is very different from calendar management in a large urban area. The formal design of the management structure must be able to accommodate such differences or it will bear little relationship to the actual operation of the court.

These two sets of contingencies provide the criteria for assessing the design of the management structure implied by the unification reforms. Three general questions will guide the discussion. First, under what circumstances is a judicial management substructure appropriate? The unification reforms assume that the courts cannot continue to operate as a simple organization, but rather must develop complex coordinating mechanisms, support services, and boundary maintenance units to be effective. This assumption cannot be taken as a given, but rather must be considered in light of the technology and task environment of the courts.[2]

Second, to what degree can uncertainty in the courts be managed through reliance on bureaucratic controls? A major component of court unification reforms is the need to reduce the managerial discretion of individual judges by imposing a uniform set of operating standards on their behavior.

Third, where should the locus of managerial decision making be located? A central issue in the debate over judicial reform has been the wisdom of the centralized design implied by the several components of court unification.

There is no single answer to each of these questions. In classic public administration literature there was a search for the "one best way" to structure an organization (Gulick and Urwick, 1937; Taylor, 1947). This search for a single orthodoxy has been replaced with a recognition that the appropriate design is a relative one (Thompson, 1967; Blau and Scott, 1962; Mintzberg, 1979). It is unlikely that a single organizational design will be appropriate for all courts or all state judicial systems. Therefore, the thrust of this assessment is to identify the circumstances under which alternative managerial designs are appropriate, including the designs implied by court unification, not to accept or reject the validity of a particular judicial reform.

CORE TECHNOLOGY

The concept of core technology has had a checkered career in organization theory literature. Like the concept of power, it is an intuitively appealing concept which seems to evaporate when attempts are made to define it in precise terms (see Mintzberg, 1979: 240-250). Nevertheless, the concept is extremely useful in the current endeavor. First, it facilitates distinguishing between that part of an organization involved in the direct, purposive production process from other activities. Second, the concept allows one to distinguish among issues of complexity which arise (1) from the actual process of deciding legal issues; (2) from outside the organization itself; and (3) internally in the management of the first two.

The Technology of the Courts

There have been many attempts to define the concept of technology in a form which can be used to distinguish organizations. Woodward (1965) focused on the relative complexity of the production process and the predictability of control operations; Perrow (1967) distinguished between routine and nonroutine processes; and Hunt (1972) abandoned the concept of technology altogether, using, instead, the notion of a technical system. One problem with the work of these authors is that their primary concern is with organizations which bear very little resemblance to the courts, for example, manufacturing plants, universities, and hospitals. Thompson's typology, however, seems much more relevant to the judiciary. He identifies three types of technologies:

(1) long-linked technology—one part of the production process is dependent upon a previous step for completion, such as an assembly line
(2) mediating technology—the primary activity is linking individuals who are or wish to be interdependent, for example, the commercial bank linking depositors and borrowers
(3) intensive technology—a variety of techniques are used to produce a change in the object but the selection of the techniques depends upon feedback from the object itself, for example, patients and a general hospital [1967: 15-18].

This typology is especially useful for our purposes because it facilitates distinguishing between the dominant activity of the courts and that of other organizations.

The primary technology employed by the courts can probably be best characterized as one of mediation, that is, linking individuals who, voluntarily or involuntarily, need to be interdependent. In criminal cases the individuals are represented by the prosecutor and the defense; in civil cases, the plaintiff and defendant. The means for bringing them together will vary according to the stage of the process involved, for example, preliminary hearings, plea bargainings, motion filings, negotiated settlements, or trials. But throughout the process the technology remains constant—linking individuals. This characterization captures most of the activities of judicial personnel involved in the adjudication process, and reflects the primary focus of most courts. There are exceptions to this general pattern, however.

The activities involved in sentencing and determining civil remedy are more akin to Thompson's description of an intensive technology than that of mediation. In both instances, the judge (or jury) must select a course of action based on an interaction with the individual. When a judge sets sentence, he or she is expected to take into account the peculiarities of the case, the person charged, and what will best serve the good of the individuals as well as society.

Several special jurisdiction courts employ an intensive technology as their primary core activity rather than limiting it to one part of the process. Juvenile courts provide a clear example of this point. The role of the judge in these courts is to act upon the individual in much the same way a doctor acts upon the patient. The action taken is expected to be for the good of the juvenile or the family, that is, it is therapeutic (Fox, 1971).

It is more difficult to find examples of a long-linked technology on the courts. There are some authors, especially those concerned with criminal justice issues, who have argued that the movement of criminal cases from arrest to adjudication to incarceration to release is analogous to the movement on an assembly line. This characterization treats the courts as an integral part of this long-linked process (President's Commission on Law Enforcement and the Administration of Justice, 1967). However, this characterization ignores the fact that criminal cases are only part of the judiciary's responsibilities (Parker, 1972). Moreover, a long-linked process assumes that a sequential set of steps must be followed to produce a successful product. However, there are several ways for a court to successfully resolve a case, including dismissal at an early stage in the proceedings, recognizing a bargain struck elsewhere for a plea or sentence, or settlement of a dispute out of court altogether. It is only in a small proportion of the cases that resolution of the dispute requires all steps in the adjudication process from filing to disposition by sentencing or determining the remedy.

The management issues involved in the technological core lie in the need to coordinate the activities taking place at this basic production level in order to reduce the uncertainties associated with it. The three technologies differ in the degree to which a subdivision of tasks is appropriate, and the appropriate form which those subdivisions may take. These differences in the complexity of the core have critical consequences for organizational design.

Complexity of the Core

A traditional one-judge court produces little uncertainty in the core of the court. Whatever uncertainty there may be which arises out of the process of deciding cases is purely idiosyncratic to the judge. The judge personally directs his own calendar, manages his time, and coordinates court activities. All tasks dealing with the core operations of adjudication and definition of remedies in all cases in the court are handled by him directly. Whatever support staff exists operates as a direct extension of the judge under his/her direction.

The problem of complexity in the core arises only when attention shifts from single-member to multimember courts. Under these circumstances some means must be found for allocating tasks among the members. There are three forms which the subdivision of tasks may take: segmentation, differentiation, and specialization.

Segmentation is the simplest form of subdivision as it involves adding more persons to the core without distinguishing their tasks. For example, cases may be assigned to the judges on a multimember court without regard to content. No distinction is made in the type of law or the proceedings to be followed from one courtroom to the next. Under these circumstances, the level of uncertainty associated with the core will be relatively low. If the court is small, it may operate in much the same fashion as a single-member court as coordination among the members can be handled through direct negotiations among the judges. As the size of the court increases, however, uncertainty is also likely to increase. A more complex coordination structure may be called for, even if segmentation remains the primary form for subdividing the tasks.

Differentiation of tasks in the core increases the level of uncertainty because of the increased problem of coordination of the activities of the members. In a differentiated core, the activities are divided into distinct tasks and assigned to formally defined positions. For example, a multimember court may differentiate by case type so that one judge handles criminal cases, another general civil cases, a third civil domestic, and a fourth juvenile. Alternatively, differentiation may occur by steps in the process, for example, preliminary hearings, motion hearings, and trial.

Specialization is, in one sense, a subcategory of differentiation in that it, too, is characterized by a subdivision of the core activities into distinct tasks and assignment of those tasks to formally defined positions. However, unlike differentiation, the tasks are organized around specialized skills and call for specialized personnel to fill them. The result is a much more complicated coordination problem as uncertainty may arise from the number of persons, from multiple tasks, and from differences in skills of the individuals. It is difficult to find examples of specialization among judicial actors because of the long-standing norm of judges as generalists. However, when the perspective is expanded to include support personnel such as probation officers performing presentence investigations, or counselors providing assistance to juvenile judges, the problem of coordinating specialization in the core becomes more apparent.

Mediating technologies have much less of an imperative toward a complex organization than do intensive or long-linked technologies because they are less given to task specialization. Organizations using long-linked technologies by definition begin by separating tasks and assigning them to different persons. An elaborate, formal coordinating structure is necessary to ensure the various tasks fit one with another. Intensive technologies are frequently differentiated by specialized services. For example, a surgical team in a hospital draws on a variety of specialities and support services to carry out its purpose.

Mediating technologies, by contrast, do not depend upon task differentiation for effectiveness. A real estate broker essentially works alone in carrying out his/her task. He/she may draw on others for support such as a listing service, loan officers, building inspectors, and lawyers, but these can be obtained through contract; the task itself remains undifferentiated. By the same token, a judge, like the real estate broker, essentially works alone in the adjudication process. Except for exceptional civil cases such as antitrust disputes, there is little specialized knowledge around which tasks can be structured which will increase the effectiveness of the judge.

Given this character of the adjudication process, it should not be surprising that the traditional court structure was that of a simple rather than a complex organization. On the other hand, it should also not be surprising that many courts do not conform to this simple model. The sheer size of multimember urban courts, for example, complicates the coordination problems regardless of the form—segmentation, differentiation, specialization—of the subdivisions which are used. In addition, it should be borne in mind that courts employ an intensive technology as well as a mediating one. Sentencing decisions, juvenile cases, and many family disputes are dependent upon information and skills which are different from those developed during legal training. These differences provide a logical focus for differentiating the core with the concomitant complexity in the management structure. Finally, judges are not the only members of judicial organizations. A court may be a complex organization because it offers several services outside of the courtroom such as counseling, probation, drug treatment centers, or even residential programs. Thus, like the real estate office which also provides apartment management services, a simple core may be part of a complex organization because of the support services it acquires.

INSTITUTIONAL LEVEL

The importance of the members of the immediate environment in the daily operations of the trial courts has been well-documented in the literature (Eisenstein and Jacob, 1977; Nimmer, 1975; Cole, 1970; Church et al., 1978). The uncertainties accompanying the dependence of the court on such external actors as prosecutors, defense attorneys, sheriff's deputies, civil counsel, and probation officers can only be minimized through careful management; they cannot be avoided altogether. Less well-documented, but equally important when considering the structure of the court, is the dependence of the judiciary on external sources for financial support, legal authorization to carry out certain activities, and even for acceptance of their legitimate role in resolving certain kinds of disputes (Barr, 1975; Baar, 1974; Korbakes et al., 1978; Grau, 1978).

Any consideration of organizational design must take account of the range of issues which must be resolved at this institutional level. The implications for design will vary, however, depending upon the magnitude of the dependence. At its broadest level, an organization must act to establish and maintain its claim to a functional territory, a task domain, which is accepted by critical actors in the environment as legitimate. "The specific categories of exchange vary from one type of organization to another, but in each case exchange agreements rest upon *prior consensus regarding domain*" (italics in the original; Thompson, 1967: 28; also see Downs, 1966: 212). These agreements may appear as formal contracts with outside agencies or organizations, as informal arrangements between judges and practicing attorneys, as the laws establishing an organization, or as the general norms in society. The issue is that the critical actors in the environment must be identified, a consensus must be reached, and the agreements must be maintained.

As the other end of the continuum, members of the organization must manage the day-to-day exchanges which are necessary to ensure that resources are available and the products have a market. The two sets of problems are interrelated. If there is a low level of consensus among the critical actors on the domain, the day-to-day problems are compounded. If, on the other hand, the daily operations are at odds with the general outline, the legitimacy of the claim to territory must either undergo a major shift or risk destroying the organization.

Task Domain

The dimensions of an organization's task domain are defined by (1) the activities it carries out; (2) the resources it requires; (3) the clients it serves; and (4) its competitors for markets (Thompson, 1967: 26-29). One source of definition for the courts for each of these dimensions is the legislative mandate. For example, court unification reforms attempt to shift the source of finances from local to state government, broaden the activities of the judiciary to include budgeting and managerial functions as well as judicial, expand the number and type of clients of trial courts by eliminating special jurisdictions, and reduce the number of competing organizations by consolidating most courts into a single court of general jurisdiction. An additional source of formal domain definitions can be found in broad policy statements by the organization's leadership, for example, rules and procedures established by a judicial council or supreme court, or rulings by appellate courts.

Simply defining the formal boundaries of an organization, however, does not ensure that it will be successful in laying claim to the implied task domain. This will depend upon the response of the critical actors in the environment. For example, assignment of management responsibilities to a state level office as called for by the court unification reforms implies a state-oriented domain which may not be possible given the political configuration of the environment. Berkson and Hays (1976) describe the successful effort of the elected county clerks in Florida to thwart attempts by the newly established state court administrator's office to standardize their recordkeeping operations. The clerks as independent elements in the environment of the court were able to maintain their own definition of the domain in spite of a central office attempt at changing it.

The degree of consensus about the domain will affect directly the organizational design as it will dictate the level of effort which must be devoted to managing the uncertainty. In Florida the court administrator was faced with the uncomfortable choice of either redefining the task domain of his office in much narrower terms or devoting a major part of his energies to dealing with these external actors.

Establishing and maintaining a firm consensus on an organization's domain is an important management problem. However, consensus does not eliminate the uncertainties associated with the environment. Independent of the level of agreement regarding its boundaries, task domains vary widely from one organization to the next in their complexity and, therefore, in the uncertainties they pose for management.

Environmental Complexity

The complexity of the environment surrounding the courts can be described in terms of two dimensions: its relative stability or instability and its degree of homogeneity or heterogeneity. Stability of the critical actors in the environment is a central issue in the management of the courts, as it is for all organizations (Eisenstein and Jacob, 1976). Fluctuations complicate any attempts to establish routine relationships. Uncertainty must, by definition, be high since a large proportion of the exchanges between the courts and the environment are based on ad hoc arrangements instead of long-standing agreements and accepted norms (Nimmer, 1978).

Any changes in the definition of the task domain are likely to produce instability on at least a short-term basis until consensus over the boundaries is established (Hays, 1978).

For example, if probation services are moved from a Department of Corrections to the judicial branch of government, renegotiations must take place over the auxiliary services that the Department of Corrections provided to probation officers such as secretarial assistance, counseling programs, office space, or transportation. The courts may have to find new sources for these services at the state or local level or become involved with federal money from corrections sources rather than judicial programs (Council of State Governments, 1977). In other instances the instability of the actors is a long-standing condition. In some jurisdictions certain courts of limited or special jurisdiction are used as the training grounds for neophyte lawyers. As soon as they gain experience in misdemeanant courts, or juvenile courts, they move on to other activities (President's Commission on Law Enforcement and the Administration of Justice, 1967). As a consequence, these courts must contend with a constant shift in the counsel who appear before them.

The degree of homogeneity of the environment is also related to the uncertainty which the organization must face. The more heterogeneous the environment, the greater the range of demands with which the courts must deal. In part this heterogeneity is reflected in the socioeconomic composition of the court's jurisdiction. Thus, urban areas present a much more heterogeneous set of demands on the courts than do rural areas (Eisenstein and Jacob, 1977; Scott et al., 1977). But this is only one form which heterogeneity may take. A special jurisdiction court, by definition, has a much more homogeneous set of demands than a court of general jurisdiction. Moreover, even in a heterogeneous environment, structures external to the court may narrow the range of exchanges. For example, one of the effects of the increased reliance upon public defenders offices for counsel in criminal cases is to introduce an organizational buffer between the courts and those practicing criminal law (Casper, 1972).

These two dimensions are analytically distinct. That is, a court's environment may be homogeneous and stable (a rural area); homogeneous and unstable (a new suburban bedroom development); heterogeneous and stable (a medium-sized urban center); or heterogeneous and unstable (a rapidly declining or expanding urban center). Clearly, the situation with the greatest uncertainty is that which is heterogeneous and unstable; the one with the greatest certainty is that which is homogeneous and stable; and the other two located somewhere in between.

Court unification reforms, by definition, increase the heterogeneity of the environment. Consolidating trial courts into one or two courts of general jurisdiction ensures that a wider variety of clients must be accommodated. Arguments in favor of shifting financial support from local to state government rarely include providing and maintaining courtrooms which usually remains a local responsibility (Baar, 1975; Lawson et al., 1979). As a result, the courts must deal with multiple funding sources instead of just one. Increasing the administrative and budgeting responsibilities of a state court administrator's office means that such practices cannot be tailored to a particular jurisdiction but must take account of court practices in the full range of environments, from sparsely populated rural counties to the cities and towns in the state.

Whether unification reforms will also affect the stability of the environment is more open to question. A short-term instability can be expected because of the disruption to the domain consensus which any shift in the formal boundaries of an organization is likely to produce. The long-term effect, however, is much more problematic.

THE MANAGEMENT STRUCTURE

The two preceding sections of the chapter have attempted to establish the sources of uncertainty for formal organizations as they relate to the courts, which give rise to the needs of a management substructure. These needs provide the substance for designing a court structure. This section of the essay addresses three questions: (1) is a management substructure necessary; (2) given that it is, what are the issues to be considered in determining the approach to management; and (3) given that a management structure exists, what are the issues in determining the appropriate locus of authority?

Is a Management Substructure Necessary?

In a simple organization the managerial function seldom implies any structural subdivision (Mintzberg, 1979: 306). The person who performs the production work will also serve as personnel manager, treasurer, salesman, even bookkeeper if the organization is small enough; or he will contract out many of these services to another agency. In an organization with a more complicated technological core, however, the managerial level is likely to be differentiated from core activities. Coordination becomes a full-time job for someone rather than one of many assignments; and support services are provided by specialized staff within the organization such as budget officers, personnel directors, planners, or management information specialists rather than something done under contract with another agency.

The court unification reforms are predicated on the need to develop a managerial substructure. Trial court consolidation is expected to provide the conditions necessary in the technological core for resource management to take place. The argument is that multimember courts will lead to greater coordination, flexibility in the assignment of personnel resources and use of facilities, and sufficient demand for support services to warrant specialization. The shift of financial, budget, and management responsibilities from local courts to a state level office is based on two arguments: the increased need for such services from the courts once they have been consolidated and the increased difficulty in dealing with the environment. Most of the arguments based on the needs of the technological core parallel those in support of court consolidation: need for coordination, potential for specialization, and increased efficiency in the use of resources. The arguments relating to the environment are based on an assumption that a separate management substructure will be more effective in obtaining resources from the state executive and the legislature than will part-time judicial administrators dealing with local actors because full-time administrators will have the skills necessary to gather technical information and make an effective case (Berkson and Carbon, 1978; Baar, 1975).

From an organizational theory perspective, the link between each of these contingencies and the presence of a managerial substructure is not as clear as the arguments in favor of court unification would suggest. There is a great deal of ambiguity in the managerial needs of the technological core of the judiciary; and the variety of task environments from one court to the next and from state to state suggest that the external imperatives for a unified court system are also more problematic than the advocates have recognized.

The Managerial Needs of the Core. The internal structure of the managerial level must reflect two needs of the technological core: the need for coordination and the need for support services. We have already suggested that a multimember court, in and of itself, does not constitute a complex organization. If coordination can be achieved through direct negotiations among the members, the court may operate as a simple organization even though it has many of the external trappings of a complex formal organization. Thus, there may be a position of chief judge, but the person who fills it will also serve in a judicial capacity and the role is more akin to chairman of a committee than to manager of an organization. This is most likely to happen where all judges on a court are handling the same type of case, that is, the task has been segmented. However, if a multimember court differentiates tasks by stage in the process, or creates specialized tasks by distinguishing between case types, or includes the intensive technology of a juvenile court as well as the mediating technology of criminal or civil, it is much more difficult to coordinate through mutual adjustment among peers. A chief judge or court administrator who actively manages the allocation of time, money, and personnel on the court becomes a necessity rather than an option. (For a discussion of the role of chief judge on appellate courts, see Tobin and Hoffman, 1979, and Ducat and Flango, 1976.)

Although differentiation in the core requires differentiation in the management structure, this factor, in and of itself, does not automatically lead to task specialization at the management level. If the only need to be met for the core is coordination, this can be achieved through a limited number of management positions such as chief judge or court administrator. The need for a specialized staff within the management level will depend upon the support skills required by the core. There is a distinct difference in the courts between those employing primarily an intensive technology such as the juvenile courts and those employing a mediating technology such as civil courts. The former require a set of specialized skills such as counseling staff and probation officers, which are not required by the latter. The presence of such staff, in turn, generates a further need for an explicit coordinating mechanism.

It is more difficult to identify specialized skills that are needed by the mediating technology in the courts. At a minimum the management level must ensure there are sufficient funds, records are kept of proceedings, personnel are hired, and space is provided. However, very few of these services require a sophisticated management effort to satisfy the needs of the judges.

Recordkeeping is important for the courts primarily during proceedings. At all other times search and retrieval is significant for actors outside of the courts—attorneys, citizens, and other government officials. Space requirements are also highly standardized in most courts. That is, the number of courtrooms is largely a function of the number of judges. The primary management requirement for courts with a mediating technological core is the recruitment of support personnel—bailiffs, court recorders, and clerks. So long as the requirements can be standardized, however, such services can be handled by outside agencies as easily as in-house. They need not be part of the same organization and, traditionally, they are not. Jury management is the most demanding of the functions to be performed at this level. However, jury trials constitute a very small percentage of judicial activity and, therefore, are insufficient in and of themselves to generate a complex management structure in all but large, urban criminal courts.

The flow of cases through the courts may also be a source of impetus for a formalized, complex management structure. Some means must be found for establishing priorities among filings, scheduling hearings, and assigning cases to judges. However, in the absence of a formal deadline such as a speedy trial rule, a simple standard of sequential assignment and scheduling will suffice. An informal set of accommodations among the regular participants in the process can regulate the flow of cases (Eisenstein and Jacob, 1977; Nimmer, 1978; Church et al., 1978).

If this variation in the needs of the technological core were the only consideration, it is reasonable to suggest that the insistence of the court unification reformers on a distinct managerial substructure is at best premature and perhaps, in some instances, dysfunctional. This is especially the case since there continues to be disagreement on whether there should be one trial court level or two in a consolidated system (Berkson and Carbon, 1978: 5). Preservation of a two-tier system at the trial court level may result in a reduced need for a managerial substructure because of the reduced need for coordination. This suggestion assumes, of course, that the task environment of the court is constant. However, such is not the case. The need for a separate managerial substructure is as dependent upon factors outside of the court as it is on the internal influences.

Managerial Needs of the Institutional Level. The more difficult it is for individual members within the court to identify the critical actors outside and establish informal arrangements with them, the greater the need for a differentiated management structure. This is most likely to occur when the environment is heterogeneous and relatively unstable (Thompson 1967: 72). Eisenstein and Jacob (1976) document this effect in their study of the work group. But it holds true for other exchanges between the court and its environment such as funding levels, space requirements, records management, and personnel. So long as the source of each of these remains relatively stable and limited, it is unnecessary for there to be a separate management structure to deal with them. As these sources lose their predictability, however, more time and energy must be devoted to obtaining the needed resources.

The most obvious differences in judicial task environments are between urban, suburban, and rural settings. The limited number of political and legal actors in a small-town setting eliminates the need for a management structure. Such things as budget hearings, calendaring decisions, and personnel recruitment are likely to take place among long-time associates. A separate managerial staff would add very little to the exchanges.[3] At the other extreme, however, are the large, urban courts. The competition for financial resources in the local government is likely to be much more intense, requiring major political skills supported by specialized budget expertise. A part-time administrative judge may be at a distinct disadvantage when dealing with a full-time mayor or executive budget officer. All of these factors are compounded if a jurisdiction is undergoing a major shift in population increasing the uncertainties from the environment (Baar and Baar, 1977).

If the environment is stable but heterogeneous, the most appropriate structure may be to segment the technological core according to subsets of the population, reducing the need for a distinct management substructure. This is consistent with the rise of specialized courts. It is not specialized legal skills which have encouraged small claims courts, for example, but rather the clientele which they are to serve (Ruhnka et al., 1978).

What is the Appropriate Management Approach?

Even when the size and organization of the court are consistent with a separate management structure, the style or pattern of management is still an open question. Management is frequently confused with the behavior of those in a position of authority in a hierarchical structure. Management, however, also refers in organization theory literature to the means used to coordinate the various activities carried out in an organization. These means can be ranged along a continuum depending upon the degree to which they are dependent upon formalization of behavior to ensure coordination rather than mutual exchanges and adjustments (Mintzberg, 1979: 81-88). The appropriateness of the approach is dependent upon the core technology and the environment.

At one end of the continuum are organizations which depend almost exclusively on explicit rules and procedures, preferably in writing, to define tasks, proscribe exchanges among members, determine authority relationships, and establish criteria for positions. The objective is to render predictable as much as possible all activity affecting the organization through standardization of practices and behavior. The control mechanisms have all of the attributes of Weber's classic definition of a bureaucracy, and we will use that term to describe such an approach to management.

At the other end of the continuum are those formal organizations which depend heavily upon individual initiative and problem solving to accomplish their goals and objectives. Individuals are assumed to have the background and skills necessary to exercise a high degree of discretion. Coordination is accomplished through mutual adjustment, accommodation through teams, and review of performance after the fact (Blau, 1962; Pugh et al., 1963-1964; Burns and Stalker, 1961). This approach has been labelled organic because it assumes that the procedures and interactions will change as the problems and issues change.

There is no assumption that all parts of the management level, or all activities, conform to the same management approach. The particular mix will depend upon the circumstances. The traditional single-judge court, for example, can be characterized as organic when describing the internal operations. That is, coordination of court personnel is likely to be accomplished through either direct supervision of the judge over secretaries and clerks or through mutual adjustments with other judges and members of the work group. The relationship with those supplying support functions from outside the courts, such as recordkeeping by the county clerk, on the other hand, is usually dealt with in bureaucratic terms because it is based primarily on an explicit set of standards regarding what will be recorded, who will have access to the records, and how they will be updated. The exercise of significant discretion is less important.

There is nothing in the court unification reforms which precludes the use of an organic approach to management. However, the implicit assumption underlying most of the changes is that a bureaucratic approach will improve judicial performance. For example, among the arguments cited by Berkson and Carbon in favor of centralized management is that "intrajudicial coordination is also enhanced . . . during the implementation of policy decisions. Channels of communication are established so that managerial personnel have a clear understanding of their responsibilities" (1978: 25). Following the same logic, standardized procedures will be possible under a consolidated court system because it will simplify the process; uniformity and consistency of administrative operations will result from centralized management through the development of standardized forms, a judicial personnel plan, record management procedures, and a state-wide classification scheme for filing cases. Similar arguments are advanced in favor of state financing and budgeting. Little or no attention is given to ways of improving the courts where a bureaucratic approach is inappropriate either because of the character of the core activity or the task environment of individual courts.

Management Approach and the Core. The core technology of the judiciary is clearly more suited to an organic management approach than to a bureaucratic one. In fact, linking the adjudication process to the term *bureaucracy* almost seems a contradiction in terms. (This discrepancy may explain why there has been resistance among judicial experts to using the concept of formal organization to understand the courts. The assertion is frequently made that one cannot "administer" justice, when the objection is actually to using a bureaucratic model.) By definition, the judge must exercise large amounts of discretion. Control is achieved through professional norms, peer review, and appellate review. This characterization holds for both mediating (civil, criminal) and intensive (juvenile, sentencing) technologies. The debate over the appropriate body for establishing rules and procedures stems, in part, from the debate over the appropriate style for managing the core technology of the judiciary. Those who advocate locating such authority in the state supreme court are relying on an implicit hierarchical concept of management structure. The advocates of locating the authority in a judicial council are tending to the organic end of the continuum, that is, management through consultation and mutual adjustment among peers.

Although a bureaucratic approach to management may be inappropriate for the core itself, it may be a useful approach in structuring the other two levels of activities. Budgeting, resource allocation, personnel, and recordkeeping are commonly hierarchically structured and operated on the basis of standardized rules and procedures. The support services of the courts—probation, counseling, social services—are also compatible with a bureaucratic approach. These activities may also be organized around an organic model. For example, it is not unusual for probation officers conducting presentence investigations to be assigned to individual judges and operate on a team basis (albeit a superior/subordinate team) with the judge and other members of his staff. By the same token, the assignment of personnel, space, and equipment may be carried out through informal negotiations among the judges, on the basis of previously established priorities such as tenure on the bench, or through a hierarchically structured decision process with an administrative judge or court administrator at the top. The incidence of one approach over the other will depend upon the stability of the demand for services from the core. If the core requirements are relatively stable, a bureaucratic approach is appropriate. If there is a high degree of uncertainty, however, an organic approach must be used. This explains why efforts to improve recordkeeping have been successful using a bureaucratic model but master calendaring has had such a checkered career (Church et al., 1978). Case flow is subject to such fluctuations that it is difficult to establish procedures which will regulate it. Moreover, the objectives of such a system change and a bureaucratic model is difficult to adjust accordingly.

Management Approach and the Institutional Level. The character of the environment also strongly influences the relevance of one management approach as opposed to another. The exchanges between a stable, homogeneous task environment can be easily structured using standardized forms, procedures, and rules of behavior, that is, a bureaucratic approach. When the environment is unstable, however, with new actors and issues being raised, standardized procedures lose their utility. There must be large amounts of discretion available to those who must deal with the external actors in order to resolve the new problems as they arise. An emphasis upon formal rules will undermine the effectiveness of the process as they are designed for the previous set of issues, not the ones currently in dispute. The variation in management approaches when dealing with the environment is reflected in three strategies described by Thompson (1967: 34-36) for reducing environmental uncertainty: contracting, cooptation, and coalescing. Their utility will depend upon an appropriate environment with contracting requiring a stable, homogeneous set of external demands and coalescing at the other extreme.

The simplest strategy for managing dependency is through contracting. The term as used here refers to more than just negotiation of a legal agreement. It includes any agreement for the exchange of performance in the future. The most obvious example from the courts is their dependence upon a county clerk for recordkeeping. This relationship is usually involuntary in that it is required by law. However, the dependency is structured through either implicit or explicit negotiations between the clerk and the judiciary. On occasion, formal powers of the court are used to coerce conformity with expectations. But this approach is rare. By the same token, arrangements are frequently made between a family court and shelter care. Implicit contracts occur on a regular basis between prosecutors and the courts regarding calendaring activities (Cole, 1972).

Cooptation refers to a process by which new elements in the environment are absorbed into leadership positions in the organization or in the support mechanisms to avoid threats to its stability or existence. For example, in some jurisdictions public defender's offices were initially viewed with suspicion by prosecutors and judges. As the public defender's office gained status, it was accepted as part of the ongoing process and began to take on many of the attributes of the actors in the process (Casper, 1972).

Coalescing is the term Thompson uses to describe a coalition which may be stable or unstable. Coalescing assumes that the exchanges between an organization and its environment are regulated through joint decision making among the interested parties. The work group dynamics in Chicago and Detroit described by Eisenstein and Jacob represent a coalescing approach to institutional issues. No single actor dominates the process. Instead, the procedures are established and maintained through an ongoing bargaining process among equals.

The success of each of these strategies will depend, in part, upon which management approach is appropriate for dealing with the task environment. Contracting is part of a bureaucratic approach to reducing uncertainty as it assumes the requirements of the relevant actors can be determined in advance. Coalescing lies at the organic end of the management continuum. It is most appropriate when maintenance of the exchanges between the court and the environment require frequent explicit or implicit negotiations. In between these extremes lies cooptation, which may assume bureaucratic overtones if formally structured as in training sessions or scheduled conferences among the critical actors or be organic in nature if carried out on an ad hoc basis.

Where Should the Locus of Managerial Decision Making Be Located?

The final issue to be addressed in the design of the managerial level of a formal organization is the distribution of decision-making authority among the various units and actors. This issue is usually defined in terms of a centralization-decentralization continuum. Mintzberg describes the continuum as follows:

> When all the power for decision making rests at a single point in the organization—ultimately in the hands of a single individual—we shall call the structure centralized; to the extent that the power is dispersed among many individuals, we shall call the structure decentralized [1979: 181].

Mintzberg further distinguishes between vertical decentralization which refers to "the dispersal of formal power down the chain of line authority" (1979: 185) and horizontal which he defines as the extent to which decisional power "remain(s) with line managers in the system of formal authority, or . . . flow(s) to people outside the line structure to analysts, support specialists, and operators" (1979: 185-186).

This issue of centralization has been a major concern in the debate over court unification. However, it is usually defined along the vertical dimension only, that is, to what extent should the locus of decision making be in a state level agency (court administrator, supreme court, judicial council) instead of a local court. This is reflected in the labels Berkson and Carbon use to categorize the reforms. Centralized management, centralized rule-making authority, and centralized budgeting can all be relabelled state management, state rule-making authority, and state budgeting. The arguments in support of shifting the locus of responsibility from local to state rest on a characterization of the changing needs of the core and of shifts in the environment.

The technological core arguments focus on the growing demand for resources and support services by the courts as the volume of cases increases. According to these arguments, this demand has generated a need for more efficient use of resources across the state.

The arguments based on the technological core are reinforced by the characterization of the environment. Shifting responsibility to the state level is justified on the grounds that this is the source of most of the resources needed by the judiciary, especially financial resources. Therefore, the structure of the judiciary must be such that it can deal on an equal basis withe the key elements in its task environment and that means the state legislature and executive.

Management Centralization and the Core. As with the other dimensions, the final design must be a function of the needs of the technological core and of the task environment. And, as with the other two, it is unlikely that a single approach will accommodate all of the circumstances of the judiciary. The first axiom in the design must be that control over decision making must rest with those individuals who have the necessary information and skills to make an appropriate response. In the case of the courts, the application of this axiom must begin with the fact that by definition the technological core must be decentralized both vertically and horizontally. At the trial court level, it is the individual judge who has the requisite skills to perform the judicial function. And he does so, for the most part, in isolation rather than as part of a team. At the appellate level, judges are more likely to be acting collectively, but the principle remains the same. It is only when addressing managerial level issues that the question of centralization becomes problematic.

The decentralized character of the technological core encourages a parallel decentralization of the managerial activities. If the function of management is to serve the core, who knows better what those needs are than the individual judge. One need which cannot be defined by the individual, however, is the need for coordination and, as has been argued before, this need is a function of the degree of differentiation, specialization, and segmentation on a multimember court. Hence, large urban courts have frequently developed extensive management structures independently of state-wide management reforms. The coordination problems which accompanied their increase in size were met with local management structures.

The arguments in favor of vertical centralization, thus, have little bearing on the technological core. It is not the core requirements which encourage vertical centralization, but rather institutional issues.

Management Centralization and the Institutional Level. Centralization of the judiciary becomes a significant issue when the effect of the environment is taken into account. A centralized structure is most appropriate when dealing with an environment which poses few problems in identifying the critical elements. Thus, a centralized funding source is important in generating a centralized administrative office. Where the environment is shifting, or heterogeneous, it is important to have as many local units as possible in order to recognize the differences and respond accordingly. This is the argument used by those criticizing court unification as being unable to respond to local differences. But this is a cogent argument only if local financing is important.

One approach to managing the exchanges between the organization and its environment is to reduce its dependency on outside influences. This approach underlies many of the components of court unification reform. There are several alternative means for reducing dependency which are reflected in the structure of a formal organization. The first, and most direct, is to expand the boundaries of the formal organization to bring the critical elements of the environment into the organization. The move to vest all rule-making authority in a judicial body, excluding the legislature from such policy decisions, is a clear example of such a strategy. Consolidation of trial courts also contains elements of such a strategy. For example, in those instances where courts of limited jurisdiction hold all preliminary hearings, consolidation brings the limited court into the general jurisdiction court.

A second means for reducing dependency is to increase the status of the formal organization members relative to the critical members of their environment. A major argument in favor of court consolidation is the increased prestige which will accrue to lower court judges. There are those who bemoan this consideration as an irrelevant one. Nejelski, for example, writes: "In Connecticut, one main reason for the Court of Common Pleas merger with Superior Court was that the judges in misdemeanor cases court eat lunch at the same club as the judges who hear felony cases. . . . That such status problems creep into the judiciary is understandable but regrettable" (quoted in Berkson and Carbon, 1978: 21). However, we are arguing that such considerations are an integral part of the institutional issues facing the courts as the prestige attached to each judge affects the position of the judiciary in society. A centralized budgeting process is also expected to lead to increased resource availability because of the enhanced status of a state level office negotiating with the legislature as opposed to the various courts appearing separately to make their requests (Baar, 1975: 168).

The third strategy for limiting dependence is to leave the boundaries of the formal organization constant, but to shift the composition of the domain by expanding or contracting the task environment. In many ways this is a corollary of the first strategy as the act of changing the boundaries of a formal organization in and of itself will affect the task environment. But, independent of this effect, the courts may change the critical actors in their environment by manipulation of structure. For example, the shift of financing from local to state affects directly the relevant external actors. The composition of the environment will vary depending upon the final mix of state and local financing. If financing becomes an exclusive state responsibility, and all personnel—judges, secretaries, clerks—and facilities are supported from the same source, the number and variety of external actors are severely reduced. If financing is shared by the two levels of government, however, dependency of the courts on the environment may be reduced by permitting judicial actors to play one off against the other. This approach is directly comparable to firms which develop several suppliers of raw materials instead of one in order to reduce their dependence upon the vagaries of a single supplier (Thompson, 1967: 32-33).

Efforts to centralize on either a vertical or horizontal basis represent attempts to limit the dependence of the courts on their environment through expanding the boundaries of the organization, increasing the status of judicial actors, or redefining the task domain. Reducing dependence seems a logical response to environmental uncertainty. However, because vertical and horizontal centralization are also likely to increase the heterogeneity of the environment, the effect may be to increase the uncertainty rather than reduce it. Including additional services such as probation, counseling, records management, and personnel within the judiciary may reduce the dependence of the core technology, but it may simultaneously increase the number and range of clients it is expected to serve. Juvenile courts, for example, may find themselves in the strange position of spending a significantly larger proportion of their budget and personnel on providing what are perceived to be auxiliary services than they do on adjudication. Horizontal or vertical centralization may increase the status of the leadership of the courts—for example, the chief justice of the supreme court or the local administrative judge—but it may be at the expense of the individual justices resulting in a net decline in the position of the judiciary.[4] Finally, redefining the task domain is not a unilateral activity. It requires the acquiescence of the critical members of the potential environment as well as the previous ones if the exchanges are to go smoothly.

SUMMARY

One might characterize this essay by paraphrasing Frost: "Before I unified a court I'd ask to know what I was unifying in or unifying out, and to whom I was like to give offense." This essay has attempted to establish a framework for addressing the implied question. Several central issues have emerged.

From an organization theory perspective, two technologies were identified as appearing in the core operation of the court: mediating—which is the basis for the adjudication process in criminal and civil proceedings—and intensive—which is characteristic of sentencing decisions, juvenile courts, and many family courts. Since mediating technologies do not lend themselves to task differentiation or specialization, they are unlikely to require an extensive management structure except on a multimember court which is too large to permit coordination through mutual adjustment among the judges.

The intensive aspects of the core, on the other hand, have much greater needs for specialized support services such as counselors in juvenile courts and presentence investigations units in criminal. The presence of such specialized skills raises significant problems of coordination. As a consequence, the relevance of a separate management structure in the court is more directly dependent upon the degree to which intensive technologies are included within its boundaries than it is on the presence of adjudicative responsibilities.

While the mediating core may not produce the demand for internal mangement, the complexity of the environment has a direct affect on the need for a separate managerial structure. A high level of heterogeneity and instability among suppliers, clients, competitors, and markets of the court will require full-time managerial units which can establish and maintain the necessary exchanges. In part the composition of the environment is beyond the control of the courts. However, the organizational design can define the character of the task domain and, by so doing, affect the level of uncertainty which must be managed.

If there is a major conclusion to be drawn from this essay, it is that no single organizational design will be appropriate for all circumstances, nor is it necessary for all parts of a complex organization to conform to the same structural principles. Issues regarding the presence or absence of a management substructure, the use of a bureaucratic or organic approach to management design, and the degree of vertical or horizontal centralization must be resolved according to the needs of each organizational level of the courts. If the requirements of each are not taken into account, there is the high risk that the needs of one will be fulfilled at the expense of the other or that the operation of the court is primarily a function of ad hoc, subterranean arrangements among the immediate players rather than in response to the formal structure. The challenge in organizational design is not the neatness of the final product, but rather its utility in reducing uncertainty in a way which reinforces the purposes of the courts.

NOTES

1. For two exceptions to this general conclusion, see Gallas (1976) and Saari (1976).

2. Most organization theory literature begins with the same set of assumptions, as their primary concern is with complex organizations not simple ones. See, for example, the quick progression of the introductory chapter of Mintzberg (1979: Ch. 1) from consideration of one person producing clay pots to a large, specialized work force which requires an elaborate management structure.

3. Rural courts whose jurisdictions encompass several counties may require more coordination than those in a small town because of the need to coordinate the movement of judges from one courthouse to the next (Stott et al., 1977).

4. Justice Felix Frankfurter makes an even broader assertion in his concurrent opinion in *Lumberman's Mutual Casualty v. Elbert*, 348 U.S. 48(1954) in which he argues that simply expanding the number of judges may decrease the prestige of any one of them.

REFERENCES

BAAR, C. (1975) Separate but Subservient. Lexington, MA: D.C. Heath.
BAAR, C. (1974) "Will urban courts survive the war on crime," in H. Jacob (ed.) The Potential for Reform of Criminal Justice, Sage Criminal Justice System Annals Vol. 3. Beverly Hills, CA: Sage.
BAAR, E. and C. BAAR (1977) "Judges as middlemen?" Justice System Journal 2: 210-224.
BERKSON, L. and S. CARBON (1978) Court Unification: History, Politics and Implementation. Washington, DC: Government Printing Office.

BERKSON, L. and S. W. HAYS (1976) "Injecting court administrators into an old system: A case of conflict in Florida." Justice System Journal 2(Spring): 57.

BLAU, P. M. and W. R. SCOTT (1962) Formal Organizations. San Francisco, CA: Chandler.

BURNS, T. and G. M. STALKER (1961) The Management of Innovation. London: Tavistock.

CASPER, J. D. (1972) American Criminal Justice: The Defendant's Perspective. Englewood Cliffs, NJ: Prentice-Hall.

CHURCH, T., Jr., A. CARLSON, J. LEE, and T. TAN (1978) Justice Delayed: The Pace of Litigation in Urban Trial Courts. Williamsburg, VA: National Center for State Courts.

COLE, G. F. (1972) "The decision to prosecute," pp. 170-182 in G. F. Cole (ed.) Criminal Justice: Law and Politics. Belmont, CA: Duxbury Press. Reprinted from Law and Society Review 4: 313-343.

Council of State Governments (1977) Reorganization of State Corrections Agencies: A Decade of Experience. Lexington, KY: Author.

DOWNS, A. (1967) Inside Bureaucracy. Boston, MA: Little, Brown.

DUCAT, C. R. and V. E. FLANGO (1976) Leadership in State Supreme Courts: Roles of the Chief Justice. Beverly Hills, CA: Sage.

EISENSTEIN, J. and H. JACOB (1977) Felony Justice—an Organizational Analysis of Criminal Courts. Boston, MA: Little, Brown.

ETZIONI, A. (1964) Modern Organizations. Englewood Cliffs, NJ: Prentice-Hall.

FLANDERS, S., et al. (1977) Case Management and Court Management in United States District Court. Washington, DC: Federal Judicial Center.

FOX, S. J. (1971) The Law of Juvenile Courts in a Nutshell. St. Paul, MN: West.

GALLAS, G. (1976) "The conventional wisdom of state court administration: A critical assessment and alternative approach." Justice System Journal 2 (Spring): 35-55.

GRAU, C. W. (1978) Judicial Rule-Making: Administration, Access and Accountability. Chicago: American Judicature Society.

GULICK, L. H. and L. F. URWICK [eds.] (1937) Papers on the Science of Administration. New York: Columbia University Press.

HAYS, S. W. (1978) Court Reform: Ideal or Illusion? Lexington, MA: D. C. Heath.

HUNT, J. W. (1972) The Restless Organization. New York: Wiley International.

Institute for Law and Social Research (1976) Guide to Court Scheduling. Washington, DC: Author.

KORBAKES, C. A., J. J. ALFINI, and C. W. GRAU (1978) Judicial Rulemaking in the State Courts. Chicago: American Judicature Society.

LAWSON, H. (1979) State Funding of Court Systems: An Initial Examination. Washington, DC: American University Law Institute.

MINTZBERG, H. (1979) The Structuring of Organizations. Englewood Cliffs, NJ: Prentice-Hall.

NIMMER, R. T. (1978) The Nature of System Change: Reform Impact in the Criminal Courts. Chicago: American Bar Foundation.

PACKER, H. L. (1968) "Two models of the criminal process," pp. 35-52 in G. F. Cole (ed.) Criminal Justice: Law and Politics. Belmont, CA: Wadsworth.

PARSONS, T. (1956a) "A sociological approach to the theory of organizations I." Administrative Science Quarterly (June): 63-85.

PARSONS, T. (1956b) "A sociological approach to the theory of organizations II." Administrative Science Quarterly (September): 225-239.

PERROW, C. (1967) "A framework for the comparative analysis of organizations." American Sociological Review: 194-208.

President's Commission on Law Enforcement and the Administration of Justice (1967) The Challenge of Crime in a Free Society. Washington, DC: Government Printing Office.

PUGH, D. S., D. J. HICKSON, and C. R. HININGS (1969) "An empirical taxonomy of structures of work organizations." Administrative Science Quarterly: 115-125.

RUHNKA, J., S. WELLER, and J. A. MARTIN (1978) Small Claims Courts: A National Examination. Williamsburg, VA: National Center for State Courts.

SAARI, D. J. (1976) "Modern court management: Trends in court organization concepts—1976." Justice System Journal 2(Spring): 19-33.

SIMON, H. (1957) Administrative Behavior. New York: Macmillan.

SIPES, L. L., A. M. CARLSON, T. TAN, A. B. AIKMAN, and R.W. PAGE, Jr. (1980) Managing To Reduce Delay. Williamsburg, VA: National Center for State Courts.

SKUPSKY, D. S., R. T. MARTIN, M. J. GRUMER, and R. P. WOLFE (1980) Comparative Records Management System and the Courts. Williamsburg, VA: National Center for State Courts.

STOTT, E. K., Jr., T. J. FETTER, and L. L. CITES (1977) Rural Courts: The Effect of Space and Distance on the Administration of Justice. Williamsburg, VA: National Center for State Courts.

TAYLOR, F. W. (1947) Scientific Management. New York: Harper & Row.

THOMPSON, J. D. (1967) Organizations in Action. New York: McGraw-Hill.

TOBIN, R. W. and R. B. HOFFMAN (1979) The Administrative Role of Chief Justices and Supreme Courts. Williamsburg, VA; National Center for State Courts.

WOODWARD, J. (1965) Industrial Organization: Theory and Practice. New York: Oxford University Press.

Chapter 3

THE ORGANIZATION OF TRIAL JUDGES

DEAN J. CHAMPION

For several decades, the American judicial system has been subjected to an intensive review by many interested organizations and institutions. Inconsistent, unfair, and occasionally incompetent applications of law in civil and criminal state and federal courts have set the wheels in motion for a sweeping reform and potential unification of court administration (Hereford, 1966). As our urban populations grow and society becomes increasingly complex, "due process" and "speedy trials" cannot be assured to litigants. Crowded court calendars, unclear and often over-lapping court jurisdictions, and poor management of office affairs by court administrators and staffs have rendered our legal apparatus grossly inefficient by most reasonable standards.

This unfortunate state of legal affairs is the result of many factors both external and internal to trial court organization. Political appointments and public elections have placed many persons in court administrative positions who are clearly less qualified compared with other prospective candidates. The lack of clear-cut rules of procedure and the independence of trial judges in their respective jurisdictions have made it increasingly difficult to conduct and regulate a consistently efficient courtroom. Poorly trained staff and/or an under-staffed administration have aggravated problems of scheduling litigation and the processing of relevant pretrial and posttrial information available to defense and prosecuting attorneys. The nonexistence of a system of accountability for trial judges who are too excessive or too lenient in setting bonds, conducting trials, and sentencing the guilty has caused a growing disenchantment with the judicial system. The National Commission on the Causes and Prevention of Violence has pointed to the general failure of the trial court by observing that "it is commonly assumed that ... law enforcement (police, sheriffs, marshals), the judical process (judges, prosecutors, defense lawyers), and corrections (prison officials, probation and parole officers) ... add up to a system of criminal justice. A system implies some unity of purpose and organized interrelationship among component parts. In the typical American city and state and under federal jurisdiction as well, no such relationship exists" (National Commission on the Causes and Prevention of Violence, 1970: 128).

This essay focuses upon the state trial court and its organization. These courts have received a great deal of attention from the public. And, they are highly visible and have become "symbols of judicial disillusionment" (Gazell. 1975: 4). Gazell indicates that:

> state trial courts have long been salient because of at least three enduring ... considerations. First, the state trial court structures, especially their management problems, deserve more public attention because of their sheer magnitude; for they easily dwarf the state appellate systems as well as the entire federal judiciary. Trial courts employ thousands of judges and staff personnel, handle millions of criminal and civil cases each year, and spend several hundred million dollars annually. Furthermore, the size of these systems derives from their position as the starting and terminal points of most litigation. Because extensive time, money, and effort

are necessary, very few decisions are appealed. Second, court systems, largely because of their size, generate serious interest—academic as well as public—in their efficiency and output. In particular, scholars and public officials need to explore how numerous devices may promote greater court efficiency (as measured by the speedier termination of criminal and civil litigation). Third, the courts are worthy of thorough investigation because of their pervasive impact on public policy. Such courts usually constitute an integral segment of the local political system and, by their decisions in criminal and civil cases, often cause critical reallocations of power within that system [1975: 5].

Often, scholars must glean information about trial courts and their organization from reports and commission surveys of court reform and unification. "Old" court organization is frequently contrasted with proposed "new" court organizational formats in an effort to highlight organizational arrangements which will simplify and streamline existing court systems. We can learn a great deal about trial court organization from this literature. More important, we may be able to discover organizational structural and processual changes which will have positive implications for the courts of tomorrow.

AN OVERVIEW OF COURT ORGANIZATION

Attempts to unify state court systems share at least one characteristic. They are directed toward greater simplification of existing judicial systems. In order to place trial courts in proper organizational perspective relative to other courts, consider the "traditional model" of court organization for Texas illustrated in Figure 1. The Supreme Court oversees the court of Civil Appeals. The Court of Civil Appeals reviews decisions of lower courts including the

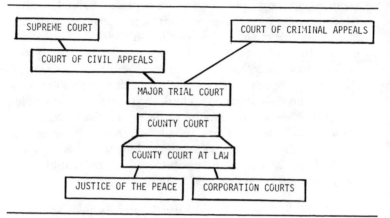

Figure 1   The Texas Model (Traditional)
Source: Henry R. Glick and Kenneth N. Vines, STATE COURT SYSTEMS.
Englewood Cliffs, N.J.: Prentice-Hall, Inc., 1973, p. 32.

Major Trial Courts and County Courts. A County Court at
Law oversees various Justices of the Peace and Corporation
Courts. A Court of Criminal Appeals, on par with the Court
of Civil Appeals, deals with criminal cases and reviews
decisions made in criminal court proceedings of Major Trial
Courts.

A significant simplification of court organization was
proposed by Pound (1940), and several modifications of it
have been made by the American Bar Association (ABA) in
subsequent years. Pound's simplified model is shown
together with two additional ABA modifications in Figure 2.

According to Volcansek, Pound:

cited four principles as controlling all efforts of court reform:
unification, flexibility, conservation of judicial power, and
responsibility. Basic to achievement of these principles is the
establishment of a single three-tiered state court system. At
the top sits the ultimate court of appeal (the supreme court).
A trial court of general jurisdiction for all major civil and

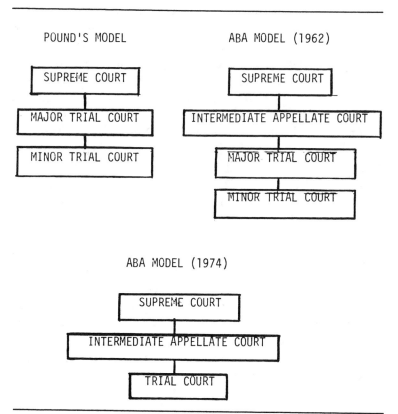

POUND'S MODEL   ABA MODEL (1962)

SUPREME COURT

MAJOR TRIAL COURT

MINOR TRIAL COURT

SUPREME COURT

INTERMEDIATE APPELLATE COURT

MAJOR TRIAL COURT

MINOR TRIAL COURT

ABA MODEL (1974)

SUPREME COURT

INTERMEDIATE APPELLATE COURT

TRIAL COURT

Figure 2   Pound's Simplified Model and Two ABA Models
Source: Henry R. Glick and Kenneth N. Vines, STATE COURT SYSTEMS.
Englewood Cliffs, N.J.: Prentice-Hall, Inc., 1973, p. 32.

criminal proceedings constitutes the second level. Depending
on the volume of litigation or on the traditions of the state,
this tier might be organized into divisions specializing in
certain types of litigation. Finally, the lowest tier of the court,
a minor trial court, hears cases of lesser magnitude [1977: 18].

Pound's model placed considerable systemic authority in
the hands of the chief justice. The chief justice would have

broad authority and responsibility to sanction judges and to generally correct abuses at all court levels. This person would also assign judges to particular divisions or localities and determine whether cases ought to be transferred from one jurisdiction to another. The chief justices' behavior would, in turn, be monitored by judicial councils and a unified bar (Volcansek, 1977: 19).

The ABA model of 1962 expands Pound's original model to include an intermediate appellate court which is designed to alleviate the burden of "appellate litigation at the highest court" (Volcansek, 1977: 20). The ABA model of 1974 simplifies the 1962 version further by providing for only one level of trial courts. These trial courts are "consolidated along district lines with multi-judge courts. Within these districts, flexible divisions that specialize in various types of litigation may be established" (Volcansek, 1977: 21).

Regardless of the model of court systems we may examine, the trial court is by far the most important and the most complex element of the judicial system (American Bar Association, 1975: 1). Most matters which come before the courts are initiated in trial courts, including issues of fact, determinative issues of law, and receiving evidence and resolving conflicting evidence" (American Bar Association, 1975: 1).

On a much smaller scale, we may examine briefly the organizational arrangement of courts (below and excluding the appellate court level) in a county of moderate size. In Knox County, Tennessee, for instance, there are two general court divisions: civil and criminal. Figure 3 shows a diagram of Knox County court organization. There are three criminal court judges, each presiding over a separate criminal court. Within the civil court arrangement there are various specialty courts. A chancery court or court of equity includes two judges who alternate the conduct of chancery court affairs. The circuit court has three judges conducting court business.

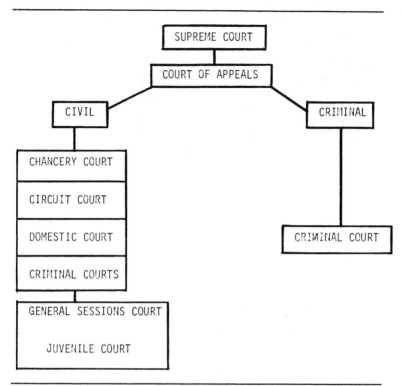

Figure 3   Tennessee State Court System Showing Knox County Tennessee Court
         Organization

A third court, the domestic court, is presided over by one
judge who handles divorce and child custody questions.

At the lowest level of the administration of justice are
general sessions courts consisting of four elected judges (and
occasional alternates) and the juvenile court. Needless to say,
larger jurisdictions would have a more complex court system.
In smaller communities, we would expect to find little
formalization of court structure. Presiding over jurisdictions
in rural areas would be justices of the peace and/or fee
judges.

THE FUNCTIONS OF TRIAL JUDGES

State and federal laws occupy many volumes on judges' shelves. While rules of procedure in administering the law are fairly clear and provide individual judges with prescribed behaviors while they are on the bench, each judge has considerable latitude regarding the conduct of the court and the behaviors of the litigants. Not all cases which come before the trial judge are clear-cut, however. In many respects, each case has individual merits, and it is difficult to achieve fairness under every condition, regardless of how closely judges adhere to procedural rules and administrative policies (American Bar Association, 1975: 1).

In 1975, the American Bar Association set forth standards relating to trial courts and their administration. While such standards are not binding on individual trial courts, judges have been increasingly persuaded to abide by them fairly closely. According to these standards, the trial court performs three primary functions:

(1) it is required to decide conflicting contentions of law and disputed issues of fact
(2) it is required to formulate sanctions and remedial orders
(3) it is required to supervise the activity of persons subject to the authority of the court [American Bar Association, 1975: 1-2].

The judges who eventually carry out these functions are expected to have only the highest personal and professional qualifications.

In an earlier statement on court organization, the ABA outlined the selection and qualifications of judges as follows:

Persons should be selected as judges on the basis of their personal and professional qualifications for judicial office. . . . All persons selected as judges should be of good moral character, emotionally stable and mature, in good physical health, patient, courteous, and capable of deliberation and decisiveness when required to act on their own reasoned judgment. They should have a broad general and legal education and should have been admitted to the bar. They should have had substantial experience in the adversary system, preferably as judges or judicial officers in other trial courts, or as trial advocates, and in any event should have had experience in the preparation, presentation, or decision of legal argument and matters of proof according to rules of procedure or evidence [American Bar Association, 1974: 40].

These objectives of trial courts and characteristics of trial judges are designed to provide the public with a fair and efficient method of administering justice to all. At the present time, however, there is little uniformity from one state to the next regarding the qualifications of persons conducting trial courts. Within any given state, there may be a wide range of competence within the judicial aggregate. An offense in city A may not be resolved as rapidly and in the same manner as the same offense committed in city B. In fact, trial judges within the same jurisdiction are often known to be more or less lenient or strict compared with one another, depending upon the sorts of cases coming before their court. "Who should judge the judges?" is a question which raises the issue of accountability.

THE BUREAUCRATIC PARALLEL

In many respects, judicial organization from the Supreme Court to the lowest municipal tribunal resembles closely the bureaucracy of the business world. Traditional treatment of bureaucracy in the context of Weber's (1946) model would include a description of an authority hierarchy. Weber was the first to formally introduce the notion of bureaucracy to the modern world. It was his intention to describe and promote the ideal model of organization. Such a model would be arranged in such a way so as to maximize the efficiency of organizational members. A significant outcome of increased individual and departmental efficiency would be the overall maximization of organizational effectiveness. The following characteristics of an ideal type of organization, the bureaucracy, were presented by Weber as follows:

(1) a hierarchy of authority
(2) spheres of competence
(3) specialization of tasks
(4) selection by test and promotion on merit
(5) impersonal implementation of abstract rules governing organizational roles
(6) office holding as a career.

It is clear from Weber's work that he envisioned an ideal organization as one where an explicit authority hierarchy exists, where obedience to rules in an impersonal fashion would be expected, where persons would be selected for tasks on the basis of test in order that the most qualified persons would occupy positions, that each person would be a specialist and operate in a department which would have clear control over a portion of organizational decision making, and where persons would have a strong commitment to organizational goals and a high degree of loyalty to the general organization.

Weber was adamantly opposed to political machinations and to nepotism. He believed that persons should perform jobs which reflected their expertise rather than their close association with significant and influential "others." Impersonality would objectify the implementation of rules and affirm the hierarchy of authority. Persons who were incompetent in their task performance would automatically be sanctioned, reprimanded, and possibly removed from their positions and replaced by more competent personnel. All of this would be accomplished in an impersonal fashion, putting aside totally all sentiments and personal feelings one might have for incompetent friends.

It seems that the judiciary would be a particularly suitable organization for applying Weber's bureaucratic principles. Important decisions are made on all occasions, and these decisions must be made in an impersonal manner, at all reasonable costs. Our legal system prides itself in the objectivity it theoretically possesses. Judges and court administrative staffs are usually assumed to be the most competent in carrying out the affairs of the court, and there are many specialists and spheres of competence.

Unfortunately, the same problems which contaminate and adversely affect business organizations and their effectiveness also befall judicial organizations. It is difficult to monitor the selection process whereby judges are appointed or elected to their respective posts. Persons bring to their jobs daily "latent social identities" and personalities which influence their task performance, their relations with other employees, and over-all organizational effectiveness. Frequently, duplication of function occurs, especially when spheres of competence of different organizational divisions or departments are not clearly delineated from one another in terms of their authority and functions. The organization is inundated by excessive paperwork, as each department or division seeks to absolve itself of potential blame from higher-ups if improper or incompetent decisions are made. In instances where decisions are necessary but no individual department is clearly charged with these specific decisions, there is the propensity to defer to "some other department" which "may be more appropriate" for such decision making. Decision making is therefore delayed and organizational effectiveness suffers accordingly.

Judges are sometimes assigned to courts where they preside over cases which they dislike and/or which fail to fit their particular areas of expertise. A judge may be particularly sensitive about drug and drug-related offenses, and a harder line might prevail against offenders at the time of sentencing. This would be an example of the influence of "latent social identities and personalities" in an otherwise objective courtroom situation.

Because of partisan politics and the routine preservation of the incumbent judge system and incumbent judges in many states, it is nearly impossible to exercise any formal control and sanctioning power over the judiciary. Judges who are corrupt or senile or who make decisions which are frequently reversed in higher courts clearly contribute to the ineffectiveness of judicial organization. Mandatory retirement of judges at fixed ages is nonexistent in many jurisdictions. There are several solutions which have been proposed, designed to "clean up the act" of the state trial judiciary. But because of the pervasiveness of the political institution in our society and its close relation with judicial organization, stating what *should* be done and *doing* what should be done are usually two quite different things.

Some proposals which have been advocated and successfully implemented in business organizations will be presented below, however. Several scholars of judicial organizations have endorsed such proposals as well.

BUREAUCRACY IN THE JUDICIARY: THEORY AND PRACTICE

The ABA has already taken several significant steps toward revamping standards governing the selection of trial judges and the conduct of courtroom procedure (American Bar Association, 1975, 1973). Certainly the specification and endorsement of general principles governing trial judges and their conduct by the ABA should encourage the judiciary generally to take serious notice of existing problems and work toward their effective resolution. What people have done with bureaucracy has given it a bad name in the business world among professionals and laypeople alike. In its ideal form, bureaucracy as outlined by Weber is a viable system of organization. If an organization only partially operates according to Weber's outline, it is a given that only *partial* organizational effectiveness will be achieved. The judiciary is not an exception in this regard.

A major effort of many state judicial systems has been and continues to be the unification and centralization of state courts (Saari, 1976; Lowe, 1973; Uhlman, 1968; Ashman and Parness, 1974). This will be the business organizational equivalent of centralized management. An explicit hierarchy of court authority with centralized control will be one means of resolving the perrenial problem of duplication of function and overlapping and superfluous jurisdictions. Gazell (1975: 71-73) recommends the abolition of "fee offices" and the absorption of their personnel into a unified system. This is a substantial step toward the reduction of subjectivity and vested interests within the lower echelons of our legal systems.

Since the matter of court delays (because of inefficiency of record-keeping and poor scheduling and/or maintenance of trial calendars) is one of the more observable problems which is associated with trial court structure and process, methods should be explored which facilitate recordkeeping. Currently, a number of information retrieval and data processing systems are available for use by the courts. In fact, many state and federal court systems are increasingly turning toward the use of computers, not only for storing and retrieving information about a defendant's offense record, court agenda and scheduling data but also for material about judges themselves. In a matter of seconds, information can be made available about a judge's courtroom record, his/her sentencing profile by offense and any number of other relevant categories, decisions which have been reversed by higher courts because of irregularities committed by the judge in the course of litigation, and a multitude of additional information about the judge's behavior. Thus, a quick and efficient method for assessing any given judge's competence and fairness is available for review by any qualified board of higher court officials. Accountability is enhanced greatly by turning to the computer for use in the courtroom (Sherman, 1977).

All trial courts can benefit significantly by the selection of competent judicial personnel initially. The philosophy that a good employee leads to a good organization is relevant here. While numerous plans for selecting and appointing judges to the bench have been proposed and used in recent years, one plan has continued to survive as a "standard" for over seven decades. Kales proposed a plan in 1914 which has survived in various forms in a number of states up to the persent time. Known as the "Kales Plan," it requires a nonpartisan aggregate of lawyers, judges, and nonjudicial personnel to acquire a list of the most qualified candidates on the basis of their records and expertise. This list is then submitted to the governor for use in making appointments. Vacancies because of death, retirement, or removal because of incompetence or any other reason can be filled with qualified personnel without prejudice and without reference to political affiliations or associations.

Ideally, any choice a governor might make from a list provided by nonpartisans will, by definition, be a good choice. It might be argued that committees are incapable of making consistently perfect choices in their compilation of qualified candidates. But the element of politics is removed to a large degree from the selection process. Political hacks are less likely to wind up on such distinguished lists of proposed candidates in the context of greater objectivity in selection (Kales, 1914).

Current ABA proposals (American Bar Association; 1974) which outline the qualifications of judges in various trial court settings and specifications for their conduct of court procedures are deemed sufficient guidelines worth following by state court systems. The major hurdle to overcome is public acceptance of change in one of its major institutions. Incumbent politicians who are interested in preserving the status quo will not be expected to contribute to proposed changes which will undermine their overt and covert power within the legal apparatus. Perhaps greater public awareness of the benefits which can accrue to them as a result of such drastic changes in court structure will lead in the long run to the removal and replacement of self-serving politicians with a more professional class of leaders. But changes of such magnitude are not likely in the near future. We can only hope that change in state judicial systems will occur, either rapidly or slowly, and in the desired objective direction. We have the theory at our disposal to make our state trial courts and court systems efficient and effective bureaucratic administrations with competent personnel. But the will to actually bring such changes about must ultimately come from the people themselves acting in their own best interests at the polls. "The right employee will create the right organization" may be rewritten to read, "the right voter will create the right judicial organization, in time."

REFERENCES

Advisory Commission on Intergovernmental Relations (1971) For a More Perfect Union: Court Reform. Washington, DC: Government Printing Office.

American Bar Association (1975) Standards Relating to Trial Courts. Washington, DC: American Bar Association Commission on Standards of Judicial Administration.

American Bar Association (1973) Standards Relating to Court Organization. Washington, DC: American Bar Association Commission on Standards of Judicial Administration.

American Bar Association (1972) The Function of the Trial Judge. Washington, DC: Author.

American Bar Association (1967) "ABA model state judicial article (1962)" as reprinted in Task Force Report: The Courts. Washington, DC: Government Printing Office.

American Judicature Society (1977) Courts of Limited Jurisdiction: A National Survey. Chicago: Author.

ASHMAN, A. and J. PARNESS (1974) "The concept of a unified court system." DePaul Law Review 24: 1-41.

BERKSON, L. C., S. W. HAYS, and S. J. CARBON (1977) Managing the State Courts: Text and Readings. St. Paul, MN: West.

BRENNAN, W. J., Jr. (1971) California Unified Trial Court Feasibility Study. San Francisco: Booz, Allen, and Hamilton, Inc.

BRENNAN, W. J., Jr. (1957) "Does business have a role in improving judicial administration?" Pennsylvania Bar Association Quarterly: 28: 238.

COYNE, R. (1975) "Has court management changed since Vanderbilt? Alternate models of court organization." Judicature 58: 266-268.

DOAN, R. and R. SHAPIRO (1976) State Court Administrators. Chicago: American Judicature Society.

FRIESEN, E. C., Jr., E. C. GALLAS, and N. M. GALLAS (1971) Managing the Courts. Indianapolis: Bobbs-Merrill.

GALLAS, E. C. (1968) "The profession of court management." Judicature 51: 334-336.

GAZELL, J. A. (1975) State Trial Courts as Bureaucracies: A Study in Judicial Management. New York: Dunellen.

GAZELL, J. A. (1971a) "State trial courts: An odyssey into faltering bureaucracies." San Diego Law Review 8: 275-332.

GAZELL, J. A. (1971b) "Three principle facets of judicial management." Criminology 9: 131-153.

GAZELL, J. A.)1968) The Future of State Court Management. Port Washington, NY: Kennikat.

GLICK, H. R. and K. N. VINES (1973) State Court Systems. Englewood Cliffs, NJ: Prentice-Hall.

HALL, R. (1967 "Court organization and administration." Alabama Lawyer 28: 148-152.

HEREFORD, W. (1971) The Judicial System of Tennessee. New York: Institute of Judicial Administration.

HEREFORD, W. (1967) "The professionalizatoon of court administration." Judicature 50: 256-257.

HEREFORD, W. (1966) "Why not one court?" Florida Bar Journal 40: 1068-1072.

KALES, A. H. (1914) Unpopular Government in the United States. Chicago: University of Chicago Press.

KLEIN, F. (1967) "The position of the trial court administrator in the states." Judicature 50: 278-280.

KLEPS, R. N. (1972) "State court modernization in the 1970's." Judicature 55: 294-295.

LEVINTHAL, A. (1965) "Monor courts—major problems." Journal of the American Judicature Society 48: 188-192.

LOWE, R. S. (1973) "Unified courts of America: The legacy of Roscoe Pound." Judicature 56: 232.

MCCONNELL, E. (1968) "The administration of a state court system." Judicature 51: 253-256.

National Commission on the Causes and Prevention of Violence (1970) To Establish Justice, To Insure Domestic Tranquility. New York: Bantam.

NELSON, D. W. (1974) Judicial Administration and the Administration of Justice. St. Paul. MN: West.

NELSON, D. W. (1973) "Organizational concepts for a unified court system in the state of Michigan." (unpublished)

POUND, R. (1962) "The causes of popular dissatisfaction with the administration of justice." Journal of the American Judicature Society 46: 62-63.

POUND, R. (1940) "Principles and outlines of a modern unified court organization." Journal of the American Judicature Society 23: 230.

POUND, R. (1927) "Organization of courts." Journal of the American Judicature Society 11: 81-82.

SAARI, D. (1976) "Modern court management: Trends in court organization concepts—1976." Justice System Journal 2:19-33.

SAARI, D. (1971) "Management and courts: A perplexing nexus." American University Law Review 20: 601-619.

SAARI, D. (1967) "New ideas for trial court administration: Applying social science to law." Judicature 51: 82-87.

SHERMAN, N. W. (1977) "Obstacles to implementing court reform," pp. 64-71 in L. C. Berkson et al. (eds.) Managing the State Courts: Text and Readings. St. Paul, MN: West.

TOMPKINS, D. C. (1973) Court Organization and Administration: A Bibliography. Berkeley, CA: Institute of Governmental Studies.

UHLENHOPP, H. (1964) "The integrated trial court." American Bar Association Journal 50: 1061-1064.

UHLMAN, W. (1968) "Justifying justice courts." Judicature 52: 22-26.

U.S. Department of Justice (1973) National Survey of Court Organization. Washington, DC: Government Printing Office.

VINES, K. N. (1965) "Courts as political and governmental agencies," in H. Jacob and K. N. Vines (eds.) Politics in the American States. Boston: Little, Brown.

WEBER, M. (1973) "Courts," pp. 171-177 in National Advisory Commission on Criminal Justice Standards and Goals. Washington, DC: Government Printing Office.

WEBER, M. (1946) "Bureaucracy," in H. H. Gerth and C. W. Mills (eds.) From Max Weber: Essays in Sociology. New York: Oxford University Press.

Chapter 4

TRIAL COURTS ON TRIAL:
EXAMINING DOMINANT ASSUMPTIONS

ARLENE SHESKIN

Trial courts have long been a subject of analysis for social scientists and practitioners. Constructing explanations for the workings of an institution whose components seem quite disparate has been a challenge, as has been developing cures for its perceived deficiencies. Researchers responding to this challenge have shared a number of assumptions about the nature of courts, the roles of the actors who operate within them, and the relationship between the legal system and the larger social order. These assumptions have made the collection of data possible by delineating the important questions and suggesting methods by which appropriate data may be collected to answer them. But ways of seeing are also ways of not seeing; taken for granted assumptions which render the world nonproblematic often extend too far, precluding the discovery and examination of alternate views. Unexplicated, such assumptions are an intuitive part of the researcher's worldview—acting as "silent partners" (Gouldner, 1970) in the research enterprise. Although such assumptions are often unspoken, they are political and are grounded in a larger theory of how the world does, and

Author's Note: *I would like to thank Charles Grau for his comments on a previous draft and Tony Ragona for the title.*

should, operate. In a world where researchers assume the value of social stability, for example, institutions devoted to its preservation are not, and cannot be, challenged. Interested researchers, at best, can only "see" ways of understanding and improving the institution as legitimate research questions. It is our contention that research on trial courts has been limited by such assumptions.

Given the air of objectivity emanating from those who do research on trial courts, it is especially important for the theoretical substructure of their work to be explicated. Not merely neutral reflections on the social world, theories may instead be seen as ideologies which influence the parameters of the problems they are said to explain. As such, they exist in a "theory marketplace" and the predominance of one is an important indicator of dominant ideologies in the society (see Shover, 1975: 96). When this notion is applied to trial courts, and the special nature of their role and the clients they process is recognized, one can note the political impact of theoretical assumptions about them. These assumptions both dictate the problems to be explored and the parameters in which they must be solved. Because theoretical assumptions regarding trial courts assume their necessity, they also underscore their legitimacy. In assuming such, research on trial courts has significance beyond the confines of particular academic disciplines. When findings are favorable to, or do not question, the existing order, they help create a general explanatory scheme, becoming master symbols—symbols of justification—which are used to justify and sanction institutional authority (Gerth and Mills, 1953). Assumptions which preclude a challenge to the existing structure of trial courts contribute to the likelihood of their maintenance.

Because of the important relationship between theory and the generation of research, this article will delineate and assess the theoretical assumptions upon which research on trial courts has been based. Much of this research has focused upon two issues—the internal dynamics of the courts (how work is done) and the reform of court practices (how to make the process work more quickly and efficiently). Given this emphasis, we will selectively review research on the workings of trial courts and suggest the extent to which a revised framework might result in a better understanding of them and their role in society.

FUNCTIONALISM: THE GUIDING FRAMEWORK

Functionalism, long a guiding perspective among social scientists, provides the theoretical basis for much of the research on trial courts. Premised on answering the question "how is social order possible," it begins with the assumption that such order is the natural and desirable state for societies and organizations. Left unexamined is the notion of order itself and the extent to which equilibrium—or its appearance—may mask fundamental conflicts and inequality (see Skolnick, 1969).

For functionalists, societal stability is based upon the theoretically assumed existence of a common pattern of shared norms and values which societal members acquire through socialization (Parsons, 1951). Particular roles are thought to have clearly defined expectations and obligations attached to them, and it is the task of socializing agents to insure that they are properly internalized by societal members in their charge. Those who deviate are thought to be inadequately socialized; the possible relativity of social roles or the desirability of protest is not generally considered, rendering a relatively static conception of social life where societal members learn what is expected of them and then perform their roles accordingly. Social change is then seen as an unwelcome disruption—often a dysfunction—and when it appears the system is thought to exert adaptive mechanisms which propel it toward equilibrium again. On the occasions that these natural mechanisms do not appear, functionalists admit the necessity, and desirability, of state intervention and engineering to restore stability (see Gouldner, 1970).

With its assumption of consensus and already agreed upon expectations attaching to particular roles, functionalism precludes imagination of a world in which meanings are not already agreed upon or where actors are engaged in creating social worlds. It also precludes consideration of power and coercion as significant variables affecting social life. By accepting institutions as given, rather than imagining fundamentally different alternatives, and through its concern with the immediate rather than with a critical examination of the surrounding social structure, functionalism establishes itself as a conservative social theory (Gouldner, 1970; Mannheim, 1971). When such conservative theoretical assumptions guide problem solving, it is no surprise that problems are not easily solved. As Quinney (1972: 331) has noted, no amount of research can solve social problems as long as the research that relates to the problem ignores (or tacitly supports) the values underlying the problem. When research accepts such values, problems and solutions tend to be tautological, leaving observers frustrated by the lack of "progress" attained. Thus, if one is to understand this lack of progress and be able to relate it to the knowledge produced about, and solutions proposed for, trial courts, an examination of the assumptions guiding research is in order.

COURTS AS BUREAUCRACY

In an early study of criminal courts in a metropolitan area, Blumberg (1967) depicted them as bureaucracies, dispensing a type of assembly line justice based upon plea bargains achieved by prosecutors and defense attorneys who depended upon each other's good will to accomplish their tasks. Bureaucratic due process was decried because it placed the goals and continued maintenance of the court over legal imperatives, thereby replacing the adversary system. We were thus reminded of a supposed past where individual rights and treatment were not sacrificed for the needs of the organization. In keeping with its view of the court as a bureaucracy, this work emphasized the ways in which procedures and social relationships were rationalized in an effort to achieve predictability. Describing the result of this process, Blumberg maintained that

> greater faith (is) placed upon symbiotic relationships and structured expectancies to meet the individual and group needs of the court participants, rather than a working through of legal abstractions such as due process. The deviant or even maverick individual who predicates his official conduct solely on accepted notions of due process, or chooses possibilities of action which run counter to normatively established routines, is quickly isolated, neutralized or resocialized [1961: 10].

Later works have quarreled with this emphasis upon courts as bureaucracies. Feeley (1980) notes that unlike bureaucracies, courts are not organized to pursue clear goals and have no formal means available to discipline recalcitrant members. He likens courts to marketplaces and asserts that the assembly line metaphor ignores the complexity of the process. While one may argue with this early insistence upon the court as a bureaucracy, or with its assumption that there was once a day when the adversary system reigned supreme, or even with its belief that adversarial techniques are necessary to the dispensation of justice, it is clear that more recent research uncritically accepts the efforts to achieve the predictability which Blumberg decried. Another differentiating feature of this early work is its concern for defendants and the effect of rationalized procedures on their legal rights. In later works, defendants receive short shrift (see Casper, 1978, for an exception) as does consideration of the ways in which their racial or economic composition may affect the operation of trial courts.

This latter point, although rarely mentioned, is of considerable importance, especially given Gordon's (1974) work on the relationship between law enforcement efforts and the actions of law violators. He argues that differences in crime may be related to the structure of class institutions in society (an individual's access to particular types of "wrongdoing") and the class biases of the state and the extent to which it rates as serious and punishes particular types of action. Greater surveillance is attached to those activities which are severely punished—usually those committed by members of the lower class—and since individuals who are apprehended for such actions have a lot to lose, they are likely to arm themselves against the possibility of capture, thus making their activities more violent.

It is not unlikely that state biases exert a similar influence on the operation of criminal courts. To the extent that their clientele is not highly valued, we may expect to see particular activities in the operation of trial courts, and suggestions for their reform, that are not present in courts dealing with a "better" clientele. Unfortunately, few analyses of trial courts, or recommendations to reform them, deal systematically with the class composition of its clientele. This absence—to which we will return—is revealing, especially since defendants are uniformly considered to be poor, male, young, and black—characteristics which are usually thought to be important explanatory variables in other contexts.

COURTROOM WORKGROUPS

One work which suffers from the limitations described here is *Felony Justice* by Eisenstein and Jacob (1977). Focusing upon courtroom practices in Detroit, Chicago, and Baltimore, they provide vivid descriptions of the everyday activities of courtroom actors. Their explanation of these activities, however, is limited by functional assumptions.

Because they find no evidence of a hierarchical structure, they reject the bureaucratic metaphor as an explanation of courtroom activity. Portraying it instead as an organization, they maintain that work is accomplished through the efforts of "courtroom workgroups," which are defined as "a complex network of ongoing relationships which determine who does what, how, and to whom." By recasting courts in this way, they develop a view which emphasizes incentives and shared goals as the motivating forces in workgroup activity. Because each member of the workgroup, consisting of attorneys, judges, and prosecutors, is thought dependent upon the other for the completion of common tasks, they are said to develop values and work patterns which allow them to complete their work expeditiously and to achieve predictability, a goal which, in contrast to Blumberg, Eisenstein and Jacob laud. This mutual dependence is also said to protect individual members by restricting the ability of any one to impose unilateral decisions on the group. While Eisenstein and Jacob are cognizant of the importance of individuals creating their own ways of managing work, they also realize that they do not do so in just the way they please. The professionals of whom he speaks all belong to sponsoring organizations which influence their representative courtroom members and the courts themselves are subject to external pressures.

When one begins with a view that equilibrium is necessary and desirable and that it is maintained because societal members share common norms and values which ensure reciprocal interdependence (Walsh, 1972), it is no surprise that Eisenstein and Jacob find the activities of workgroup members essential to the maintenance of the system. Unfortunately, they provide neither clear empirical support for the consensual nature of these relationships nor the meaning of these relationships to the actors engaged in them. The problem resides in the very notion of a courtroom workgroup. Eisenstein and Jacob assume its existence, along with common norms and values on the part of actors, because they see individuals interacting with work being accomplished, but interaction does not necessarily lead to feelings of belonging. Eisenstein and Jacob appear to acknowledge this when they note that although team members share common norms and values, "they (workgroup members) may not realize it." If they do not realize it, how can others assume it exists? The issue of whether the individuals described actually experience themselves as being members of a group is an empirical question which cannot be resolved a priori. The concomitant emphasis on interdependence and shared values also limits our understanding of how work is accomplished because it ignores both the possibility of conflict as a motivating force and the ways in which courtroom actors may shape their activities.

In assuming the shared values of workgroup members, for example, we have no sense of how they are created. And given the ahistorical bent of functional theory, we have less sense of what these were prior to Eisenstein and Jacob's arrival on the scene, or how any variety of future events may affect them. Because a shared universe of discourse is assumed to exist between researchers and those they observe, actors are not asked to speak for themselves, thus obviating the possibility of knowing what their work roles actually mean to them or whether their arrangements are seen as being free from coercion. Vocalized support of the system, however, does not mean the end of the research process. The support of the prosecutor for the system, or for the disposing of cases, may be very different from that of a defense attorney, which may in turn differ from that of a judge. One can also imagine important differences within these general categories. Because they look only at end points, rather than the process by which they are arrived at, such complexities are ignored.

If cases are processed, and if people work together everyday in ways which allow them to fulfill the requirements of their jobs, one cannot conclude that it is shared values which allow this to be done. It is also dangerous to assume that because no rigid hierarchy is observed and because individuals *appear* to work together for a final goal that all are equal partners to the process. At particular times, some members of the court have the power to impose new rules and procedures upon the others. While those others have the *potential* power to band together and subvert those actions, and while this may sometimes limit the other's willingness to impose new procedures, it does not negate the reality of differential power. What appears as shared may really be the only option available to powerless parties.

This is not to say, however, that there are no shared values among courtroom actors. As members of a society operating under a particular ideology of justice, we would expect courtroom actors to reflect the educational and ideological processes to which they have been party. The issue is not to conclude there is agreement and then celebrate it as the best of all possible worlds, but to establish which beliefs are shared, why, and with what effect. To do so, however, would move us outside the courthouse to a consideration of the ways in which consciousness is shaped, a task which most who research courts have not found necessary.

The authors are unable to deal with notions of power and coercion because they ignore the ways in which meanings are created. When such meanings are taken as problematic and then delineated, a different version of trial courts emerges. The abolition of plea bargaining in Alaska, for example, enabled researchers to chart the ways in which actors adapted to change—a change which was imposed by the Attorney General, in part, to make courtroom actors work harder and which was not welcomed by them (Rubenstein, 1976). The differential interests and powers of various courtroom actors became apparent in their adaptations. Instead of being guided by common group norms which might stress inter-dependence, those who had an advantage used it. Prepaid attorneys were able to resort to trial more often because of their greater resources, while prosecutors had an edge over defense attorneys with regard to what they could offer under the new system. That such a change could be instituted also speaks to the importance of considering power and coercion as factors affecting the content of courtroom work. Although actors may be interdependent, some may be more independent than others, allowing them to exert their will and control situations at critical times. In keeping with such differentials, Levin (1975) notes that although actors work together, their goals are often in conflict. He further observes that actors primarily try to serve their own interests first. When these interests converge with those of other actors, a system of exchange and equilibrium may seem to be operating. When they diverge, the wishes of the most powerful one in that particular instance becomes apparent. Because research assumptions about the reality of trial courts dictates a world which is nonhierarchical and consensual, we are deprived of the opportunity to judge the ways in which that reality was constructed, thus casting doubt upon its very validity.

Similar problems appear when Eisenstein and Jacob delineate the goals of the court. The expressive goals, which are said to serve symbolic functions, include doing justice and maintaining group cohesion while the instrumental ones, which serve material functions, include disposing of cases and reducing uncertainty. The difficulty presented by this typology is that one can neither be certain of its meanings nor sure of its inclusiveness. For example, while the disposition of caseloads may be measurable, it cannot be assumed that all would agree on the proper speed by which they should be disposed. In addition, while this may be thought of as an instrumental goal, an argument can be made for its expressive function as well. Perhaps there are courts where the disposition of cases "infuses more meaning into activity" than in others. In Ohio, for example, judges win awards for complying with the dispositional standards established by the State Supreme Court (Sheskin and Grau, 1980). In public ceremonies, they are praised for expeditious service and rewarded with plaques citing their "superior judicial performance." In subsequent elections, some of those who have been so praised and rewarded cite their commendation as an example of their judicial worthiness. Clearly, in Ohio the disposition of cases serves an important symbolic goal, at least by Eisenstein and Jacob's standards. Using their criteria one could also argue that maintaining group cohesion has an instrumental function. Its absence, in a system where work is accomplished because of the shared norms of participants, would seem to deal a fatal blow to the ongoing process. Most activities can be seen to have both expressive and instrumental components and the issue to be addressed is how and why they come to be defined in a particular way. In addition, a discussion of court goals which is limited to those which allow actors to accomplish their tasks ignores the context in which courts operate and their larger role in society. Courts have goals which are created and extend outside courthouse doors but to discover them one must move beyond an examination of courtroom activity.

Finally, by noting the affect of external agents and sponsoring organizations in fostering courtroom goals and activities, Eisenstein and Jacob provide an important contribution. Unfortunately, they ignore the ways in which courtroom actors may, in turn, fashion the expectancies or ideologies of their sponsoring groups, thus engaging them as allies rather than merely accepting their dictates as constraints. Thus, in their work a dialectical view of interaction and change is eschewed in favor of a unidirectional one. This can be done only when actors are not viewed as active participants in the construction of social reality and are not interviewed to test their interpretations against those of the researcher. Things are not always as they appear in social life, and without penetration of actors' worldviews we are left wondering as to the meaning of what we see.

Eisenstein and Jacob are not alone in their failure to apprehend the process by which a semblance of order may be created. Lipetz (1978), in a study of a misdemeanor court dealing with prostitutes, applies the workgroup model, telling us that "members have devised a set of norms that allow work to be accomplished quickly, efficiently and with a minimal amount of uncertainty" and that "the commitment of the group to the routine was so strong that any attempts to modify it failed." While one may not quarrel with the notion that individuals establish routines at work, one can take issue with the notion that this routine rests upon shared norms and values and serves the best interests of all. Only because the author is bounded by assumptions which accept the legitimacy and necessity of the present system can she conclude this, thus rendering a variety of other issues nonproblematic.

The existence of a separate court for women, and the possibility that those who must process low-status women have particular feelings which might affect their work routines and the ways in which they dispose of their charges is not considered. These considerations are ignored because the outcome—the speedy disposition of cases and the avoidance of unpredictability—is assumed to be a social good. They are important, however, because the author's conclusion that everybody wins does not mean that no penalties are paid. The finding that no one spent *much* time in jail or paid fines, and that women were *harrassed* but not deterred from their occupation is not the type of finding which leads one to conclude that defendants were necessarily pleased with the results of workgroup activity. Because interviews with them were not conducted, we can only speculate whether their analyses agree with the author's. Even if defendants shared the view that things could be worse, it is the task of the researcher to relate the activities in court to the social structure outside it.

The author also does not comment upon the ways in which making work predictable may interfere with "justice." A defense attorney who "insisted on following the letter of the law" is characterized as asserting himself above the court's norms. Attorneys like this were punished; their cases were called late and they were made to wait for questions to be answered. This use of power against "recalcitrants" is cited to emphasize the importance of proper socialization to court-room roles rather than to question the propriety of such practices. The assumed necessity of equilibrium and the belief that roles have clear expectations attached to them again precludes additional analysis.

Nardulli (1978), in a cogent critique of early literature on the courts, delineates the problems posed when mistaken theoretical assumptions guide the analysis of data. He notes that studies which adopted a legalistic perspective "failed to consider inter-relationships and the functions practices served for the court actors." Those stemming from a crime survey tradition were also deficient due to their uncritical acceptance of the belief that the basic structure of criminal justice was an optimal one. In his own analysis of trial courts, however, he falls victim to a similar problem. Although his analysis is more complex than those we have noted, his general emphasis on the collective and cooperative efforts of judges, prosecutors, and defense attorneys falls squarely within the functionalist tradition.

Nardulli's work appears different from the others we have noted because he seems to deal more directly with the issue of power. By categorizing the main courtroom actors as an elite, we have an immediate impression of a system where some are able to impose their will upon others, a key component in the definition of power (see Weber, 1954). But while Nardulli notes differences between the elite and those beneath them (i.e., bailiffs, clerks), he seems unwilling to apply the same perspective to the elite itself. He assumes that the discretionary power accorded them is distributed in such a way that none can dominate criminal court operations. Because the necessity to dispose of cases is identified as a shared goal, he finds it unnecessary to explore the types of contingencies which might fly in its face. What happens, for example, when one party thinks a case is too important to be disposed of in the "normal" matter? Whose will prevails? What happens, too, when the coalition he describes disagrees? Who does what, to whom, and with what consequences? Unless we accept a functionalist view of professional socialization—one stressing adherence to already existing and carefully defined rules—we should be able to imagine circumstances which are, at best, unordinary, requiring negotiation and interpretation on the part of actors. Because Nardulli accepts such a view, he sees unordinary situations only in terms of deviant actors who do not know, or do not accept, the rules. Not addressed are the ways in which the interdependencies among one courtroom elite may be graded, leaving one group more independent than another at particular times.

This is a curious omission because Nardulli's own data suggest a reality less grounded in consensus, and more problematic, than he admits. He notes that court consensus is sometimes marred by displays of hostility, but instead of analyzing who is hostile to whom and with what consequences, he maintains that hostility is "functional because it tends to reinforce the virtues of cordiality in the minds of trial court participants" (Nardulli, 1978: 183). Stripped of functionalist assumptions, these data may be interpreted differently. Outbursts of hostility may reflect the disadvantageous position of particular court participants, particularly when their charges are not resolved in a way desirous to them. The data may also suggest that cordiality exists only so long as actors are unwilling to challenge the powers that may be. Much like the civil liberties which are strongly guaranteed, but which become problematic when they are utilized (see Quinney, 1974), the cordial atmosphere in the court may be more apparent than real. While Nardulli (1978: 183) maintains that a cordial atmosphere reigned in the courts because its maintenance was in the interest of the courtroom elite, it may have appeared to reign because unequal partners did not have the power to challenge it without further undermining their positions. Gentlemanly prerogatives may thus mask a system based on something other than gentlemanly reserve.

This seems apparent in Nardulli's description of the way in which court business is handled. He notes, as does Lipetz, that continuances are easily granted, and cooperative attorneys have convenient times scheduled for their cases. While this may be the ordinary way of doing business, the fact that it can be changed at the behest of one member of the elite rather than another means that issues of differential power must be addressed. Given an apparent lack of conflict, one cannot conclude that social harmony has been achieved; one should instead be made all the more cognizant of the existing mechanisms which keep conflict from erupting.

In considering the relationship between trial courts and their environment, Nardulli moves beyond the impact of sponsoring organizations to an analysis of input and output regulators, the former referring to witnesses, victims, and police, with the latter to the chief judge, state's attorneys office, and the state legislature. Nardulli then notes, quite correctly, that the environment in which the trial court operates has an important impact on internal dynamics. While Nardulli shares with Eisenstein and Jacob a disinclination to imagine, or examine, the ways in which the court may affect its external environment by reacting to it, or anticipating its stance and attempting to shape it in accord with its policies, there is an even more important omission in this type of analysis. Trial courts are related to, and affected by, an external environment which extends far beyond the local and state level. They are products of a particular legal system which is itself a reflection of a particular state apparatus. Without understanding the larger structure in which these courts operate, and to which they are addressed, we are left with a disjointed view, even when conflict among courtroom actors is considered. By missing the possibility of differential power within the court, however, the literature we have reviewed does not imagine the impact of its existence outside it.

COURTS AS PROCESS

We have so far suggested several problems which characterize research on trial courts. A consistent critique has been their assumption of consensus and stability, and their failure to consider a version of reality where actors are not attached to clear-cut norms and programmed to do what is expected. Work has appeared which addresses these issues, and from it we gain a view of courtroom activity which is at odds with the one presented thus far. Mather (1979), in a comprehensive, qualitative study of the Los Angeles Superior Court, examined how determinations were made with regard to plea bargaining. Rather than assume a mechanistic system where the needs of courtroom actors determine dispositions, she aimed for a "cultural description" based upon the native point of view, hoping to reveal the extent to which actors shape the reality of their lives. She found, along with the other researchers we have considered, that common understandings with regard to work did exist but the nature of the understandings she delineated differs from the ones we have seen. They are neither engraved in stone nor the result of some eternal, indelible consensus. Instead, these understandings are a product of a continuous negotiation and construction of reality. Order is achieved, but not forever, as it is subject to new circumstances which must be interpreted anew by actors from different vantage points. In keeping with this more problematic view of courtroom activity, Mather notes:

> The social reality of the court is one where even facts are negotiated matters. To discover what really happened in a case and then to determine the legal significance of the suspect's behavior is a very complex and ambiguous task [1979: 141].

Given such complexity, actors are continuously attempting to reconcile diverse, and sometimes competing, versions of reality. Echoing Sudnow's (1965) work on normal crimes, Mather shows the ways in which expectations with regard to particular types of crimes and dispositions are achieved. Distinctions are made on the basis of seriousness and the strength of the prosecutor's case, all of which are open to negotiation and interpretation. Thus, in Mather's scheme, the interdependence and consensus of courtroom actors is no longer taken to be an independent variable, affecting the disposition of cases and courtroom activity. In addition, the exclusion of defendants from decisions affecting their fate is found distressing rather than taken as a necessary part of business as usual.

In keeping with this emphasis upon actors' roles in shaping social life, Heumann (1977) examined the ways in which courtroom actors learn about their tasks. Although he was interested in adaptation and assumed a consensual view of how courts should operate which newcomers eventually accept, he uncovered more conflict than might be assumed in a system where consensus prevails. He shows, for example, that while most participants accept plea bargaining, many do not believe in its inherent virtues. They comply because to do otherwise would be foolhardy, given their awareness of the coercive techniques available to those with more power. To an outside observer, their actions may reflect consensus; but when their motives are probed, a different picture emerges. While this work is a helpful antidote to the static, conflict-free view of courts to which we have been witness, it does not go far enough to explain the larger role of courts in the society. It shows us the similarities between courtroom activity and other social processes, but ignores the special role of courts and the ways in which their activities differentiate them from other institutions. For example, courts may be compared to hospitals in that both are filled with workers who must negotiate a reality if their work is to be accomplished. They differ dramatically, however, because of their special relationship to the state and their role as the purveyor of social order. As Day and Day (1977) note, research which

focuses upon the ways in which actors negotiate and con-
struct reality is deficient because the conceptualization of
negotiation and bargaining presented suggests a cooperative
and usually smooth process involving temporary disruptions
in normal routines and new tacit understandings, with little
actual domination or oppression emanating from different
bases of power within and without the organization. So while
Mather (1979) and Heumann (1977) suggest a world which is
more conflictual than other researchers, it is still one that
does not adequately address the parameters within which actors constrict their modus operandi. The power relationships
within courts is important in understanding who does what to
whom, with which results, and why. But while this micro
political analysis is interesting, it cannot explain why certain
classes of defendants are treated in the way they are or why
particular laws are upheld, with transgressors being severely
punished, at some times more than others. To understand
these processes we must move away from the court and the
institutions immediately surrounding it (i.e., police, sponsoring organizations) to an examination of the material forces
which surround it and impinge upon it.

CRITICAL VIEWS

While this article has attempted to remedy the emphasis
upon stability and consensus in earlier literature by pointing
to possible conflicts among courtroom actors, it is important
to emphasize that conflict and differential power are not sufficient explanations for courtroom activity either. Just as
participants are not always united in wanting to dispose of
cases in the same way, or in their ability to always have their
will recognized, neither are they continually engaged in combat. This lack of combat can, in part, be attributed to actors'
shared belief in defendants' guilt. That a presumption of guilt

allows them to process cases expeditiously is not questioned. What remains to be explained is why this belief takes hold. We must also wonder why there are few financial or professional incentives motivating courtroom actors to spend more time on their cases. The lack of such incentives (see Nardulli, 1978) and the belief in defendants' guilt—in clear violation of the presumption of innocence upon which criminal law is based—alert us to the special role of trial courts, a role which cannot be understood by focusing only upon the differential power of actors or the relationship between the court and its immediate environment.

The demographic characteristics of defendants processed in trial courts is an important indicator of the court's mission, and the type of internal operations which has arisen to fulfill it. Although defendants are generally young, male members of minority groups, these characteristics have been given short shrift in the literature we have cited. The failure to consider them in the operation of criminal courts is striking. Galanter (1974), for example, has distinguished in the civil area between one-shotters, who rarely resort to litigation, and repeat players, who make frequent use of the courts. Repeat players are usually richer and more powerful, with these attributes bestowing advantages upon them, not least of which is the purchase of legal talent.

If the civil system works best for those with advantages, we should not be surprised to find that the criminal side does, too. On the occasions when the wealthy or powerful are charged with criminal acts, they, too, are able to work the system to their advantage (Cartwright, 1979; Thompson, 1977). But such parties rarely appear in criminal courts, thus leaving the system to deal with a mass of social refuge who can neither exert control nor work the system to their own advantage. Given their position, this clientele attracts representation from the lower echelons of the legal profession (Wice, 1978; Blumberg, 1967) who have neither the will nor economic standing to sacrifice too much for a particular case. The lowly are thus served by the lowly, further substantiating their disadvantageous position and allowing the class nature of justice to become apparent.

The disadvantaged nature of defendants helps shape relationships among courtroom actors. Because defendants are generally assumed guilty and unworthy—attributes easily applied to members of minority groups—courtroom actors can easily agree upon dispositions. Thus, the important agreements among actors are not ones of how to shape work, but ideological ones based on the necessity for social order and the need to control particular elements of the population. Even when courtroom actors conflict over strategies, or when one party is better able to make the other's job more difficult, they are all united in administering outcomes; an assumption of the law's legitimacy and the obligation to attend to those who violate it is shared by all. When conflicts occur, however, they may alert us to something other than inadequate socialization among courtroom actors. The occasional appearance of wealthy defendants with motivated, well-paid attorneys, for example, may threaten agreements regarding proper dispositions for particular crimes.

Generally, the social control work of the court can be accomplished despite the systemic inequalities it fosters. This can be done, without protest from attorneys, because the doctrine of legal thought to which they are subject allows these inequities to be assuaged. Actions which might conflict with ethical traditions are shrouded in notions of the laws legitimacy, thus insuring perpetuation of a system of domination and social control (Tushnet, 1978). The system is further legitimated by a courtroom drama which pays "symbolic homage to the adversary tenets of legal rationality" (Balbus, 1973). Judicial assurances of defendants' rights not to be pressured are examples of such symbolic homage.

The literature we have cited has not attended to these factors because it has generally ignored the special role of the court. That the court must control certain activities and individuals and then legitimate the actions it takes with regard to them are factors affecting the courts operations which are not generally considered. Since Balbus (1973) and Heydebrand (1979) have specifically addressed these issues in their work, the deficiencies of other research on courts become apparent. Balbus, for example, examines the structure of the court by linking it to the court's historic role in the preservation of order. He sees the court's role as maintaining order, achieving formal rationality, and perpetuating the organization. Striking a balance among these functions—which are contradictory—is the work to which courtroom actors are addressed. The vast differences between the ideal and the real, however, are masked, because to do otherwise would undermine the ideal of law and equal justice which the court is to uphold. If this mask were dropped, the legitimacy upon which the court—and by extension the state for whom it is a representative—rests would be endangered, with the possible provocation of assaults upon it by individuals no longer mesmerized by assurances of equality. Courtroom actors, then, are neither primarily nor solely responsible for charting the direction of the court, as some of the literature we have cited suggests. The goals of the court, in addition, are not matters of individual whim, nor are they the result of aggregates of people pursuing different and often antagonistic interests (Feeley, 1979: 278). They are linked to the court's repressive role and the need for it to appear legitimate if the state's mandate is to go unchallenged.

Focusing upon the treatment accorded blacks arrested during the "riots" of the 1960s as evidence of the court's conflicting functions, Balbus concludes that, because of their color:

> the interest of court authorities—as well as the defense community—in formal rationality was simply not as manifest as it would otherwise have been. The blatent abrogations of legality which did occur during and immediately following the revolts would have been more difficult to justify, and therefore far less likely to have occurred, had whites, rather than blacks, been the object of the sanctioning process [1973: 257].

Thus, in striking a balance among the court's functions, the maintenance of order took precedence. If the system is to survive, however, repression cannot always dominate. In the instances in which order is emphasized, increased attention is directed toward the court's ability to fulfill the requirements of formal rationality, thus endangering agreements regarding the allocation of work and the disposition of cases which depart from the legal ideal. Factors like these can obviously not be considered when the court is viewed as a mechanism existing solely for the disposition of cases, without inquiry into the value or purpose of the work or the necessity for speed, apart from the will of the workers.

The movement to make courts more efficient can also not be understood by focusing upon the internal dynamics of courtroom activity, even if potential power differentials and processual aspects are stressed. These explanations are incomplete because the movement has arisen outside the court, with its proposed innovations often implemented over the desires of courtroom actors. Many of these innovations, such as Speedy Trial statutes, and Rules of Superintendence, have been implemented to expedite court practices and some, if fully adopted, would require greater accountability and effort from professionals who had previously been thought autonomous (see Sheskin and Grau, 1980). Technical strategies directed at changing the nature of courtroom tasks, such as video technology and forecasting models, have also been introduced (Heydebrand, 1980). These new strategies emanate, in part, from the fiscal crisis of the state which directly impinges upon the court. Faced with declining resources, with increased demand for court services, the court must change to become more cost-effective. But because its basic functions do not change, adherence to the ethos of formal rationality and legitimacy cannot just be forsaken. Thus many new procedures are couched in their value and concern for defendants; speedy trial statutes, for example, are said to keep defendants from languishing in jail but, at the same time, they reduce operating costs to counties which had previously warehoused large numbers of individuals awaiting trial. Because the court must maintain order, innovations cannot be adopted which lay bare the repressive role it plays for the state. Legal actors cannot just dispose of cases, ignoring due process guarantees, even if it is less expensive to process cases that way. To adopt this strategy—one, as Balbus notes, that is adopted after large-scale disturbances— invites public scrutiny, thus undermining the court's imperative for organizational maintenance and the need for its actions to appear legitimate. But to the extent that the court is a vehicle of the state, it is affected by, and must respond to, the state's fiscal problems in ways which may not suit the immediate interests of legal actors. Thus, although their perceptions of reality are important, they provide only a partial view of the factors affecting them. To understand these, trial courts analyses must be placed in a larger social and historical perspective. Changes in work, relations among legal actors, adherence to due process guarantees must all be viewed as processes affected by historical factors and economic demands.

That a preponderance of the research on trial courts has failed to deal with these factors can be attributed to the assumptions which have guided research in the area. Such relationships are ignored because the desirability of the already given social order is not questioned; thus the need to critically examine the relationship between trial courts and the state is not realized. Instead, we see a variety of insular analyses which seek to understand trial courts apart from the larger social structure in which they are imbedded.

REFERENCES

BALBUS, I. (1973) The Dialectics of Legal Repression. New York: Russell Sage.

BLUMBERG, A. (1967) Criminal Justice. Chicago: Quadrangle.

CARTWRIGHT, G. (1979) Blood Will Tell. New York: Harcourt Brace Jovanovich.

CASPER, J. (1978) Criminal Courts: The Defendant's Perspective. Washington, DC: Law Enforcement Assistance Administration.

DAY, B. and J. DAY (1977) "A review of the current state of negotiated order theory." Sociological Quarterly 18.

EISENSTEIN, J. and H. JACOB (1977) Felony Justice. Boston: Little, Brown.

FEELEY, M. (1979) The Process Is the Punishment. New York: Russell Sage.

GALANTER, M. (1974) "Why the "haves" come out ahead: Speculations on the limits of legal change." Law and Society Review 9.

GERTH, H. and C. W. MILLS (1953) Social Theory and Social Structure. New York: Harcourt Brace Jovanovich.

GORDON, D. (1974) "Capitalism, class and crime in America," in C. Reasons (ed.) The Criminologist. Santa Monica, CA: Goodyear.

GOULDNER, A. (1970) The Coming Crisis of Western Sociology. New York: Basic Books.

HEUMANN, M. (1977) Plea Bargaining. Chicago: University of Chicago Press.

HEYDEBRAND, W. (1979) "The technocratic administration of justice," in S. Spitzer (ed.) Research in Law and Sociology. Greenwich, CT: Jai Press.

LEVIN, M. (1975) "Delay in 5 criminal courts." Journal of Legal Studies 4.

LIPETZ, M. (1980) "Routine and deviations: The strength of the courtroom workgroup in a misdemeanor court." International Journal of the Sociology of Law 8.

MANNHEIM, K. (1971) "Conservative thought," on K. Wolff (ed.) From Karl Mannheim. New York: Oxford University Press.

MATHER, L. (1979) Plea Bargaining or Trial Lexington, MA: Lexington Books.

NARDULLI, P. (1978) The Courtroom Elite. Cambridge, MA: Ballinger.

PARSONS, T. (1951) The Social System. New York: Macmillan.

QUINNEY, R. (1974) The Critique of Legal Order. Boston: Little, Brown.

QUINNEY, R. (1972) "From repression to liberation: Social theory in a radical age," in R. Scott and J. Douglas (eds.) Theoretical Perspectives in Deviance. New York: Basic Books.

RUBENSTEIN, M. (1976) "Plea bargaining in Alaska." Judicature 10.

SHESKIN, A. and C. GRAU (1980) "Judicial responses to technocratic reform," in J. Cramer (ed.) The Judiciary. Beverly Hills, CA: Sage.

SHOVER, N. (1975) "Criminal behavior as theoretical praxis." Issues in Criminology 10(Spring): 95-108.

SKOLNICK, J. (1969) The Politics of Protest. New York: Touchstone.

SUDNOW, D. (1965) "Normal crimes." Social Problems 12.

THOMPSON, T. (1977) Blood and Money. New York: Dell.

TUSHNET, M. (1978) "A Marxist interpretation of American law." Marxist Perspectives 1.

WALSH, D. (1972) "Functionalism and systems theory," in P. Filmer et al. (eds.) New Directions in Sociological Theory. Boston: MIT Press.

WEBER, M. (1954) Max Weber on Law in Economy and Society. New York: Touchstone.

WICE, P. (1978) Criminal Lawyers. Beverly Hills, CA: Sage.

Part II

THE JUDICIARY

Chapter 5

LEARNING ABOUT TRIAL JUDGING:
THE SOCIALIZATION OF STATE TRIAL JUDGES

LENORE ALPERT

The socialization of judges on the bench—the process by which judges learn in office and the effect of this adaptation upon their behavior—is an unexplored area of judicial research. While the idea of growth on the bench is neither startling nor recent, we know relatively little about the actual process by which newcomers are transformed into sitting jurists. Other than anecdotal or biographical works,[1] only a handful of studies have examined on-bench socialization and most have concentrated on specific areas of learning.[2] For example, Cook (1971) studied the impact of federal judicial seminars on docket management of federal district judges; Luskin (1976) explored preliminary hearings in Detroit courts; and Heumann (1978) investigated plea bargaining among Connecticut court judges, prosecutors, and defense attorneys. Only Carp and Wheeler (1972) explored on-bench learning as a general phenomenon rather than a narrower focus on one specific area of learning. In their study of federal

Author's Note: *The author expresses her appreciation to the judges of Florida who participated in this study. She also wishes to thank Professor Herbert Jacob who provided critical comments on earlier versions of this article.*

Computing work utilized the facilities of Vogelback Computing Center located at Northwestern University. This work was carried out under a doctoral disser-

district judges, they described the areas and sources of on-bench learning that these trial judges experienced in their socialization into judging.

Unlike these studies, this research will rely upon the literature of the organizational behavior field on socialization within work organizations,[3] linking the socialization of state trial judges with the theoretical literature of that field. In this context, judicial socialization is conceptualized as a form of organizational socialization involving "the social and psychological adjustment of men to their work settings," whereby "knowledge, abilities, and motivation" are transmitted to the newcomer (Van Maanen, 1976: 67; 77). As in other organizations, newcomers to the bench are "taught and learn 'the ropes' of a particular organization role" (Van Maanen and Schein, 1979: 209-264). During socialization new judges learn organizational goals, preferred means for achieving these goals, responsibilities of their role, required behavior, and rules for maintaining the courts as an organization (Schein, 1968: 3). In short, those who are socialized learn to perceive the organizational world similarly to others already in the organization.[4]

Like the Carp and Wheeler (1972) study, this research will focus on more general aspects of trial judging and how they are learned. It will explore problems associated with trial judging and the resolution of these problems during socialization to the bench. The specific concern is how judges become socialized into their role as organizational members—what they learn, when they learn, who they learn from, and how they learn. I shall begin with a formulation of stages of socialization on the bench, a description of activities

tation grant from the Graduate School at Northwestern University and under grant #80-IJ-CX-0005 from the National Institute of Justice, U.S. Department of Justice. The views expressed are those of the author alone and do not reflect opinions of the National Institute of Justice nor the Graduate School of Northwestern University.

in each stage, and the outcomes of each stage, in order to develop the context within which socialization occurs for state trial judges.

STAGES OF JUDICIAL SOCIALIZATION

Because on-bench socialization developed in this article is closely linked to the stages of judicial socialization, it is appropriate to describe them at this point. These stages were developed from a set of interviews with Florida trial judges and provide the basis for this study of on-bench socialization. These stages rely upon those formulated in studies of organizational socialization.[5] Five stages of socialization were identified for trial judges: Professional socialization—a pre-bench stage—and four on-bench stages—Initiation, Resolution, Establishment, and Commitment stages.[6]

The Professional Socialization stage is analogous to the Anticipatory Socialization stage of organization studies. During this period, individuals receive formal legal training in law schools and informal legal training in legal practice. Some also hold public offices that may help prepare them for the bench, for example, as prosecutors or local government attorneys. Impressions that are formed about judging during this period may not be entirely accurate; Heumann's recent study found that newcomers do not have "a realistic perspective on the operations of the criminal court" (1978: 153). While legal norms and values may be widely shared as a result of legal training, judges may not be prepared for the conflict between their idealized views of the office and the reality of their actual experiences on the bench.

Upon becoming a judge, the Initiation stage begins, analogous to the Encounter stage of organization studies. Here the newcomer judge first encounters judging; it is a period of rapid initial adjustment to the bench during the first year, characterized by role definition and reality shock as the judge realizes judging may not be all that he expected. The concerns of "being a judge" are immediate—learning how to behave in the new position, how to maintain order in the course of hearings or trials, how to administer the docket, and how to make proper rulings. During this period the newcomer judge may experience an identity crisis, as he seeks to mold his self-identity to fit the new role. Further, it is also a period of bewilderment and confidence building.

This initial stage is followed by the Resolution stage, analogous to the Accommodation stage of organization studies. From about years 1 through 4, intensive learning occurs on the bench, such that by the beginning of year 5, most are comfortable with all aspects of trial judging. Roles become more clearly defined during this stage as the judge completes his transformation from advocate to arbiter. He begins to deal with role conflict during this stage, learning to handle isolation on the bench and to manage pressures from within the court as well as from the community outside the court.

Management of this role conflict continues into the Establishment stage, or "settling in" period, analogous to parts of the Role Management stage of organization studies. From about years 5 through 9, more long-term coping with judicial life occurs, for example, handling social and political isolation. Judges are confronted not only with conflicting demands from within the organization but also from within their personal lives. In particular, during this stage many judges experience a "midcareer crisis" in which personal needs and family needs must be managed and resolved in order to remain on the bench. This is a decision period when some decide not to make judging their career, preferring to use their remaining years to better themselves financially in non-judicial pursuits. Most, however, decide to remain on the bench, looking forward to a pension as they complete their judicial career. These are the judges who have adapted to judicial life and are comfortable with a more isolated lifestyle. They find judging personally fulfilling—"It's a decision that this is what you think you do well and you like it better than anything else."

From this period of introspection and thinking about the future, judges enter the final stage, the Commitment stage, analogous to some aspects of the Role Management stage of other studies. It is a period of great satisfaction and involvement with judging; identification with the court increases. Comradeship and dedication mark this final stage, accompanied by a sense of serenity and accomplishment.

In the context of these stages, we will now develop themes of judicial socialization as we explore how the judicial career evolves.

AN OVERVIEW—
THEMES OF ON-BENCH LEARNING

Carp and Wheeler (1972) identified three areas of on-bench learning in their study of federal trial judges—learning about legal issues, administrative issues, and personal issues. Legal issues involve matters of substantive law and legal procedure, an area in which most judges would be expected to be well-prepared by virtue of their legal training and attorney experiences. Administrative issues involve supervising court staff, organizing and planning the docket, and managing judicial time, an area in which judges might be somewhat less well-prepared since administrative training is rarely covered in legal coursework either during law school or afterward in continuing legal education. Finally, personal issues involve shifting from attorney to judge and managing the isolation of the office and community pressures, an area in which prebench experiences might offer little guidance, consequently raising more unexpected problems for the newcomer judge.

These three areas of on-bench learning were explored in this study of Florida circuit judges to determine their relevance for the socialization of state trial judges. Florida judges were asked about each of these areas of judicial learning, first in focused interviews and later in a statewide survey, to ascertain what these state trial judges learned on the bench, from whom they learned, and in what manner they learned.[7] According to one judge who was interviewed, learning about these areas of judging occurs in cycles throughout the judicial career:

> I think that they [these issues] probably permeate to some degree all of what we do, and with me, I would graph it for you with a bunch of wavy lines . . . sometimes other ones would be high and another would be low. You go through short cycles and long cycles . . . for example, there's always some degree of administrative problems. They increase at times when you're involved in having to make administrative decisions. Like if I were administrative judge or chief judge . . . they would be right at the top of the cycle. . . . Legal problems were much higher at the beginning of my career. . . . Administrative is not quite as high at that point of time either. And I don't think the psychological existed . . . I probably wasn't aware [of it] because I spent so much time and energy just getting [myself] grounded substantively and procedurally.

Before turning to the survey data, several key themes articulated by trial judges in focused interviews will be examined.

WHAT FLORIDA JUDGES LEARN
ABOUT TRIAL JUDGING

Legal Issues

Almost immediately newcomer judges are confronted with procedural and substantive legal matters, although concern for these matters also continues throughout the judicial career. Varied legal backgrounds do not always prepare new judges to assume their specific assignments on the bench. One recurrent theme from the interviews is the self-education required to adapt to judging, although sources of help do come from fellow judges, court staff, and attorneys. According to one newcomer judge, self-education was coupled with formal coursework and help from knowledgeable friends:

> It was a period of adjustment for me to go from being a 95-98% civil practice to a 75-80% judge of essentially criminal cases. . . . I have also gone through the stage of learning a relatively, for all practical purposes, a new area of law to me, which is the search and seizure issues and the *Miranda* area and a number of the other issues involved in criminal cases, and incidentally the discovery proceedings under the new criminal proceedings in juvenile, which were new to me, and I had to learn the rules of that. And so I've gone through a learning process . . . I had to educate myself. . . . I went to the course that's run by the judges . . . the new judges' conference . . . And I went to some continuing legal education courses that involved criminal practice that were helpful, but I would say the education process was 75-80-90% on my own. . . . Basically I educated myself [on] the juvenile system and the criminal system. I relied on the courses to some extent but not a great deal, just really to confirm that I wasn't far off the mark. And then I had friends from practice who were in criminal and when I had a new issue and one in which my

decision made me feel uncomfortable, I called them, to confirm that there wasn't anything I wasn't overlooking.

This focus upon learning by doing is due in part to the nature of trial judging, in which the trial judge is confronted with unfamiliar legal territory in a relatively isolated judicial setting early in the socialization process. The prevailing pattern involves little formal training for newcomer judges. In Florida a one-week seminar is offered for all newcomers through the state trial judges' organization.[8] Formal courses through the National Judicial College are usually attended later in the judicial career. Further, though help is available from others within the court organization, this sharing of information is usually supplemental to that which the judge himself experiences on the bench. In the course of a trial or hearing, it is difficult to seek advice at the moment it is needed; consequently, much of what is learned on the state trial bench, just as Carp and Wheeler found on the federal trial bench, is "learning by doing"—what Carp and Wheeler called "sink or swim."

This trial-by-error process that characterizes judicial socialization was summarized by one judge, who recalled how he became more self-assured on the bench as a result of his experiences as judge:

I think after awhile I felt more comfortable and I am more self-assured after doing it [judging] more ... after awhile becoming knowledgeable about the legal and administrative responsibilities that were expected [that] allows you not to have as many "up in the air" kind of feelings that you have when you began. But I think that would take place with anybody with time—I think it is a "learn by doing" kind of thing.

While focusing generally on this theme of self-education, trial judges did report other sources of learning about legal issues. One judge recalled guidance he received from fellow trial judges during his introduction to the bench:

> I think that the most extensive learning period came the first year. Almost every day and certainly every week, a judge, even in the civil division, is likely to run into a facet of procedure or law . . . that he doesn't feel very comfortable with . . . I was fortunate to have assistance from other judges; that's primarily the way you learn a great many things—by doing and by osmosis and by listening and [by] watching them . . . There wasn't time to do any essential research; you had to ask a judge you knew.

Another judge mentioned informal talks with fellow judges and observation of their courtroom techniques to remedy his inexperience with domestic cases:

> I had no experience with domestic relations at all, so before I came to the bench I came down to a few of the brother judges and sat in on some of their divorces and then over lunch . . . asked them questions. And they told me their philosophy.

Many judges model themselves after judges they practiced before as attorneys before becoming judges. One judge recalled his emulation of judges he respected:

> I've been influenced by the judges that I've practiced before, and those that I respected and thought were good judges, I've tried to emulate in my own way. I try to run my court on time . . . I used to be disturbed as a lawyer about a judge who would be . . . late to court. . . . I don't run it that way.

Several judges relied upon court staff in helping them learn to handle trial judging:

> When you first go on the bench you don't know how to open a court, you just kind of grit your teeth and go along with it. And in juvenile—here juvenile is isolated because you're down there and you had counselors there and everybody there—oldtimers that you kind of rely on, court staff.

Surprisingly, many judges recalled that attorneys were not entirely helpful during their initial period of adjustment to the bench. Instead, the attorneys played "lawyer games" with the judges, testing them to see how far they could go with a particular judge. One judge summarized the role of attorneys in his socialization:

> I think all lawyers sort of test a new judge, the new guy on the block, to see what they can get away with to begin with, and as soon as the parameters of conduct and everything are felt between the judge and the lawyers, then it all settles down very quickly. Yes, the lawyers were helpful, but they didn't go out of their way, I wouldn't say that. You see, if the judge has got problems, all he has to do is ask the lawyers to submit a brief and then they're gonna have to look up the law and give the cases and the judge can study it.

Coping with attorneys is like a marriage of necessity, with judges requiring the legal expertise of attorneys in their daily tasks, yet not quite confident to what extent they may rely upon these attorneys. During the initial adjustment to judging, judges must shape the parameters for appropriate behavior in their interactions with attorneys. As part of this adjustment, they learn which attorneys they can trust and which ones will mislead them.

In contrast to help from those within the court organization, few judges mentioned formal training as aiding their adjustment to trial judging. Formal courses are not widespread and those in which judges participate are often attended later rather than earlier in their tenure. For example, the National Judicial College was referred to by several judges as helpful, but only in the context of having been on the bench a while and already being knowledgeable about judging. This mode of formal training is viewed as a means to perfect techniques and learn different approaches to judging rather than to learn the basic tools of judging. One judge summarized this contribution of the Judicial College:

We have our judges' conferences and these are educational programs. I've attended three sessions at the National College of the State Judiciary. . . . Really you need to have a little time on the bench before you attend the National College because when you get out there you see how it's done throughout the country, and they don't have a program for really teaching you something. It's more a place where you go and discuss ideas and approaches and if you've been on the bench long enough to understand the problem, then you can appreciate the solutions from Oregon or somewhere else.

Evidently judges are largely on their own in learning about legal issues, with whatever help they can secure from those in the court organization. Reliance on others, however, is not the net result of learning about trial judging, but rather, as one judge emphasized, only the first step in a continuing growth process that occurs throughout the judicial career:

When I entered a totally new area where I had never been involved before, after I had been a judge . . . I went through a second—another period of initiation . . . That happened to me after four years after I'd been a judge. . . . Somebody in the field is recognized as knowing what is the answer and what should be done, and there's almost a reliance upon them, either as people or even as an institution. . . . Then you go through that period, cause that period is I think a grow-through period . . . where you get to the point where you recognize that that person or that institution or whatever it is just doesn't have the answers. They think they've got the answers, but they really don't have the answers and if they present it to the effect that they have the answers [and don't] . . . then there's a tremendous disillusionment that sets in. . . . and then that's when the real growth begins and you really start to struggle and try to put the pieces together. [After 5 years], I was getting to the point where now I see where the process is, now I see why I'm doing these things.

In summary, learning about legal issues is largely an informal process of self-education—"do it yourself but rely on others when you can." It is one in which members of the court organization—fellow judges, court staff, and attorneys—can aid newcomer judges if they are so inclined. It is also one in which judges learn whom to trust, while ultimately building self-confidence and reliance upon their own personal resources to become independent of advice from others that characterizes their early adjustment to trial judging. With this newly found confidence, judges continue to grow on the bench and shape their own responses to legal issues they encounter as trial judges.

Administrative Issues

Along with legal matters, newcomer judges are also confronted with administrative concerns early in their socialization. They must quickly learn to manage their dockets and handle their court staffs. One prevalent theme from the interviews is that pre-judicial experience does not adequately prepare newcomers for this aspect of judging. One newcomer judge described his adjustment to this area of judging:

> Administratively I've had a new ball game because my secretary and I are responsible for all calendar setting. We set the hearing dates and that's something that we've never—we learned as much as we could before we came in here and unfortunately we didn't spend enough time in transition to grasp it, although I was out here for three days, primarily watching what the judge did in court. She spent a full day with the person's secretary, but we just didn't grasp the concept of calendaring having never done it before. That is the biggest problem we've had. . . . The judge is ultimately responsible for—while he doesn't employ the clerk or employ the state attorney or public defender—he is still responsible for the official functions in his court and he's got to direct those other people and not just leave it to them to direct him.

As in learning about legal issues, learning to handle administrative issues also requires much self-education and "learning by doing," although there is apparently more guidance available from other court staff than in other areas of judging. And like legal matters, adjusting to administrative tasks is a continuing process that occurs throughout the judicial career. Adapting to administrative issues involves not only the initial adjustment but also shifts in division assignments that raise new administrative tasks throughout the career. For example, one judge recalled how helpful the staff of the clerk's office had been in his adjustment to the probate division:

> We had excellent clerks—we still do. I am now in the probate department and I just transferred there. We have good girls there, really paralegals. They are so good, they know the

statutes better than I do, and they send up notes with each file so you just look at that and see whether you approved this, and they give me that statute which concerned it. It is just wonderful the way those girls are. I have always found that the help was not a problem. The only problem we really had was an overload of cases. You just can't keep up with it.

A third aspect of learning administrative issues involves devising new strategies to handle the judicial workload. Like the adjustment to a new division, this is also a continuing process throughout the judicial career. Trial judges appear concerned with caseload statistics, one of the more visible measures of their performance in office, and much energy in the administrative area is directed toward achieving more effective disposition of cases. For example, one judge described his efforts to manage his workload through controlling the cancellation of hearings by attorneys:

Administering the workload—that's probably the biggest problem that judges have, more at our level than at the appellate level because it is the custom to allow the lawyers who set the hearing to cancel it, and that means that ordinarily unless the judge instructs otherwise or has a different routine, you can come in at the time of the hearing and cancel it or you can call anytime before. So in this manner, you can take hold—if something seems to be being dragged for reasons you don't understand and the court can set a hearing, the lawyer must attend. . . . [I] require the lawyers to attend when the lawyers set the hearing unless it's cancelled about 10 days ahead or unless you file a formal motion for continuance . . . if you have a good cause to continue it. But today, the lawyer has no good cause. He shows up if he wants to or cancels it. If he doesn't cancel it and does not show up and doesn't have a good reason, I fine him. So he doesn't do that more than once.

Another aspect of managing the judicial workload involves making efficient use of judicial time in planning for trials that are settled too late to permit scheduling another proceeding. Again, administrative strategies can be formulated to handle this contingency, strategies that judges develop both early and late in their judicial career. One judge illuminated one such scheduling technique to circumvent this administrative problem:

> In _____ County, roughly half your time is in hearings and half of it is in trials. So the other half that's in trials is also a difficult administrative problem because probably 75% of the continuances or settlements take place too late, and again you can only guess. Now I deal with that in this matter—I have, except for dissolution matters and custody matters, I try jury and nonjury cases every other two-week period and I try the jury cases first ordinarily. The way that I deal with it is I accept far more cases than I think I will get to and normally it works out all right. . . . In the beginning I believed if two weeks before the trial everybody felt that they were going to trial, they probably would go and so I would wind up with more days of no trials and no hearings becaufe . . . cases were settled [at the last minute].

In sum, learning to handle administrative issues is similar to legal issues. Members of the court organization are instrumental, especially court staff, but the major responsibility for resolving administrative problems rests with the trial judge. Ultimately, success in handling administrative concerns depends upon the ingenuity of the trial judge and his willingness to develop techniques to manage the workload, techniques that are formulated throughout the socialization process. Most important, little formal training is provided to aid the trial judge in managing his workload; he primarily learns through experimenting with means to handle administrative problems—learning by doing—just as with legal issues.

Personal Issues

Personal issues, like legal and administrative issues, surface both early and late in the judicial career, but in contrast to the two latter areas, receive less attention from others in the court organization. Judges must make this psychological adjustment to office largely on their own without help from their brethren or from other members of the court staff. For this reason, this area of judging may pose more difficult adjustment problems than either of the other two areas of judging. Personal issues raise two major sets of problems for trial judges—coping with social and political isolation and handling the authority of the office.

Coping with social and political isolation and underlying norms of judicial impartiality raises psychological problems that arise early in the judicial career. Judges must strive for total objectivity in their administration of justice, for behavior that is beyond reproach. To achieve this objectivity requires severing social relationships with members of the bar, those that by training and background judges are closest to, and replacing it with a "cult of the robe" or camaraderie among fellow judges. It also involves reconciling ideals of justice with the political reality of the judicial system, a system that is not entirely separated from the political arena.

The problem of social isolation from attorneys was mentioned repeatedly by judges, suggesting it is a key adjustment to trial judging. Knowing intellectually that judging is circumscribed is not the same as experiencing that isolation from former friends, as this one example illustrates:

The isolation, while I knew intellectually that there would be a great deal of isolation emotionally I hadn't sought, I hadn't perceived myself as a gregarious person that liked people, talking to a lot of people. As a judge, you have very few confidantes, nearly none in judicial matters and in personal matters very few. A judge has the political, in the generic sense, the political problems of election and office-holding. In addition, he has the problems with the confidentiality of matters he hears, avoiding even the appearance of impropriety by contacting improperly different people. There is a great deal of isolation; I found out very quickly that a judge and his conduct is more circumscribed than I had thought. . . . It's a lonely profession. . . . You don't socialize much with lawyers. . . . I think you become more family-oriented. I spend more time with my wife and we do things together. . . . Essentially a judge is an island.

Further, while social restrictions of the position were anticipated, the general confining nature of the job was not, as one judge quickly pointed out:

Almost no judge ever realizes the personal changes that are required when he becomes a judge, the personal adjustments. . . . To be a judge is very restrictive personally because at once you virtually have to discard your friendships with lawyers. You have to be very careful about that and of course as time moves along, the activities of judges in personal business have been very seriously restricted. Plus it is a much more confining job than anybody who is not a judge realizes. That is, if you take it seriously and most of the judges that I know do take it seriously. . . . Well, I understood that being a judge [required] that my contacts with lawyers would have to be very limited and very careful, [but] as far as being confining, no, I didn't think about that. . . . The economic restrictions were imposed some good length of time after I became a judge, the social restrictions are immediately noticeable and so is the confining nature of the job. . . . You adapt or you quit, supposedly, or you are certainly extremely unhappy.

To overcome this isolation, judges subscribe to a kind of "cult of the robe"—a fraternal brotherhood that one judge likened to a fraternity:

> The judiciary is a fraternity and it has initiation rites, and it has a uniform that you wear, and it has books that are worshipped by the fraternity. Maybe it's a religion almost, and once you belong it's almost like you have a private group, you know, and you go wherever you want to go or go to one of these meetings with judges, and you find yourself accepted by people as a brother—literally as a fraternity brother. . . . By joining the fraternity it is necessary from their point of view that I subscribe to their ritual if you will, to their fraternal, their common ideas that the fraternity espouses.

Another aspect of this isolation involves coping with political isolation, adjusting to the judicial system, and reconciling the realities of that system with norms of political independence. Court reformers have long argued that norms of impartiality demand such independence from the political system—a key argument against a partisan elective judiciary. In Florida, trial judges are elected on a nonpartisan ballot, but as one judge observed, politics still remains an integral part of that system, making it sometimes difficult to bridge the gap between ideals and reality:

> I felt it myself, and I noticed that new judges kind of find it difficult [to] get comfortable with what you're doing and relate to the judicial role. You're within a system and you have, like I had an ideal—you had the ideals when you come in as to what a judge is and you think a judge as being above politics—he rules on the law and makes independent judgments and that's what I strive for, and that's what you're supposed to strive for. But you begin to see at some point in

the system how it's not always that way. There are a lot of politics involved in the judicial system.... Your ideals confront the reality or the practicality of it ... in criminal, especially, a person can be—you don't realize the pressures that come to bear on you from the public, say if you're doing what you think is fair and right in a case and the remedy someone doesn't like is appealed.

Yet not all trial judges ascribe to such ideals of political isolation. For example, one judge rejected the need for isolation from political matters, noting his continued political activism on the bench that he felt aided his judging:

I don't feel as isolated as some judges. I was for most of my career actively involved in politics ... The only thing that I stopped doing [upon becoming judge] was raising money. But I didn't drop a single community membership and that ranges all the way from the NAACP to the American Civil Liberties Union back across the board to the Criminal Justice Committee, Judicial Council, for the State of Florida ... I have continued to be an activist as a black person in our community and as a politician in our community. I did drop all direct political affiliations and committees because that is required by law, and I would not participate in any direct politics as it pertains to law ... But in expression of ideas I can't find that there is any conflict.... You see, I am a human being first, I am a citizen as it pertains to this country second, and I am incidentally a judge. That is what I do for a living. I am going to do it and do it well. I am not going to let it get me in a position where I am backed off into a corner so that I don't hear the world ... I think judges get caught in that and then when you are not in tune with the times, when you are not in tempo, you are not giving forth a full range of what happens in life with people when giving a decision. I don't find myself isolated.

In summary, isolation is a phenomenon that trial judges must cope with upon coming to the bench. It is immediately restrictive of their interaction with attorneys and later in their political activity. Both appear to pose psychological problems for judges as they learn to cope with personal issues of judging. But unlike learning to handle legal and administrative issues, judges receive little guidance from those in the court organization in handling this aspect of judging.

In addition to coping with social and political isolation, trial judges are also confronted with awesome authority and power over the lives of other persons as they learn to handle personal aspects of judging. Learning to handle this authority poses one of the more difficult problems of judging, for managing the authority of the office ultimately structures not only relationships with attorneys, litigants, and court staff but also relationships with the community at large. It is often a disconcerting experience, as illustrated by one newcomer's initial adjustment to this authority:

> I am aware that very significant changes took place during my first year. When I started, when I first sat on the bench, I was very uneasy, I suppose was the feeling, I was very uncomfortable. Sitting in a position of authority does not come easily to me; I don't like that kind of role as a personality. I am more of a reflective person . . . so I found it very uncomfortable to exercise the role of authority. . . . I grew with time to be more comfortable with the authority that I had. . . . I felt I was being reasonable but I grew more and more confident with the position and the power that I had which at first I was pretty uncomfortable with. I was very shocked at the impact of everything I said had on people, not only on the individuals who were there for the litigation—the parties— but on the lawyers, on the court personnel, and others. I was not accustomed to that being an individual practitioner for the past 8 years—that people would hang on every word I said. But I grew more and more accustomed to that.

Another judge described the interaction between power and authority in trial judging and the necessity for recognizing the power of self in office in order to constructively structure that authority. Reconciling self with office—or power with authority—may be linked to a judge's self-concept and his own personal fulfillment, suggesting intricate psychological interaction in resolving this key socialization dilemma. The general norm seems to be that "the more authority you have, the less you have need to use it," as illustrated in the reflections of one trial judge:

I think it's an interesting phenomenon—power and authority—how they interact—whether or not there's almost a dependence that develops in us . . . [on] that authority, in order to build our pseudo power, our security . . . our self-confidence, our self-concept . . . The authority is there . . . a tremendously uplifting kind of thing . . . the same thing I would . . . say [about] a minister or priest. . . . Judges must be measured in the area of power and their ability to cope with their own power. I believe that the less power that a person perceives himself deep inside having, if they are fortunate to ascend to a position of judge, the worst judge they are . . . because they tend to fill in that authority that they have in the position . . . and you see things that are very abusive by judges. . . . On the other hand, my theory is that the person who is more self-fulfilled and has a strong sense of power and can use the power, knows how to use it, knows how to own it . . . knows that they're using it and why they're using it, that they would tend to be better judges because they would not rely upon the authority of their position. In fact they would use their power much less as a judge. They would need to use it less because the authority is cloaked over them and it's not necessary. I find that I rarely have to really use power in order to achieve anything in the judiciary. . . . The question is 'How much of my power as an individual is tied into my authority and how much of my power as an individual is owned by me?'

A more senior judge phrased the problem in more graphic language, suggesting the negative aspects of wielding authority of judging:

> We have to be careful of that psychic development—getting "judgitis." That's the fellow that sooner or later feels that he's not appointed, he's anointed, that [he] can do no wrong . . . You have to practice humility at all times . . . I think you have to seek out some things to involve yourself [in] other than strictly judging, to grow, or to stay effective really. . . . Now I personally feel that they should be court-related or judge-related. . . . There is kind of a fine line in how far to go.

The pitfalls of ineffective socialization in learning to handle the authority of judging were alluded to by several judges, suggesting that this aspect of judging may reflect not only on individual judges but also on the judiciary as an institution. For this reason it is a concern of no small importance to trial judges during their socialization to the bench.

As with isolation, trial judges learn to manage the authority of judging in large part independently of others within the court organization, adjusting by themselves. In general they are "on their own" in handling personal issues of judging to a greater extent than when learning about either legal or administrative issues, and they may well experience greater difficulty in coping with these personal issues as a result. Personal aspects of judging raise many interesting problems that may have more far-reaching implications for the judiciary as a democratic institution than the technical and task-related aspects of judging found in legal and administrative problems. In resolving personal problems, the interviews suggest that judges have difficulty in relating to the community from the cloistered environment of the bench and in wielding the authority of the third branch of government. While judges have apparently devised ways to handle problems resulting from legal or administrative aspects of judging, they mentioned fewer techniques for dealing with the personal aspects of judging, for which easy solutions are not available. But in maintaining the judiciary as a coequal branch of government, socialization of judges in the personal aspects of judging may be just as important, if not more important, than learning about legal and administrative aspects of judging. Each area of socialization raises different dimensions of judging that impinge on responses to on-bench learning. Further, each are equally important for understanding this socialization process.

While the interviews are suggestive and rich in individual socialization experiences, the extent to which these individual experiences apply to trial judges in general needed to be tested in a broader quantitative study. Interview data were useful in describing the three areas of on-bench learning that occur during judicial socialization; survey data were gathered to test these findings statewide on a set of trial judges in Florida. The focus of the survey was on learning about judging in each of these three areas as an initial and continuing socialization process, the timing of this socialization for each area, the nature of the role sources, and the way that learning occurred in each area. With this in mind, we now turn to the survey data to determine the generalizability of socialization themes suggested in the interviews.

THE SURVEY DATA—
EXTENT OF ON-BENCH LEARNING

The nature of on-bench learning in each of the three areas of judging—legal, administrative, and personal—was investigated in the questionnaire sent to all Florida circuit judges sitting on the bench in 1979. As suggested in the interviews, the survey data confirm that learning occurs both initially and throughout the judicial career in each of these areas. Two patterns of learning emerge in the data, as shown in Table 1. First, more judges learn initially about administrative issues to a greater extent than about either legal or personal issues. Nearly 60% of the respondents report substantial initial learning about administrative issues, but only 40% report substantial initial learning about legal or personal issues, suggesting newcomer judges are better prepared to handle legal or personal issues than administrative ones. Administrative issues may require more initial learning in part because the specific nature of legal training does not prepare judges for handling these concerns. In contrast, experiences in law school and in legal practice may prepare newcomer judges for handling legal questions or psychological adjustments to office; it may also be that personal issues do not surface until later in the judicial career when more immediate concerns have been dealt with successfully.

Second, more judges continued learning about legal issues throughout their career to a greater extent than about either administrative or personal issues. Nearly 70% of the respondents report substantial learning about legal issues throughout their tenure, compared to only 30% to 40% who report substantial learning about administrative or personal issues during their tenure. Legal issues may become more important over time in office because they reflect the core tasks of trial judging—deciding cases and adapting to new legislation—that occur throughout the judicial career. They are also the focus of most formal training that judges participate in during their tenure. Administrative concerns may surface early and receive attention at that time, becoming less problematic for judges later in their career. Apparently personal concerns are not subject to as much learning on the bench as legal or administrative concerns, even though the interviews suggest that personal concerns require an adjustment during judging. Judges learn less about handling this

TABLE 1 The Extent of On-Bench Learning for Florida Trial Judges

| | Extent of On-Bench Learning | | | | |
	Not at all	To a very little extent	To some extent	To a considerable extent	To a very great extent
	(n)	(n)	(n)	(n)	(n)
Initial Learning *					
Legal Issues	2%(2)	23%(28)	37%(45)	27%(33)	11%(13)
Administrative Issues	3%(4)	6%(7)	34%(42)	34%(42)	22%(27)
Personal Issues	5%(6)	19%(23)	35%(42)	28%(34)	13%(16)
Continual Learning +					
Legal Issues	0	6%(7)	28%(34)	44%(54)	22%(27)
Administrative Issues	2%(2)	22%(26)	37%(45)	33%(40)	7%(8)
Personal Issues	4%(5)	26%(32)	36%(43)	29%(35)	5%(6)

*Question: To what extent did you have to learn something almost entirely new about these three aspects of judging upon coming to the bench?

+Question: To what extent has learning about each of these issues been a continuing process throughout your judicial career?

TABLE 2   Type of Learning During On-Bench Socialization for Florida
           Trial Judges

	Legal Issues	Type of On-Bench Learning Administrative Issues	Personal Issues
Socialization Stage	(n)	(n)	(n)
Initiation (within 1st year)	25% (30)	28% (33)	31% (37)
Resolution (Years 2-5)	42% (51)	46% (55)	46% (55)
Establishment (Years 6-10)	12% (15)	12% (14)	8% (10)
Commitment (after 10 years)	1% (1)	0	0
Never	9% (11)	4% (5)	5% (6)
Not Yet	11% (13)	10% (12)	9% (11)

Question: When in the course of your tenure on the bench did you feel that you had
learned enough not to worry much about these three aspects of judging (e.g., as you
became experienced in dealing with these issues)?

problem in their career than about other problems; only 30%
to 40% of the respondents report substantial learning about
personal issues at any time during their career—either early
or throughout their tenure. Survey data generally tend to
support the findings of the interviews, with the exception of
personal issues that are subject to less on-bench learning than
expected.

With regard to the timing of their socialization, most
judges report they were comfortable with all three areas of
judging by the end of the fifth year in office (after the
Initiation and Resolution stages). As shown in Table 2,
nearly three-quarters of the respondents were experienced
with all issue areas by the end of year 5 in office, suggesting
the importance of these early years on the bench. In
particular, about one-quarter were experienced with all areas
of judging after the first year of office, suggesting a rapid

learning period for some trial judges. It may be that particular backgrounds facilitate adjustment to judging, for example, holding lower court judgeships, a hypothesis that will be explored below. Slightly fewer judges learn about legal issues as quickly as they do about administrative and personal issues, fitting the findings that legal issues require continual learning throughout the judicial career. The general pattern is that most judges quickly adjust to trial judging; consequently, it seems plausible that most effective judicial training would occur during this early period of the judicial career. Other training later in the career may also be helpful, as suggested by the data on continuing learning, but this first five years is the crucial learning period when judges may benefit most from their training.

Survey data on sources of learning also confirm those findings suggested in the interviews. As expected, most judges reported that fellow judges were instrumental in aiding adjustment to trial judging. Judges known before coming to the bench were also relied upon by many judges in finding out about judging. Fewer judges felt either court staff or attorneys aided their socialization, with the exception of the administrative area where many judges report that court staff were helpful. Many judges indicated that two professional organizations that offer formal courses for judges—the Florida Circuit Judges Conference and the National Judicial College—facilitated their learning in all areas. Formal training thus appears to be more helpful than suggested in the interviews, and only one member of the court organization—fellow trial judges—emerges as a key role source for most trial judges.

As shown in Table 3, the type of role sources that trial judges rely upon varies little across areas of judging. Most judges report the same role sources, regardless of the area of judging. For example, in learning about legal issues, more judges rely upon fellow trial judges, followed by the Florida

TABLE 3   Role Sources Relied Upon By Florida Trial Judges During
           Socialization

		Type On-Bench Learning	
	Legal	*Administrative*	*Personal*
Type Role Sources	(n)	(n)	(n)
Fellow Trial Judges	86% (104)	81% (98)	79% (96)
Judges Known Before	62% (75)	49% (59)	58% (70)
Fla. Circuit Judges Conf.	84% (101)	63% (76)	55% (66)
National Judicial College	60% (73)	52% (63)	47% (57)
Court Staff	7% (8)	46% (55)	7% (9)
Pre-Judicial Experience	38% (46)	25% (30)	16% (19)
Written Documents	32% (39)	17% (20)	11% (13)
Professional Training	32% (39)	17% (21)	14% (17)
Attorneys in Court	31% (38)	16% (19)	12% (14)
Attorneys Known Before	28% (34)	12% (14)	26% (32)
Professional Organizations	21% (25)	10% (12)	9% (11)
Appellate Judges	12% (15)	3% (4)	9% (11)
Personal Associates	5% (6)	5% (6)	9% (11)

Question: Who did you talk with about these issues?
         What other sources were helpful to you in learning these aspects of judging?

Circuit Judges Conference, judges known before coming to
the bench, and the Judicial College. In learning about
administrative issues, more judges also rely on fellow trial
judges, followed by the Circuit Judges Conference, the
Judicial College, judges known before, and court staff. In
learning about personal issues, more judges also rely on
fellow trial judges, followed by judges known before, the Circuit Judges Conference, and the Judicial College. In general,
more judges learn from their fellow trial judges in all three
areas of judging; other common sources are the Florida Circuit Judges Conference, the National Judicial College, and
judges known before coming to the bench. Only in the ad-

ministrative areas is there a deviation from this pattern; here, court staff aid judges in learning, according to 46% of the respondents. But in general the pattern is to rely upon fellow trial judges and judges known earlier, as well as two professional organizations that conduct training sessions for judges.

In order to determine which sources aided trial judges most in their on-bench learning, respondents were asked to rank their two most important sources of learning for each area of judging. As shown in Table 4, most judges ranked fellow trial judges highest compared to those who felt the National Judicial College, pre-judicial experience, or written documents were most important. Choices for the next important role source were fairly evenly split among fellow trial judges, the Florida Circuit Judges Conference, and the National Judicial College. Some variation does emerge in this second choice, however, with some judges reporting that court staff are important for administrative learning, professional training for administrative and personal learning, and written documents for legal learning.

In sum, it appears that fellow trial judges play a key role in helping new judges, as does professional training received through the Florida Circuit Judges Conference and the National Judicial College. Other sources of less importance are court staff, written documents (such as bench books), pre-judicial experience, and other professional training. These finding support the notion that on-bench learning about trial judging is primarily a self-education process although sources of help are available from fellow trial judges and, to a limited extent, court staff, as well as from certain formal training courses available to trial judges. That only one member of the court organization—fellow trial judges—is reported to be an important source of learning suggests that judges are not "taught" about judging but "learn by doing" in their daily work on the bench.[9] They may seek out formal courses

TABLE 4   Most Important Role Sources for Florida Trial Judges

	Legal Issues	Type Learning Administrative Issues	Personal Issues
Most Important Role Sources			
Fellow Trial Judges	31% (34)	41% (43)	41% (41)
National Judicial College	15% (16)	19% (20)	13% (13)
Pre-Judicial Experience	17% (18)	0	10% (10)
Written Documents	10% (11)	0	0
Next Important Role Sources			
Fellow Trial Judges	16% (14)	14% (11)	15% (11)
Court Staff	0	15% (12)	0
Circuit Judges Conference	12% (11)	13% (10)	12% (9)
National Judicial College	14% (13)	17% (13)	11% (8)
Professional Training	0	10% (8)	11% (8)
Written Documents	13% (12)	0	0

Question: Of the above persons and sources that aided you in learning about judging, rank the two most important ones.

offered through professional judicial organizations or accept guidance from other judges, but are largely on their own in their socialization to trial judging.

HOW FLORIDA JUDGES LEARN ABOUT TRIAL JUDGING

It was expected that trial judges would learn about judging in a variety of ways. This study explored six tactical dimensions that affect the socialization process within organizations, developed by Van Maanen and Schein (1979) in their theory of organizational socialization. These six dimensions include collective versus individual socialization, formal versus informal socialization, sequential versus random socialization, fixed versus variable socialization, serial versus disjunctive socialization, and investiture versus divestiture socialization.

The collective/individual dimension refers to the extent to which recruits are processed as a group sharing socialization experiences (collective) or singly in isolation from each other (individual). While collective processes enhance demands of socialization agents, individual processes produce more heterogeneous socialization. Judicial socialization may involve group and individual learning; although there are usually few newcomers and role behavior is amenable to individual interpretation, constrained by a lengthy antici-patory socialization period that prepares attorneys for specific task performance, formal group training reflects collective learning. The formal/informal dimension indicates the degree to which formal or informal processes dominate. Formal processes involve segregation from regular organi-zational members, for example, in professional schools, that focus on attitudes rather than on behavior in promoting newcomer acceptance of appropriate role expectations, while informal socialization provides more variant socialization in situ. Judicial socialization may involve more informal, experiential learning, although formal programs may be somewhat important.

The sequential/variable dimension distinguishes learning in discrete, identifiable steps (sequential) from that in ambiguous, shifting phases (random). While judicial socialization may be a function of random experiences that include legal education, political involvement, and often public officeholding, once on the bench, judges may encounter discrete stages of learning. The fixed/variable dimension refers to whether a specific timetable exists for socialization (fixed) that is communicated to newcomers or whether uncontrollable factors mark the learning process (variable). The uncertainty of variable learning would likely result in greater conformity to organization norms. Because the time frame for judicial socialization is often poorly communicated to newcomers, judicial learning may be characterized by the variable process. The serial/disjunctive dimension distinguishes whether experienced organization members serve as role models for newcomers and provide information about role performance (serial) or whether the newcomer lacks role models for guidance in assuming roles (disjunctive). Because guidance in learning judicial roles is not provided by role agents, although role models are present, judges may experience only a modified or weak form of serial socialization. The investiture/divestiture dimension refers to whether the process confirms (invests) or disconfirms (divests) the newcomer's identity. Investitute builds upon the newcomer's skills, values, and attitudes acquired prior to organizational membership while divestiture replaces these with ones more appropriate to the new role. Judging may rely upon investiture since new judges are expected to utilize skills they learned as attorneys.

Each of these modes of socialization was examined to determine to what extent it applies to learning on the bench. A total of seven items operationalized the theoretical concepts formulated by Van Maanen and Schein (1979). These items asked judges to place themselves on a continuum for each of the process variables to determine whether judges learn in groups or individually, formally or informally, with or without incumbent judges, by building on past experiences or by replacing old standards with new ones, with or without flexibility, in ordered stages or randomly, and by being able to predict or unable to predict their learning time. The measures were scored 1 to 5, depending on the point circled on each continuum.

Van Maanen and Schein propose that the six tactical dimensions of learning will result in either custodial or innovative responses to socialization experiences within an organization. Those tactics that they suggest would result in maintenance of the status quo, or custodial responses—group learning, formal learning, learning in ordered stages, with incumbents, without flexibility, by replacing old standards with new ones, and by being unable to predict learning time—were examined to measure their effect upon on-bench socialization, using the three areas of judicial learning and seven judicial norms (decisiveness, caseload and procedural efficiency, precedent, neutrality, isolation, and maintenance of the status quo) as sites of potential influence.

The findings reveal that Florida trial judges learn in a variety of ways, as shown in Table 5. Among respondents, more judges learn informally than formally, in ordered stages than randomly, with incumbents than without incumbents, by building on past experiences than by replacing the past with new standards, and without being able to predict the length of learning time than by being able to do so. About the same number of judges learn in groups as learn individually. Finally, more judges are ambivalent about the amount of flexibility they have in defining judging, although more learn with flexibility than without flexibility.

Thus we find that judicial socialization is characterized by both custodial and innovative processes. It involves both collective and individual processes; although there is much individual adaptation, formal group training reflects the collective dimension. It is also characterized by the informal mode of learning involving experiential learning since most judges learn without formal coursework. Further, while judicial socialization is affected by random prebench experiences—that may include a career pattern of legal education, political involvement, and public officeholding—judges learn in discrete, identifiable steps once they reach the bench, or se-

TABLE 5   Dimensions of the Socialization Process Among Florida
            Trial Judges

Custodial Processes		*Innovative Processes*	
Collective (Group)	37% (44)	Individual (Self)	36% (43)
Formal (Formal)	20% (24)	Informal (Informal)	47% (56)
Sequential (ordered)	46% (55)	Random (Random)	29% (34)
Variable (Inability to Predict Learning Time)	58% (68)	Fixed (Ability to Predict Learning Time)	25% (29)
Serial (With Incumbent's help)	61% (72)	Disjunctive (Without Incumbent's help)	17% (20)
Serial (Without Flexibility)	22% (26)	Disjunctive (With Flexibility)	36% (43)
Divestiture (By Replacing Old Standards)	5% (6)	Investiture (By Building on Past Experiences)	67% (80)

*Totals do not average 100% because judges could also indicate a third response for each item—that socialization occurred by both modes and was neither one nor the other process exclusively.

quential socialization. Even though stages of judicial socialization follow a loose timetable, this timetable is often not
communicated to organizational members, resulting in individual career aspirations that are idiosyncratic without
generalizable patterns, or variable socialization. Trial judges
experience a modified form of serial socialization, with role
models to guide in learning roles but no formal role agents to
transmit information about judging. This weak communication linkage between role models and newcomer judges
makes uniform learning difficult, with variation among
courts. Finally, judicial socialization builds upon the newcomer's skills, values, and attitudes acquired prior to becoming a judge, or investiture.

The data tend to support Van Maanen and Schein's
hypotheses about custodial processes being more important
in preserving organizational norms, processes that result in
more learning in all three areas of judging.[10] But only certain

processes involved in socialization of judges emerge as crucial for insuring adherence to prevailing norms and for encouraging more on-bench learning. For example, judges who learn in ordered stages adhere more closely to norms of the status quo than those who learn randomly.[11] Other differences among process variables and adherence to judicial norms are not statistically significant, suggesting that the type of learning process alone does not insure norm adherence.

With regard to the extent of on-bench learning, those judges who were unable to anticipate the length of their learning time learned more initially about administrative[12] and personal issues[13] and more throughout their career about legal,[14] administrative,[15] and personal issues[16] than those who were able to predict their learning time. This variable mode of socialization is a custodial process, suggesting it fosters learning conventional approaches to trial judging that assure perpetuation of the court as an organization. Further, those who learned in this manner had longer learning times than those who did not.[17] Those who also learned in ordered stages learned more initially about personal issues than did those who learned randomly.[18] Judges who learned informally deviate from this pattern, learning slightly more initially about administrative issues than those who learned formally.[19]

Apparently the level of on-bench learning is affected by this ability to anticipate learning time, where courts communicate a specific timetable for socialization to newcomers. Judges tend to be able to predict the length of learning time on courts with collective learning processes, suggesting that larger, urban courts are slightly more likely to communicate this timetable.[20] These are the same courts where judges tend to learn with the help of incumbents.[21] Perhaps interaction among judges on larger courts facilitates on-bench learning by focusing on particular areas, while the lack of interaction among those on rural courts lengthens the learning time.

Accepting judicial norms and conventional approaches to judging may vary according to the type of court organization. It may also be that judges need to learn more to achieve a "caretaker" response to socialization and assume "customary" strategies and norms associated with conventional modes of judging. This may require rejecting past experiences and learning more by expanding those horizons by relying upon more role sources. Indeed, judges who adhere more closely to norms of precedent, decisiveness, and procedural and caseload efficiency, tend to rely upon a greater number of formal and informal role sources than those who reject such norms.[22] However, those who violate norms of isolation and the status quo also tend to rely upon more formal and informal role sources than do those who accept such norms.[23]

Those judges sitting on smaller, rural courts may have a more "parochial" orientation to trial judging, suggested by their moderate reliance upon more local role sources for learning about judging, such as local attorneys[24] and other judges.[25] Pre-judicial experiences also appear important to somewhat more judges sitting on smaller courts than for judges sitting on other courts.[26] In contrast, those judges sitting on larger, urban courts may have a more "cosmopolitan" outlook as noted by their moderate reliance upon the National Judicial College in their socialization.[27] Perhaps different legal cultures exist on different size courts within different population areas. Such differences in legal culture may affect the nature of the role sources involved in on-bench socialization and ultimately the outcomes of that process. These findings suggest that variables other than the learning process, for example, local legal culture, may affect on-bench socialization. Individual characteristics of trial judges, particularly their backgrounds, may also affect the learning process, to which we now turn in the final section.

ANTICIPATORY SOCIALIZATION
AND LEARNING ON THE BENCH

Experiences prior to becoming judge, or anticipatory socialization, may help explain differences in the patterns of learning on the bench. Judges come to the bench with a variety of legal and other public officeholding experiences, as well as private practice. For example, 84% of the respondents held prior legal offices, half as lower court judges and a quarter as prosecutors or local government attorneys. Another half of the respondents held nonlegal public offices, such as local government positions. Evidently trial judges are a politically active group with a penchant for public officeholding. With regard to legal practice backgrounds, about three-quarters of the respondents had general practice experience, compared to 45% with civil law and 30% with criminal law experience. Perhaps more attorneys in general legal practice find judging more appealing than those in legal specialties.

It was expected that those who held lower court judgships or other legal officeholding would be better prepared for the trial bench than those who lacked this experience, resulting in greater norm adherence. In contrast, public officeholding would have an opposite effect, requiring greater adjustment to trial judging for those who share this experience. As expected, we find a slight tendency for judges with legal officeholding experience to adhere more closely to norms of isolation than for those without legal officeholding.[28] Although this provides some support for the legal officeholding hypothesis, there is only mixed support for the public officeholding hypothesis. Judges with fewer public officeholding experiences show a slight tendency to adhere to norms of the status quo compared to those with public officeholding,[29] while those with public officeholding tend to adhere more closely to norms of precedent than those without public officeholding.[30] Likewise, the nature of the legal practice tends to affect the acceptance of judicial norms; those with criminal law backgrounds show a slight tendency to adhere more closely to norms of caseload efficiency[31] than those without this background. These findings suggest that these particular backgrounds foster norms on the bench—isolation, precedent, and efficiency in handling caseloads as chief administrative judge. But apparently these backgrounds do not uniformly prepare judges for the trial bench and for adherence to all judicial norms, although they may sensitize judges to specific norms.

It may be, however, that adherence to norms does not completely reveal the impact of anticipatory socialization. The extent of on-bench learning may also reflect the effect of background experiences. In general, there is slightly less awareness of learning associated with adherence to norms of decisiveness,[32] precedent,[33] and isolation[34] but slightly more awareness of learning associated with adherence to norms of neutrality[35] and caseload efficiency.[36] Judges with public and legal officeholding and attorney experiences in general practice or criminal law learn slightly more about most areas of judging,[37] suggesting that these backgrounds sensitize judges to learn more in specific areas of judging.

With regard to length of learning time on the bench, only judges with a civil law background learn in less time (about legal issues) than do those without civil law experience.[38] Perhaps the specialist nature of the civil law practice fits most closely with the type of legal issues judges handle on the bench. Attorneys in civil law practice are often involved in prolonged litigation that requires adherence to legal procedures and legal rules (e.g., commercial litigation); it is entirely plausible that they are more aware of certain aspects of judging than are judges without this background.

On the other hand, a criminal law background may uniquely qualify a judge for the criminal bench, but its scope may be too narrow to prepare him for the broader range of cases on the civil bench. As well, a general practice background would seem to prepare a judge for the generalist nature of judging, but not necessarily so if one considers that many general practitioners are involved in office work such as real estate, divorce, or probate that neither fosters extensive contact with the courts nor breeds familiarity with court procedures. Thus the nature of the legal practice, specifically the extent of contact with courts in general and trial judges in particular, may facilitate learning on the bench. But the extent of contact with courts is not itself sufficient to enhance on-bench learning if it is limited to relatively narrow areas of the law.

The same reasoning may also explain why legal and public officeholding do not prepare an individual for judicial office as well as expected. Public officeholding neither facilitates contact with the courts nor encourages a "judicial approach" to issues. Instead, a public office background might be expected to impede learning on the bench since it requires more dramatic shifts in role from public norms to legal norms. In contrast, legal officeholding might be akin to narrow legal backgrounds that foster familiarity with only a specific area of the law. For example, even if a judge has served as prosecutor, local government attorney, or lower court judge, he has not necessarily been exposed to the broad range of civil law issues that confronts the circuit courts. So while he may be familiar with certain criminal court procedures and law, he may not be as informed about the full range of other legal issues.

From a policy perspective, this suggests that those involved in recruiting state trial judges should give equal consideration to private attorneys and those with legal officeholding, examining the specific background and type of legal practice as measures of competency. The evidence suggests that an aspiring judge may be as well-prepared for the circuit bench by remaining in private practice as he would by holding legal office, with the qualification that this depends upon the nature of the legal practice. Practical reasons may explain the more conventional career path of legal office-holding, however, since those in legal offices may well have greater opportunity for recruitment to the bench. That so many respondents have held legal offices suggests legal office-holding does enhance opportunities for judicial office-holding.[39]

In sum, in developing a theory of judicial socialization, the data suggest several influences upon the outcomes of on-bench learning. Not only does the learning process itself affect these outcomes but also so do the local legal culture and the background experiences of judges. The local legal culture seems to influence the choice of role sources that judges rely upon during socialization; background experiences appear to affect adherence to judicial norms. Custodial learning processes tend to result in adherence to conventional norms of judging. Further, the process of judicial socialization may be uniform, involving adjustment to the same three areas of judging regardless of whether judges sit on state or federal benches. And while judges may seek guidance from fellow trial judges in learning about life on the bench, they are generally on their own in adjusting to trial judging. Thus judicial socialization emerges as largely a self-education process in which trial judges learn by doing, as they progress through stages of the judicial career.

NOTES

1. Anecdotal works are quite popular among judges, see, for example, Satter (1979).

2. See, for example, Carp and Wheeler (1972), Heumann (1978), Luskin (1976), and Cook (1971).

3. See Van Maanen (1976) for an extensive review of the organizational socialization literature.

4. Relying on the organizational literature provides a theoretical basis for this inquiry, but only with the caveat that courts, and particularly trial courts, do not fulfill all of the formal requirements of organizations. Recognition of the differences between courts and other organizations, especially the informal character of courts, requires caution and selective application of the organizational literature to courts. But while not all features of organizational socialization are relevant to courts at the trial level, sufficient aspects are applicable to make this a fruitful endeavor.

5. See, for example, Feldman, (1976); Hall and Schneider, (1973); Katz and Kahn, (1973); Van Maanen, (1975); and Wanous, (1977).

6. This information of judicial socialization stages, based upon focused interviews with 43 trial judges in Florida, is elaborated in Alpert et al. (1979).

7. In addition to focused interviews with 43 circuit judges in Florida, two surveys were mailed to all 291 circuit judges sitting on the bench during 1979 in Florida. The response rate to the first survey was 42% (n = 122) and 75% (91 of 122 initial respondents) for the second survey, a follow-up survey sent to all respondents of the first survey. Respondents were not significantly different from nonrespondents with regard to tenure group or type of initial selection, although they did differ by size of court and population of circuit. Respondents overrepresent smaller, rural courts, $\chi^2(2) = 7.51$, p = .05, and underrepresent larger, urban courts, $\chi^2(2) = 7.51$, p = .05.

8. The training for new judges has been conducted in Florida for every year since 1972 except one and periodically since 1960. At these seminars judges learn the basics of trial supervision, case management, and court administration. The Circuit Judges Conference also holds semiannual conferences during which training also occurs for all judges.

9. Heumann (1978: 3) found that Connecticut trial judges adapt to the bench by learning "about an environment that differs from what they expected" rather than from any specific teaching agent, suggesting this finding is a general phenomenon of judicial socialization.

10. Nine different Pearson correlations (p = .05) reveal that custodial processes result in slightly more learning on the bench; only one correlation shows that these processes result in less learning.

11. $F = 3.3$, n = 112, p = .04.

12. $F = 3.6$, n = 118, p = .03.

13. $F = 4.5$, n = 117, p = .01.

14. $F = 3.9$, n = 118, p = .03.

15. $F = 3.9$, n = 117, p = .02.

16. $F = 5.9$, n = 117, p = .004.

17. $F = 5.4$, n = 95, p = .006 for learning legal issues; $F = 5.8$, n = 100, p = .004 for learning administrative issues; $F = 6.1$, n = 100, p = .003 for learning personal issues.

18. $F = 3.7$, n = 117, p = .03.

19. $F = 4.3$, n = 119, p = .02.

20. The correlation of size with process is: r = .20, n = 118, p = .02; of population with process: r = .17, n = 118, p = .03.

21. r = .14, n = 119, p = .06.

22. Twelve Pearson correlations (p < .10) associate higher norm adherence with more role sources for all norms except neutrality during trials, isolation from press, and maintaining the status quo.

23. Three Pearson correlations reveal this association pattern (p < .10).

24. Crosstabulation analyses support this interpretation of the data. $\chi^2(2) = 8.6$, Cramer's V = .27, n = 121, p = .01 for administrative learning.

25. $\chi^2(2) = 5.8$, V = .22, n = 121, p = .06 for personal learning.

26. $\chi^2(2) = 7.8$, V = .26, n = 120, p = .02 for legal learning.

27. $\chi^2(2) = 8.8$, V = .27, n = 120, p = .01 for legal learning; $\chi^2(2) = 10.4$ V = .29, n = 120, p = .006 for administrative learning.

28. r = .21, n = 116, p = .01.

29. r = −.14, n = 128, p = .06.

30. r = .20, n = 111, p = .02.

31. r = .15, n = 115, p = .06.

32. r = −.23, n = 116, p = .006 for initial administrative learning; r = −.14, n = 115, p = .07 for initial personal learning.

33. r = −.16, n = 90, p = .07 for initial administrative learning.

34. r = −.31, n = 90, p = .002 for initial administrative learning; r = −.24, n = 90, p = .01 for continual legal learning.

35. r = .21, n = 90, p = .02 for initial legal learning; r = .16, n = 90, p = .07 for initial personal learning.

36. r = .16, n = 90, p = .06 for initial legal learning; r = .15, n = 91, p = .07 for continual legal learning.

37. Nine breakdown analyses with F scores (p < .10) support this interpretation of the data.

38. $F = 3.6$, n = 91, p = .06.

39. A total of 99 respondents (84%) held legal offices prior to coming to the bench. A similarly high proportion of unsuccessful judicial candidates (79%, n = 27) also held legal offices.

REFERENCES

ALPERT, L., B. ATKINS, and R. ZILLER (1979) "Becoming a judge: The transition from advocate to arbiter." Judicature 62: 325-335.

CARP, R. and R. WHEELER (1972) "Sink or swim: The socialization of a federal district judge." Journal of Public Law 21: 359-393.

COOK, B. B. (1971) "The socialization of new federal judges: Impact on district court business." Washington University Law Quarterly 253-279.

FELDMAN, D. C. (1976) "A contingency theory of socialization." Administrative Science Quarterly 21: 433-452.

GRAEN, G. (1976) "Role-making processes within complex organizations," in M. D. Dunnette (ed.) Handbook of Industrial and Organizational Psychology. Skokie, IL: Rand McNally.

HALL, D. T. and B. SCHNEIDER (1973) Organizational Climates and Careers. New York: Seminar Press.

HEUMANN, M. (1978) Plea Bargaining. Chicago: University of Chicago Press.

KATZ, D. and R. L. KAHN (1973) The Social Psychology of Organizations. New York: Wiley.

LUSKIN, M. L. (1976) "Determinants of change in judges' decisions to bind over defendants for trial." Presented at the meeting of the American Political Science Association, Chicago.

SATTER, R. (1979) "The quality of a judge's experience." American Bar Association Journal 65: 933-935.

SCHEIN, E. H. (1968) "Organizational socialization and the profession of management." Industrial Management Review 9: 1-16.

VAN MAANEN, J. (1976) "Breaking in: Socialization to work," in R. Dubin (ed.) Handbook of Work, Organization, and Society. Skokie, IL: Rand McNally.

VAN MAANEN, J. (1975) "Police socialization: A longitudinal examination of job attitudes in an urban police department." Administrative Science Quarterly 20: 207-228.

VAN MAANEN, J. and E. H. SCHEIN (1979) "Toward a theory of organizational socialization," pp. 209-264 in B. Staw (ed.) Research in Organization Behavior (Vol. 1). Greenwich, CT: Jai Press.

WANOUS, J. P. (1977) "Organizational entry: Newcomers moving from outside to inside." Psychology Bulletin 84: 601-618.

Chapter 6

JUDICIAL SOCIALIZATION:
THE PHILADELPHIA EXPERIENCE

PAUL B. WICE

Students of judicial behavior are thought to be offered an excellent opportunity to observe the process of adult socialization. In contrast to judges from most other countries, the United States has failed to create a career judiciary (Karlen, 1966). Instead, American judges, who rarely receive any training or education prior to assuming office, learn their craft through a form of on-the-job training. The beginning judge in the United States must therefore be "socialized" into his new position and be dependent upon his colleagues on the bench and other "socializing agents" for the necessary information and informal training.

This essay will reexamine the process of judicial socialization by applying the major theories of this process, which have been developed primarily from previous studies of state appellate and federal court judges, to the socialization experiences of felony trial court judges from a large eastern city. The first section of this essay will review the theoretical foundations of judicial socialization and discuss some of the most important recent studies on this subject. The second section will present the perceptions of judges from the Philadelphia Court of Common Pleas who handle criminal matters concerning their first years on the bench. Because the impressions of these Philadelphia judges contrasted so sharply with the earlier research discussed in the first section, a third, and final section of the study will attempt to explain these differences and possibly identify explanatory variables which could lead to greater understanding of the problem through enlightened future research.

Before proceeding further the reader should be made cognizant of the heuristic nature of this essay as well as its rather narrow scope. This study is part of a larger research project in which many more judges from several additional jurisdictions will be interviewed on a wide variety of issues related to professional life. The forthcoming research may replicate these initial findings or may prove Philadelphia to be a unique jurisdiction. Nevertheless, the initial perceptions of these criminal court judges contrasted drastically with previous studies of judicial socialization, so that it appears to warrant this seemingly premature analysis.

JUDICIAL SOCIALIZATION:
ITS THEORETICAL FOUNDATIONS

As initially noted, American judges are prime candidates for analysis by students of adult socialization. Adult socialization has been defined in the *Encyclopaedia of Social Sciences* as a learning process which occurs when "the individual is confronted with a new role and knows virtually nothing about what he should do. In such a case society will require new socialization" (Stills, 1968: Vol. 14, p. 555).

It is true that nearly all American judges have shared the common experience of a legal education. However, once completing law school, lawyers then specialize in divergent areas of the law and many almost never venture inside a courtroom. In contrast to most European countries, the Unites States has not chosen to develop a body of career judges where one enters the profession at an early age and works his way up the judicial hierarchy. Instead, we have opted for what Neubauer has described as "essentially judicial amateurs . . . who have no practical experience or systematic exposure to the judicial world" (1979: 168).

What seems to exacerbate the problem even more is that we seem to have a penchant for selecting judges, especially to the criminal bench, who are highly deficient in litigation experience. The problem was highlighted by the President's Commission on Law Enforcement and Administration of Justice which stated: "It is possible for a judge who the day before had made his living drafting corporate indentures to be called upon to rule on the validity of a search or to charge a jury on the law of entrapment" (1967: 68).

If we do not have many experienced trial lawyers being selected for judgeships, who are receiving these appointments? Of the two major empirical studies surveying judicial backgrounds, the most recent data collection was by Volcansek-Clark and concluded that from her sample of Florida judges, "most come from civil or general legal practices . . . 46% of the sitting judges interviewed did however previously hold a governmental position" (1978: 175). Clark also found that most lawyers were discouraged from becoming a judge because of the low salary and resulting loss in income as well as the necessity of entering into political campaigns.

The second study was a more comprehensive survey by the Institute of Judicial Administration (1965) in New York City which constructed a national profile of the American judge. Their major findings described a typical judge being 54 years of age and having held his position for about 8 years. More than half of the judges surveyed had served in some public office prior to reaching their present position as judge with more than a third having been formerly with the prosecutor's office. Almost half of the judges practiced alone or with a handful of associates, while one-quarter worked in large firms. A substantial number of judges reported legislative service, primarily at the state level. Both of these studies, as well as the work of Schmidhauser on the federal system, seem to substantiate the generally accepted belief that most judges have emerged from fairly successful civil law firms or business enterprises and are predominantly upper middle class, White Americans.

As a result of the lack of litigation experience as well as the absence of any viable orientation or training program, the newly selected judge is thrust into a rather alien environment. It is at this point that the "judicial socialization" process goes to work to teach the beginning judge the accepted modes of behavior of his new profession. Feldman has offered an excellent model for this process of "individual socialization into a new organization" and has identified three distinct stages leading to four possible outcome variables. Although Feldman's (1976) study was conducted at a hospital rather than a courthouse, its applicability to the judicial scene will be readily apparent.

The first stage is defined as "anticipatory socialization," which occurs before the recruit enters the organization and begins to form expectations about his job and starts to receive some preliminary information from his prospective employer. At the next stage, entitled "accommodation," the individual sees what the organization is actually like and attempts to become a member of it. The final stage, which is termed "role management," finds the recruit now having resolved some of his newly emerging problems in his work group and now begins to mediate conflicts within the organization.

The Feldman model soon proved to be a workable paradigm for the study of judicial socialization and was recently utilized by Alpert et al. (1979). Although they modified the Feldman model, its influence was noted by the authors and was readily apparent. These authors developed a four-stage process which carries the judge completely through his judicial career. It begins first with "Professional Socialization" before he becomes a judge, where he primarily is a product of his early legal experiences, including law school. The second stage, "Initiation and Resolution" includes the judges' first five years on the bench where he typically has an altruist or legalist role orientation and begins to learn the reality of his newly accepted profession. The third stage is the "Establishment Period" which lasts from years 6 through 15 and has the judge adopting the role orientation of "guardian of the law" and begins a long-term process of coping and possible role redefinition. The final period is the "Commitment Period" after the judge has served 15 years. He has now chosen to become a legalist and guardian of the law and experiences increased satisfaction with his judicial life.

Alpert et al. conclude that "our model of socialization indicates the effect of organizational tenure upon both the individual judge and the individual-organization fit" (1979; 335). They have thus offered a theoretical schema of judicial socialization which may be applied to varying levels of courts.

The final article to be reviewed in this section is an important and oft-quoted study of 30 federal district court judges. This is the work of Carp and Wheeler (1972). Although the Carp and Wheeler study utilized a rather small sample of judges from a particular court system, their findings are generally considered to be the definitive work on most facets of judical socialization. In contrast with Feldman (1976) and Alpert et al. (1979), Carp and Wheeler (1972) moved away from simply categorizing the various stages of socialization and instead focused upon the major problems facing judges during their early years on the bench. They found that socialization problems for the judges were either legal, administrative, or psychological. Legal problems were substantive or procedural and were usually caused by the inexperience of the judge in handling criminal cases. The procedural problems ranged from a shaky understanding of the pretrial arraignment process through difficulty in drawing up proper charges to the jury. The administrative problems were presented as an unexpected difficulty. Most beginning judges had little appreciation for the complexities of managing a budget, staff, or docket. The psychological problems facing the judge were summarized by the authors as being mainly "the loneliness of the office, sentencing defendants, forgetting the adversary role, local pressure and maintaining a judicial bearing both on and off the bench" (Carp and Wheeler, 1972: 373).

With so many problems facing the beginning judge, where can he turn for help? It was previously noted that there is almost no formal educative or training process currently available. The judge must therefore turn to a group of "socializing agents" who can informally educate him as to the legal and social prescriptions of his newly acquired position. Carp and Wheeler as well as others have usually rated the judge's colleagues as the foremost training agents. They accomplish this task both through formalized professional meetings and seminars as well as informal exchanges during the workday. A second source of information are the lawyers who appear in their courtrooms. Blumberg (1967) believes that, based on his observations in the Kings County (Brooklyn), New York, Criminal Courthouse, the judge's staff—law clerks, secretary, stenographer, and bailiff—commonly provide him with critical advice on administrative and procedural matters. Despite all of this possible help, Neubauer is probably correct in concluding that "In the end, the judges must rely on themselves. Through reading in the law library and seeking out knowledgeable persons, judges engage in self-education" (1979: 169).

Law reformers, legal scholars, and other students of our nation's judicial system have long been aware of the absence of meaningful education programs for the beginning judge as a substitute for this "self-education" process. Although most judges still receive at best only a cursory orientation and continue to be dependent upon an informal socializing process, the past 20 years have witnessed many new bold programs and the prognosis for the future appears positive. The concept of judicial education was first translated into actual training seminars in 1961. Fifty sessions were conducted between 1961 and 1963 for state trial judges. The program was financed by both the American Bar Association and the W. K. Kellog Foundation. Prior to these initial efforts, the idea that a judge needed to go back to school as not widely accepted and viewed by many as an insult to the judiciary, inferring that judges did not know how to do their jobs (Neubauer, 1979).

By the late 1960s the necessity for judicail education was accepted by bench and bar. By the end of the decade, the Federal Judiciary had opened its own academy in Washington, D.C. The American Academy of Judicial Education had begun conducting its National Trial Judges Academy, and the National College of State Judiciary had initiated its extensive training programs in Reno at the University of Nevada. In addition to the commencement of these specific programs, a national consensus of professional opinion had agreed upon the necessity for creating and implementing a widespread program of education for all levels of judicial officials. Standard 7.5 of the National Advisory Commission on Criminal Justice Standard and Goals exemplifies this national commitment. This standard urges each state to "create and maintain a comprehensive program of continuing judicial education" and recommended that these programs have the following features:

> 1. All new trial judges within three years of assuming judicial office, should attend both local and national orientation programs as well as one of the national judicial educational pro-

grams. The local orientation program should come immediately before or after the judge first takes office. It should include visits to all institutions and facilities to which criminal offenders may be sentenced.

2. Each state should develop its own judicial college which should be responsible for the orientation program for new judges and which should make available to all state judges the graduate and refresher programs of the national judicial educational organization. Each state also should plan specialized subject matter programs as well as two to three day annual state seminars for trail and appellate judges [1973: 157].

Despite the growing awareness of these programs and encouragement from national commissions and organizations, there continues to be a lack of total commitment by all state and local court systems to institutionalize training and orientation programs. As of 1980, five states have no training programs at all (Maine, Montana, Vermont, West Virginia, and Wyoming) and of states with programs, only half are mandatory. The National College of the State Judiciary in Reno, Nevada, and the American Academy of Judicial Education in Washington, D.C., however, are two organizations which are aggressively attempting to improve the quality of judicial education. The American academy, for example, states in their organizational material that they are currently able to "design and operate a state judicial academy, provide organizational support to the state educational officer, function under the supervision of a state education committeee as the training arm of the state supreme court or develop whatever kind of special program is useful or necessary. Always with the judge in clear focus and the judicial system as the primary benefactor" (1980). Turning to the work of the National Judicial College, its former Dean, Laurance M. Hyde, sums up the significance of the college's program by stating: "The most important thing we offer is the chance to exchange viewpoints and experiences and to give them a sense of a national picture" (quoted in Jackson, 1974: 19).

Before moving on to the discussion of the socialization experiences of Philadelphia criminal court judges, it would be instructive to briefly reconstruct the major theories of judicial socialization. The major theoretical premise for the necessary existence of such a process is that when one enters the judiciary, because there has been no prior training, the new judge undergoes a rather severe socialization process in which his views of proper role conduct will be significantly shaped. Since we have so few formal socializing processes (educative orientation programs), a variety of socializing agents, dominated by his colleagues on the bench, engage in an informal yet effective socialization/education process. Additionally, professional organizations have recently responded to the absence of these formalized educative structures and are rapidly beginning to develop a wide range of orientation and continuing education programs.

Since all of these new programs and recent research projects have been based upon what might be a questionable premise—that all new judges know almost nothing about their jobs and are in drastic need of educative programs—this study has attempted to investigate a group of criminal court judges in Philadelphia, Pennsylvania's Court of Common Pleas, to learn if their early years on the bench do, in fact, fit these premises. Let us now turn to the second section of this essay and the Philadelphia socialization experience.

THE PHILADELPHIA EXPERIENCE

As a result of spending four weeks during the summer of 1980 observing and interviewing judges in the Philadelphia

Court of Common Pleas, the process of judicial socialization as described in the preceding section did not occur. Because of either inherent self-confidence, easy adaptability, or prior experience and training, these judges did not believe or act as if they had undergone any evident socialization process. Although they admitted they received virtually no orientation or training, they generally thought they were quickly able to do a competent job, often independent of the aid from any socializing agents such as colleagues or law clerks.

This second section of the essay will attempt to closely examine the limited socialization experience of these judges. Topics for analysis will be their prior background, how they were selected, first days on the job, possible socializing agents, and initial adjustments to the job. In the final section of this study two important variables will be offered to account for the Philadelphia phenomenon, and an assessment of whether their socializing experience was actually so unique.

Methodology

In the review of earlier studies of judicial socialization, it is significant to note that nearly all of the major works have focused upon judges from either the state appellate or federal systems (Alpert et al., 1979; Carp and Wheeler, 1972). This emphasis upon appellate and federal courts has permeated not only studies of judicial socialization but also the entire study of public law. In an attempt to shift the focus down to the overcrowded, overworked, and understudied trial courts, I designed a study with the sponsorship and cooperation of the Institute of Judicial Administration. The study will involve approximately 75 criminal court judges from five major urban jurisdictions and will hopefully provide a realistic portrait of the professional behavior of these judges.

The Philadelphia judges selected for this study form a pretest for the expanded version to be completed within the next two years. Nearly 45% of the active judges hearing criminal cases in the Philadelphia court of Common Pleas were interviewed. This court has jurisdiction over the disposition of all felony cases and has a total of 35 judges involved in a homicide program (8), calendar program (14), and criminal list program (13).

The judges were randomly selected and represented all three of the court's special programs (homicide, criminal list, and criminal calendar). Interviews averaged two to three hours and ranged from one to seven hours. All of the judges except three were willing to participate. The interviews were typically conducted in the judge's chambers after completion of his day's caseload, which usually meant from 4 to 6 p.m. Several of the busier judges were only able to be interviewed during their lunch hour (12:00-1:30). In order to promote candor and relieve possible tension, all judges were promised confidentiality. Although specific questions were asked of all respondents, the structure of the session was kept informal and flowed from a spontaneity of response which necessitated the abandonment of a fixed interview schedule. Whatever may have been lost in scientific rigor was hopefuly gained in the quality and frankness of the information collected. In addition to conducting the personal interviews, many hours were also spent observing the judges as they performed their professional responsibilities. This accomplished several things: (1) it frequently improved the rapport with the judge indicating increased interest in his courtroom; (2) it was a possible way to measure any blatant conflicts between the judge's perceptions of his behavior on the bench and the observed performance in the courtroom; and (3) it permitted the researcher to gain fuller appreciation of the milieu in which the criminal court judge must operate.

Their Background. The underlying premise in justifying the existence of judicial socialization is primarily the belief that most judges lack the necessary courtroom experiences to adequately prepare them for their forthcoming judicial responsibilities. This seems especially true in the federal courts where appointments are frequently made of high-quality corporate lawyers who rarely have litigation experience and are even less likely to be prepared to handle the inevitable criminal cases soon to appear on their calendar (see Goulden, 1976, and Schmidhauser, 1979, both of whom draw similar conclusions).

It was interesting to note that even though Philadelphia's Court of Common Pleas handles both civil and criminal matters, nearly all the judges, through a self-selection process generally related to their intellectual interests and previous legal experiences, have stayed either within the criminal or civil side without the expected rotation. This contrasts sharply with the Federal District Courts where the judges will be faced with all types of cases and have no control over which category of dispute they will be deciding.

The explanation for the Philadelphia's judges self-confidence upon taking office is most likely related to their prior experience. In contrast to the generally accepted belief that most judges come ill-equipped for the job with little litigation experience, 80% of the Philadelphia sample stated that they had trial experience with over half having served in the prosecutor's office. One of the judges had even been a law clerk for 20 years. Other types of legal experiences related to trial work were negligence (40%) and general business litigation (25%). Besides 50% of the sample being former prosecutors, several others had experience with the criminal justice system as 15% were formerly employed in the city's prestigious public defender office and 25% had experience as a private criminal lawyer. Nearly all of the judges interviewed, with but two exceptions, started out on the criminal side and have spent their entire judicial tenure on the same type of cases.

Another trend within the Philadelphia judiciary was their similarity of educational background. This, combined with the decidedly inbred nature—born and raised within the city limits—gave the court a homogenous grouping rarely found at the appellate or federal level. It is also a finding consistent with my earlier work on criminal lawyers in which 22 of the 23 Philadelphia sample were raised and educated locally (Wice, 1978).

The Selection Process: The Political Path. Despite the surprising amount of trial experience, particularly in the practice of criminal law, it clearly was the presence of political connections and activities which seemed to propel nearly all of the judges through the selection process. Common Pleas judges are elected to 10-year terms in Philadelphia and must be able to gain the support of the dominant leaders of the Democratic party, although a select number of "acceptable" Republicans are allowed to gain favorable backing. All judges interviewed attested to the extreme politicization of the judicial selection process. Previous studies of Philadelphia have also noted the significant impact that politics plays upon the entire criminal justice system (Wice, 1974, 1978; Wice and Suwak, 1973).

Immediately prior to running for judicial office, nearly half of the judges had held public office or were actively involved in politics (according to their own self-evaluation). Several of the judges had run (usually unsuccessfully) for congressional and mayoral positions. Nearly all had sometime in their recent past (within 10 years of receiving their judgeship) maintained a moderate level of political involvement. This manifested itself in a variety of tasks and responsibilities within the party organization. Their activities ranged from near full-time preoccupation with politics and elections at the ward, state, and national levels to a highly selective and limited participation in a few carefully chosen campaigns. Politics for most of the judges was a fascinating and important diversion toward which their formal legal careers had inevitably drawn them.

Despite the obvious interest in political affairs prior to becoming a judge, approximately 50% of the judges interviewed forcefully indicated that they did not seek out the judgeship as a political goal but rather it was offered to them by friends who were influential party officials. The reasons for being the recipient of such good fortune was thought by the judges to be derived from long friendships with these political leaders, their distinguished professional reputation, and moderate visibility on the Philadelphia political and social scene—the last two criteria being logically related to the vote-getting potential of the candidate.

The political career of one of the city's judges, Thomas A. White, was highlighted in a recent *Time* cover story entitled "Judging the judges" and offers a critical examination of the linkage between politics and judicial office in Philadelphia. The article recounts that "White was picked to fill a vacancy in 1977. Why? "I'm Irish," he says, "Of course I'm qualified," he hastily adds, but he matter of factly explains that the Democratic Party needed an Irish judge to balance the ethnic make-up of their judicial slate. One of 16 children of an IRA member who fled Ireland, he is also a lifelong Democrat who managed to be elected to the state legislature in the Eisenhower landslide. Redistricted out of his seat in 1954, he decided to go to law school and became a criminal defense lawyer. All the while, he stayed active in Democratic ward politics and his loyalty was rewarded when he was backed for a judgeship by Congressman Raymond F. Lederer whom White describes as a "close personal friend" ("Judging the judges," 1979: 52). Although the career of Judge White is an extreme example of the possible political involvement of Philadelphia's judges prior to their election, it is nevertheless a difference in degree rather than kind.

First Days on the Job and Additional Training. Traditional descriptions of the first days on the job for new judges are filled with feelings of trauma and inferiority. The Philadelphia judges, however, recounted this memorable period as one of excitement and challenge. They generally were confident that they could handle the new job. There was little that was unexpected and most felt that on-the-job training would shortly dispose of those few problems and uncertainties. The absence of a viable orientation program was noted but most judges felt that, for themselves, any extended type of training was not necessary (although many thought that some of their colleagues may have been brought along too rapidly and were in need of a lengthier indoctrination).

These sentiments should not be construed to imply a blasé attitude on the part of these novice judges. They were both flattered and sometimes puzzled by their new prerequisites and respect. Even the idea of wearing a robe was foreign to them as they strolled from their chambers to the courtroom. The bowing and scraping of City Hall functionnaires is still an annoyance and embarrassment for most of them. A disappointment for the newer judges was their less than impressive office quarters (chambers) located in an undistinguished office building across the street from the City Hall Courthouse. Most of the judges implied that their chambers were a noticeable step down in terms of size and elegance from their previous private law offices.

In Philadelphia, new judges are given a two-day orientation which concentrates upon administrative concerns. They are also urged to attend state-wide judicial conferences held twice yearly and are designed to offer an educative component for the beginning judge as well as refresher seminars for the more experienced. These conferences were described as more social than educational. The only judge interviewed who did seem to require extensive preparation because of his lack of legal experience was given a three-month stint in the Municipal Court which handles misdemeanors and less serious cases. None of the judges interviewed had been to the National Judicial College at the University of Nevada. Most were skeptical of such programs, describing them as being social affairs with little long-range value.

Philadelphia judges interviewed in this study, as a rule, exuded self-confidence in their capacity to master the art of judging in criminal cases without formalized training sessions. Any problems which did arise would be readily disposed of through informal conversations with trusted colleagues. No new plans appear to be projected in the near future to significantly alter the current limited and unstructured training process. As long as the judges continue to reach the court with such respectable litigation backgrounds, the necessity for such educative programs may not be relevant for the Court of Common Pleas.

Socializing Agents. Being consistent with the rest of this study's findings, the Philadelphia judges did not feel any urgency for consulting with or relying upon the help of socializing agents. As noted in the introductory section, these socializing agents are comprised of a group of public officials within the criminal justice system who provide advice and information for the beginning judge. They include the judge's colleagues, his court staff (law clerk, bailiff, secretary, and stenographer), lawyers, and public officials such as prosecutors, public defenders, and court administrators.

If a problem did arise most of the judges stated they would first turn to one of their more experienced colleagues whom they respected. The entire Court of Common Pleas meets two or three times a year and then only to discuss pressing administrative matters. For the 8 to 10 judges assigned to the waiver unit which conducts nonjury felony trials, their intragroup monthly meetings were viewed by most of the judges interviewed as informative and useful. Most acknowledged that these lunch-hour meetings offered the major interaction among the judges. Outside of these meetings, the beginning judge might select another judge or two that he personnally respected and contact him privately in chambers for advice. Typical dificulties for the novice judge were proper drafting of charges to the jury, judicious handling of obnoxious defense attorneys, and aiding incompetent prosecutors.

Nearly all judges interviewed were surprised by the lack of collegiality among their fellow members of the court. There was almost no socializing outside of a few official functions. Each judge seemed to have two or three close friends among his colleagues but was rather disdainful toward most of the other members of the court. It was surprising to have every judge interviewed comment so negatively upon the ability of his colleagues. The most typical descriptions involved the terms lazy, slow-witted, inadequate, and mediocre.

The second group of socializing agents used by judges is their court staff. The Philadelphia judges did not emphasize the role of their staff during their initial socialization, although they were appreciative of the many useful services that they did provide during their judicial tenure. The law clerk, typically a half-time employee with a law degree and an interest in criminal law, is the most critical member of the court staff. Although the amount and type of work delegated to the law clerk varied greatly among the judges, most seemed to rely upon them for tedious legal research. Some judges offered clerk positions to outstanding law school graduates and treated it as an honorific yearlong position similar to a clerkship at the appellate level. Many judges, however, simply viewed the clerk as a professional aide who would remain with the judge for as long as both of them could stand each other. These clerks occasionally worked with the judge prior to his reaching the bench. One judge credited his law clerk of many years experience with personally reducing the number of possible appellate reversals.

Other possible socializing agents beyond the law clerks and their colleagues were either not mentioned or noted as being ineffective. This is not to imply that judges in Philadelphia are not friendly and open with members of the courthouse community. One is immediately struck by the friendly atmosphere in both the chambers and the courthouse. But this surface conviviality has not affected the independent decision making of each judge.[1]

Adjustments. Even though most Philadelphia judges indicated that their assuming judicial office did not necessitate any meaningful adjustments in their lives, each judge did note some particular shift in his life which he had not fully anticipated. Almost without exception the judges stated that their social life and circle of friends did not change. If they were friendly with lawyers, both parties made a conscious effort to avoid topics which might prove uncomfortable and studiously avoided talking about pending litigation.

A few of the judges were surprised by their difficulty in abandoning their previously held adversarial role. Especially during the first months on the bench, several judges stated that they had to restrain themselves from jumping into the fray to aid an incompetent attorney. One judge had trouble initially stifling himself from objecting to an attorney's arguments which were drifting off the subject. Too many years as a defense attorney or presecutor leave a mark on courtroom behavior which often takes several months to erase. One judge candidly admittted that he would close his eyes in the beginning as the only way he could refrain from showing emotion. The most unusual adjustment was by one judge who stated that as a top trial lawyer he was working himself toward a nervous breakdown and he found that the pace of court life was sufficiently slow to reduce stress and lower his blood pressure.

The Future and a Miscellany of Related Comments. It was interesting to note that with few exceptions (three), most of the judges expressed a strong desire to continue working in the criminal law area despite the fact that by being in a unified court system they could easily choose to be rotated to the civil side. The administrative judge, realizing the preference of most civil judges to remain within their more familiar environs, was happy to keep things static and not coerce the judges into unpopular shifts. A possible explanation for this development may be related to the legal backgrounds of each group of judges. The civil judges in particular have been described as being quite unfamiliar with the criminal law and rarely litigated criminal matters prior to their assuming office. As previously noted, the criminal judges frequently came with experience in the prosecutor's office or an occasional criminal case as part of their general litigation practice. Several of the criminal court judges stated that they resisted a switch to the civil side because they would not know the law and they would be continually having to call their colleagues for advice. They found themselves to finally becoming comfortable handling criminal cases and did not want to complicate their lives by having to retool and learn the myriad of civil law complexities. Other judges found the civil law boring and dry and preferred the excitement and drama of criminal cases. It was frequently described as being more significant since it dwelt with peoples' lives and not merely the exchange of moneys and property. Only one judge stated a strong preference for leaving the criminal law and he believed that the civil side held the greater intellectual challenge that had been waning after his first few years on the bench.

Approxmiately 25% of the jddges interviewed were looking forward to leaving the bench at the completion of their present term of office. Another 25% were undecided about the future, while the remaining 50% had positive feelings about continuing on the bench indefinitely—either at the Court of Common Pleas or a higher court such as the state appellate branch. For those contemplating leaving the court, monetary reasons were by far the most common explanation. Depressing working conditions, declining respect, and impossible caseloads were additional reasons. It was felt by nearly all of the judges interviewed that they were losing 50% to 75% of their potential salary by remaining on the bench. One frustrated judge added that the longer he remained on the bench, the more difficult it would be for him to return to private practice where the continually changing laws would have him hopelessly out of date. He thus concluded that despite financial hardships, he had to remain on the bench.

CONCLUSIONS

It appears from the findings of this study that the criminal court judges sitting on the Philadelphia Court of Common Pleas have not undergone the type of judicial socialization process which was described in the initial section of this essay. The overwhelming majority of judges interviewed in Philadelphia possessed the self-confidence and/or prior experience to assume their judgeship with almost no reliance upon socializing agents or training programs.

The Philadelphia experience as described in this essay raises several important questions concerning the city's court system and the political environment which encapsulates and affects its operation. Is this city's criminal court system and political culture a unique situation? Is it such an anomaly that it may be discounted as merely an extreme, and therefore, isolated, phenomenon? This question can only be answered after future research investigates judicial socialization experiences in a wide variety of additional jurisdictions (i.e., federal, appellate, and trial) located within a diverse range of political cultures.

As noted initially, this Philadelphia study is part of a much larger study expanding to several additional jurisdictions and including many more interviews in each locale. It is optimistically hoped that at the conclusion of this more ambitious project, a better grasp of the factors influencing judicial socialization will be obtained and contribute to a clearer understanding of the problem.[2]

Because the study of the Philadelphia court of Common Pleas represents a different type of judicial and political milieu from the federal district and state appellate court systems which have formed the primary data base for most of the previous studies of judicial socialization, it may be hypothesized that the divergent environments are the critical explanatory variables. Thus, the Philadelphia socialization process may be typical for urban felony couuts operating within a highly politicized setting, while the Carp and Wheeler (1972) study accurately describes federal and state appellate courts within their relatively less political settings.

Recent studies of the federal judiciary by Schmidhauser (1979) and Richardson and Vines (1970) have carefully documented the fact that most of those selected have come from prestigious law firms and dominated by upper-middle-class, White, Anglo-Saxon Protestants. Although politics obviously plays some role in their selection, it is a minor factor when compared with the Philadelphia process. Even the nature of the federal court system—with its lifetime appointments and newly implemented merit panels—attempts to remove the judge from political pressure. The judges are also frequently forced to relocate in a new city, although he will remain within the same region. Coming into a new city, forced to deal with criminal (as well as civil) cases for the first time in their lives after professional seclusion within a large corporate firm, it is little wonder that these federal judges would be likely (and willing) candidates for judicial socialization.

Beyond the influence of the type of court system is the possibly even more critical factor of the type of political culture which surrounds that court system. This point was convincingly demonstated by Levin (1977). Levin's study compared the criminal trial judges in a traditional city—Pittsburgh, where judicial selections reflected a highly politicized environment—with a reform city—Minneapolis, which had a weak political machine. In Pittsburgh, Levin found that the Democractic Party machine selected judges from its own ranks and "have minority ethnic and lower income backgrounds and pre-judicial careers in political parties and government rather than in private practice" (1977: 5). In Minneapolis, however, the selection of judges had been taken out of politics and controlled more by the bar association and large, business-oriented law firms. The judges selected also were most likely to come from both of these institutions.

As a concluding note, it is urged that social scientists interested in understanding judicial socialization take into account two critical variables which appear to influence the process. The first is the type and level of the court. For too long, studies of judicial socialization (and, for that matter, most aspects of judicial behavior) have focused almost exclusively upon the federal or state appellate courts. The Philadelphia judges deciding felony cases within the Court of Common Pleas have experienced a far different socialization process than is found at these higher levels. It appears that, additionally, the professional backgrounds and style of judicial recruitment and selection also differ markedly from their federal and appellate counterparts. Obviously this is not a call to terminate the study of the federal and appellate systems, but rather a recommendation to follow the leads of Eisenstein and Jacob (1977), Neubauer (1979), Levin (1977), and Cole (1975) who have initiated serious investigations into the operation of our local trial courts.

The second variable, closely related to the first, is to take into consideration the degree and type of politicization surrounding the local court system. This variable, as Levin has pointed out, can exert significant influence upon the operation of the court system from its selection and recruitment process all of the way through critical sentencing decisions. The startling similarity between the Philadelphia political environment studied here and that of Pittsburgh studied by Levin appears to offer further evidence of the possible linkage between these sets of variables. Such similarities and trends are, of course, not being presented now as proof of the existence of a relationship, but rather in the hope that further research can begin by asking the important questions and examining the critical factors underlying the judicial socialization process.

NOTES

1. Possibly the fact that these judges operate in so political an environment in which nearly all the actors are inbred and have known each other for so long accounts for the small town atmosphere of the courthouse.

2. The most recent studies in this field have been initiated by Arthur Rosett for the Twentieth Century Fund and John Paul Ryan for the American Judicature Society.

REFERENCES

ALPERT, L., B. ATKINS, and R. C. ZILLER (1979) "Becoming a judge: The transition from advocate to arbiter." Judicature 62; 325.

American Academy of Judicial Education (1980) Publicity Handout. Washinton, DC: Author.

BLUMBERG, A. (1967) Criminal Justice. Chicago: Quadrangle.

CARP, R. and R. WHEELER (1972) "Sink or swim—socialization of a federal district judge." Journal of Public Law 21: 359.

COLE, G. (1975) The American System of Criminal Justice. N. Scituate, MA: Duxbury.

EISENSTEIN, J. and H. JACOB (1977) Felony Justice. Boston: Little, Brown.

FELDMAN, D. C. (1976) "A contingency theory of socialization." Administrative Science Quarterly 21: 433.

GOULDEN, J. C. (1976) The Benchwarmers: The Private World of the Powerful Federal Judges. Westminster, MD: Ballantine.

Institute of Judicial Administration (1965) "Judicial education in the United States: A survey." (mimeo)

JACKSON, D. D. (1974) Judges. New York: Atheneum.

"Judging the judges." (1979) Time (August 20): 52.

KARLEN, D. (1966) "Judicial education." American Bar Association Journal 52: 1049.

LEVIN, M. (1977) Urban Politics and the Criminal Courts. Chicago: University of Chicago Press.

National Advisory Commission on Criminal Justice Standards and Goals (1973) Courts. Washington, DC: Government Printing Office.

NEUBAUER, D. (1979) America's Courts and the Criminal Justice System. N. Scituate, MA: Duxbury.

President's Commission on Law Enforcement and Administration of Justice (1967) Task Force Report: The Courts. Washington, DC: Government Printing Office.

RICHARDSON, R. and K. VINES (1970) The Politics of the Federal Courts. Boston: Little, Brown.

SCHMIDHAUSER, J. R. (1979) Judges and Justices: The Federal Appellate Judiciary. Boston: Little, Brown.

STILLS, D. [ed.] (1968) "Adult socialization" in Encyclopaedia of Social Sciences (Vol. 14). New York: Macmillan.

VOLCANSEK-CLARK, M. (1978) "Why lawyers become judges." Judicature 62; 166.

WICE, P. B. (1978) Criminal Lawyers: An Endangered Species. Beverly Hills, CA: Sage.

WICE, P. B. (1974) Freedom for Sale. Lexington, MA: Lexington Books.

WICE, P. B. and P. SUWAK (1973) "Current realities of public defender programs." Criminal Law Bulletin (November).

Chapter 7

JUDICIAL SUPERVISION OF THE
GUILTY PLEA HEARING

JAMES A. CRAMER

It has been well-documented that guilty pleas comprise the bulk of convictions in the criminal justice system. The usual estimate is 90%, although variation in rates has been shown to exist (Miller et al., 1978).

Since the guilty plea process differs from trial in terms of the burden placed on the prosecution for proving the offense, it is important that procedural safeguards are carried out in order to protect the defendant from a conviction that is unwarranted by the facts of the case or achieved through violation of due process.

A major concern of critics of plea bargaining is that the process is susceptible to violation of due process and rights of the defendant (Rosett and Cressey, 1976). Conversely, proponents of plea bargaining argue that due process and fairness may, in many instances, be much more likely to occur if the process is carried out correctly and with adequate supervision (Miller et al., 1978). These proponents argue further that the primary responsibility for insuring that due process

Author's Note: *This article is a product of research funded by the Law Enforcement Assistance Administration, U.S. Department of Justice, grants 75-NI-99-0129 and 77-NI-99-0049.*

safeguards are in operation belongs squarely on the shoulders of the judiciary, and particularly the trial judge.

While there is widespread recognition of the necessity for judicial scrutiny of the guilty plea process, virtually no empirical data exist on the extent to which judges are applying the standards, rules of criminal procedure and case law in conducting and overseeing the guilty plea *hearing*. It is to this problem that the present research is addressed.

BACKGROUND

The judge has several oversight responsibilities upon formal entry of a guilty plea in court. He must personally address the defendant to determine that: (1) there is a factual basis for the charge to which the defendant is pleading; (2) the plea is both knowing and voluntary; (3) the defendant understands the consequences of the plea; and (4) that a number of constitutional rights are being waived.

Standards for performing these oversight functions are found in statutes, cases, and rule of criminal procedure. Of the 26 states sampled in this study, 22 have adopted a statute or criminal rule pertaining to judicial supervision of the guilty plea process. All of the states studied have specific case law setting forth requirements of judicial oversight (Table 1).

Additionally, there are four national models and the Federal Rules of Criminal Procedure which set forth standards for judicial supervision of the guilty plea process. The four models are:

(1) A Model Code of Pre-arraignment Procedure
(2) American Bar Association Standards Relating to the Function of the Trial Judge
(3) National Advisory Commission on Criminal Justice Standards and Goals, Court and Criminal Justice System
(4) Uniform Rules of Criminal Procedure.

TABLE 1 Judicial Supervision

	AL A	AL B	AK A	AK B	AZ A	AZ B	CA A	CA B	CO A	CO B	CT A	CT B
1. Ascertaining defendant's knowledge/understanding of nature (elements) of the charge. [ABA 1.4]	NS	NS	R	R	R	R*	NS	R	R	R	NS	NS*
2. Ascertaining defendant's knowledge/understanding of sentence possibilities. [ABA 1.4]	NS	NS	R	R	R	R	NS	?	R	R	NS	NS*
3. Ascertaining defendant's knowledge/understanding of collateral consequences.	NS	NS	NS	NR	NS	N	NS	NS	NS	NS	NS	NS
4. Ascertaining defendant's knowledge/understanding of constitutional rights waiver. [ABA 1.4]	NS	NS	R	R	R	R	NS	R	R	R	NS	R
5. Ascertaining plea voluntariness. [ABA 1.5]	NS	R	R	R	R	R	R	R	R	R	NS	R
6. Ascertaining factual basis/accuracy of the plea. [ABA 1.6]	R	NS	R	NS	R	R	NS	NS	R	R	NS	R
7. Procedural adequacy of the record. [ABA 1.7]	NS	R	R	NS	R	R	NS	R	R	R	NS	R

175

TABLE 1 Judicial Supervision (continued)

	FL A	FL B	IL A	IL B	IN A	IN B	IA A	IA B	LA A	LA B	MA A	MA B
1. Ascertaining defendant's knowledge/understanding of nature (elements) of the charge. [ABA 1.4]	NS	R	R	NR*	R	R	NS	R	R	NS	R	NS
2. Ascertaining defendant's knowledge/understanding of sentence possibilities. [ABA 1.4]	NS	NR*	R	NR*	R	R	NS	R	NS	NS	R	NS
3. Ascertaining defendant's knowledge/understanding of collateral consequences.	NS	NR	NS	NR	NS	NS	NS	NS	NS	NS	NS	NR
4. Ascertaining defendant's knowledge/understanding of constitutional rights waiver. [ABA 1.4]	NS	R	R	R	R	R	NS	R	NS	R	R	R
5. Ascertaining plea voluntariness. [ABA 1.5]	R	R	R	R	R	R	NS	R	R	NS	R	R
6. Ascertaining factual basis/accuracy of the plea. [ABA 1.6]	R	R*	R	R	R	R	NS	R	NS	NS	NS	R*
7. Procedural adequacy of the record. [ABA 1.7]	R	NR	R	R	R	R	R	R	NS	NR	NS	R

TABLE 1   Judicial Supervision (continued)

	MI A	MI B	MO A	MO B	NV A	NV B	NJ A	NJ B	NM A	NM B	NY A	NY B	OH A	OH B
1. Ascertaining defendant's knowledge/understanding of nature (elements) of the charge. [ABA 1.4]	R	*	R	R	R	R	R	R	R	R	NS	R	R	R
2. Ascertaining defendant's knowledge/understanding of sentence possibilities. [ABA 1.4]	R	NS	NS	R	NS	R	R	R	R	R	NS	R	R	R
3. Ascertaining defendant's knowledge/understanding of collateral consequences.	NS	NS	NS	NS	NS	NR	NS	NS	NS	NS	NS	R	R	R
4. Ascertaining defendant's knowledge/understanding of constitutional rights waiver. [ABA 1.4]	R	R	NS	R	NS	R	R	R	R	R	NS	R	R	R
5. Ascertaining plea voluntariness. [ABA 1.5]	R	R	R	R	R	R	R	R	R	R	NS	R	R	R
6. Ascertaining factual basis/accuracy of the plea. [ABA 1.6]	R	R	NS	NS	NS	NS	R	R	R	NS	NS	NR	NS	NS
7. Procedural adequacy of the record. [ABA 1.7]	R	R	NS	NS	NS	NS	R	R	R	NS	NS	NS	R	R

TABLE 1 Judicial Supervision (continued)

	OR A	OR B	PA A	PA B	SC A	SC B	TN A	TN B	TX A	TX B	VA A	VA B	WA A	WA B
1. Ascertaining defendant's knowledge/understanding of nature (elements) of the charge. [ABA 1.4]	R	R	NS	R	NS	R	NS	R	NS	NS	R	NS	R	R
2. Ascertaining defendant's knowledge/understanding of sentence possibilities. [ABA 1.4]	R	R	NS	R	NS	R	NS	R	R	R*	R	NS		R
3. Ascertaining defendant's knowledge/understanding of collateral consequences.	R*	NS	NS	NS	NS	NS	NS	NS	NS	NS	NS*	NS	NS	NR
4. Ascertaining defendant's knowledge/understanding of constitutional rights waiver. [ABA 1.4]	R	R	NS	R	NS	R	NS	R	NS	R	NS	NS		A
5. Ascertaining plea voluntariness. [ABA 1.5]	R	R	NS	R	NS	R	R	R	R	R	R	R	R	R
6. Ascertaining factual basis/accuracy of the plea. [ABA 1.6]	R	NS	NS	R	NS	R	NS	R	NS	R	R	NS	R	R
7. Procedural adequacy of the record. [ABA 1.7]	R	NS	R	R	NS	NS	NS	R	NS	R	NS	NS	R	R

R = required; NR = not required; NS = no statement on this issue; P = prohibited; A = allowed or suggested; * = see textual commentary which is located in Appendix to clarify or avoid misinterpretation

Despite, however, the proliferation of law and national models pertaining to judicial supervision of the guilty plea process, and research pertaining to judicial participation in plea negotiations, information on the actual oversight functions of the judge in the guilty plea hearing is virtually nonexistent. A notable exception is the work of Mileski (1971). In observation of lower court practices, Mileski observed that the presiding judge did not apprise the defendants of their constitutional rights in one of every four cases. The study also found that the seriousness of the charge affected the nature of the judicial role. Serious offenders were more likely to be apprised of their rights individually rather than as part of a group of defendants. Four forms of apprising defendants of their rights were observed: (1) in a group and out in the audience; (2) in a group before the bench; (3) in a group before the bench with individual follow-up; and (4) individually before the bench. Mileski holds that each method is progressively more effective and that the individual method may be more effective in terms of the defendant's understanding of the process. Conversely, the collective method contributes to the operation of a more efficient court bureaucracy (Mileski, 1971). She concludes that the norms of justice and organizational imperatives are contrary to one another and that the need for comprehensive judicial supervision of guilty pleas is essential.

METHODS

The data in this study were gathered as a component of a three-year national study on plea bargaining (Miller, 1978). The project was divided into two phases. The first phase was designed to develop a national overview of plea bargaining in America, including the extent, nature, and types of bargaining that existed. In the first phase, 26 jurisdictions were selected, including a 10% random sample of legal juris-

TABLE 2   Number of Guilty Plea Observations in Six Jurisdictions

	Felony	Misdemeanor
Jurisdiction		
El Paso	24	82
New Orleans	67	53
King Co.	100	38
Pima Co.	69	41
Deleware Co.	78	53
Norfolk	75	31
TOTAL 413	298	(Combined N = 711)

dictions of 100,000 population and above (20), and 6 additional jurisdictions that had special programs designed to either drastically reduce or eliminate plea bargaining. The primary form of data gathered in this phase of the study came from structured interview schedules covering judges, prosecutors, and defense attorneys.

The second phase of the study focused on the statistical analysis of data gathered in six jurisdictions.[1] The data included interview material, prosecutor case file data from guilty pleas and trials, data from a plea bargaining simulation, and data recorded from in-court observations of guilty plea hearings.

The data for this article were derived primarily from the in-court observations, which were conducted in 711 guilty plea hearings in both felony and misdemeanor courts in six jurisdictions. Supplemental interview data collected in phase 1 and 2 of the study are presented as a brief overview in the findings.

The guilty plea observations were recorded on a structured observation form by research associates during guilty plea proceedings in each of the jurisdictions. The items on the observation forms pertained to the procedure followed in the plea proceedings. Of particular concern was the form and substance of how the judge addressed the defendant during the plea acceptance in court.

This article addresses four major questions relating to judicial supervision of the entering of a guilty plea in court. They are: (1) Did the court inquire as to the factual basis of the guilty plea? (2) Did the court determine that the plea was entered by the defendant voluntarily and with understanding? (3) Did the court inform the defendant of the consequences of his plea? and (4) Was an in-court record made of any plea agreement between the prosecution and defense?

The data presented here cover felony cases only. The misdemeanor courts are, however, discussed briefly with the felony courts in the overview of the findings presented below.

FINDINGS

Overview

In all of the courts observed by project staff in phase 1 of the study, some form of explanation or general warning was given to defendants before a plea of guilty was accepted by the court. The degree of specificity and comprehensiveness, however, varied considerably between jurisdictions. The greatest variation occurred in misdemeanor cases, where in some instances the explanation was given by court personnel other than the judge.

Within particular jurisdictions it was not uncommon to see some judges using a standard written list of warnings which resembled a litany. Other judges either did not have standard litanies or varied their length depending on the defendant. In St. Louis, for example, judges indicated that they exchanged litanies in order to arrive at the most comprehensive and useful one available. Some indicated that they varied the litany depending on the ability of the defendant to understand the proceeding.

The most cursory attention given to defendants and oversight responsibilities occurred in Dallas County, Texas, where defendants charged with misdemeanors and awaiting dispositon in confinement are brought before the judge in what is referred to as a "jail chain." In one court that was observed, these defendants signed a form indicating that they were not indigent and would not voluntarily accept state-appointed counsel. A very brief litany was all the defendant heard. It was usually started before the defendant even reached the bench. It was not uncommon for 70 or more defendants to be disposed of in a matter of a few hours. Few left the court without pleading guilty.

In King County, Washington, felony court judges often merely ask the defendant if the defense attorney has explained the rights that are set forth in the Statement of Defendant on Plea of Guilty, which is signed by all parties in the court. Despite the phrase in the statement that it was read by or to the defendant in open court, this did not usually occur.

In an Anchorage, Alaska, misdemeanor court, the judicial litany was read quickly to a group of defendants sitting in the jury box. It was not easy to follow and the judge emphasized the right of the defendants to represent themselves. Waiver of counsel appeared to be routine, even when defendants were sentenced to incarceration.

At the other end of the continuum, a judge in San Bernardino County, California, expressed the belief that the court should take time to explain the defendant's rights *in court*. It took an average of one-half hour to accept each guilty plea. In yet another jurisdiction, the type of explanation depended on the seriousness of the charge. Thus, a felony judge said the explanation was given with more emphasis as the cases became more serious. He also indicated that it was given in a more sophisticated fashion in the suburbs than in the city. But once again, a wide variation was noted in the jurisdictions. One position was that the litany should be standardized and read verbatim. The other approach was that every case was different and that different questions should be stressed or expanded at different times depending on the circumstances.

Overall, then, the field observations in phase 1 revealed a divergent pattern of judicial supervision of the guilty plea hearing. Let us now turn to the data gathered in phase 2: the systematic observations of guilty plea hearings in six jurisdictions.

Guilty Plea Hearings in Six Jurisdictions

In order to determine how the factual basis was established in the guilty plea hearing, four questions were included on the observation form: (1) Did the judge ask the defendant if he was pleading guilty because he was in fact guilty? (2) Did the judge ask any additional questions relating to the defendant's guilt in the case? (3) Did the prosecutor make any statements or present evidence at the guilty plea hearing? and (4) Did the state produce a witness during the plea hearing?

As indicated in Table 3, marked variation occurred both within and across jurisdictions regarding how factual basis was established. By far, the most common method was for the judge to ask the defendant if he was pleading guilty because he was in fact guilty. This was consistently asked in over 60% of the cases in five of the six jurisdictions. The other three methods recorded for determining factual basis show a pattern of extreme variation across and within jurisdictions.

Using the methods noted above, Norfolk, Virginia, appeared to have delved into the factual basis more systematically in a larger percentage of cases than any other jurisdiction. Table 3 reflects, however, a greater role by the prosecutor in establishing the factual basis, with both evidence and witnesses being presented by him in court. In Pima County, Arizona, the judge assumed primary responsibility for deter-

TABLE 3   Method of Judicial Determination of the Factual Basis for Guilty Pleas

	Percentage of cases in which the method was used			
Jurisdiction	Judge asked defendant if he was pleading guilty because he was in fact guilty	Judge asked additional questions about offense	Evidence was presented by the prosecutor	Prosecutor produced a witness for plea hearing
El Paso	64%	57%	100%	0%
New Orleans	68%	5%	18%	13%
King Co.	60%	18%	10%	0%
Pima Co.	90%	96%	3%	0%
Delaware Co.	30%	44%	44%	16%
Norfolk	72%	8%	77%	76%

mining factual basis by personlly addressing the defendant regarding his guilt and asking additional questions in over 90% of the cases. Overall, while establishment of factual guilt appears to be carried out in a high percentage of cases in most of the jurisdictions, the judges routinely asked additional questions only in Pima County. And, only in El Paso and Norfolk do the prosecutors routinely present any evidence regarding factual guilt. Finally, only in Norfolk are witnesses commonly produced for testimony.

The interview data collected from judges in the six jurisdictions suggested that while the judges recognized the importance of establishing a factual basis, they did not want to move into the area of assessing the strength of the state's case. The most common position was that it was the responsibility of the defense attorney to establish the probability of conviction and therefore determine whether the defendant might plead or go to trial. Only one judge interviewed said that he regularly probed into the strength of the case. He maintained that this was primarily limited to situations in which the plea agreement involved an unusually lenient sentence recommendation. Such a recommendation was seen by the judge as an indicator of an extremely weak case, and perhaps one without a factual basis at all.

Overall, judges recognized the importance of establishing a factual basis in court, but felt there were other mechanisms throughout the system to assist in making that determination. Some believe that grand jury procedures provide an adequate method of achieving this. Others cited the preliminary hearing as precluding the necessity of making an extensive factual basis inquiry at the guilty plea hearing. In Virginia, where there is commonly a grand jury proceeding after a preliminary hearing, judges routinely hear a witness for the state before accepting a plea.

It was not uncommon to find variation within jurisdictions as to how the factual basis was established. For

example, in King County half of the judges interviewed indicated that they would ask defendants questions regarding
their offense behavior. However, the use of a written form,
signed by the defendant at the guilty plea proceeding,
appeared to satisfy the remaining judges that the factual basis
requirement was met. These jduges felt that the statements,
read and signed by the defendants, satisfied the requirement
of the law. Further, defense attorneys were often seen going
through the standard written court litany item by item.

Regarding the court's responsibility to ensure that the
defendant's plea is both knowing and voluntary, the rules and
cases of the states do not detail specific procedures. For
example, one case held that if a defendant answers that he is
pleading guilty of his own free will, the test of voluntariness is
met, *State v. Ellis,* 572 P.2d 791 (1977). In another case, it was
held that a signed written waiver of rights is sufficient, *State
v. Henry,* 114 Ariz. 494, 462 P.2d 374 (1977).

The data in Table 4 show a pattern of variation within and
across jurisdictions as to how judges establish that the plea is
both knowing and voluntary. Overall, judges are most likely
to ask the defendant if he understands the nature of the
charges. This was done at least three-fourths of the time in
four of the jurisdictions and about half the time in the other
two sites. By contrast, only in Pima County did judges regularly ask the defendant if additional promises had been made
to him (96%). The other five jurisdictions ranged from 6% to
35%.

Regarding the question of threats or coercion used to
induce guilty pleas, this kind of inquiry was only made regularly in New Orleans and Pima County (96% and 97%, respectively). The remaining jurisdictions range from 12% to 67%.
As a note of clarification, however, in Delaware County
defense counsel noted in court that no threats had been made
or coercion used on their clients. This occurred in approxi-
matley half of the cases observed.

TABLE 4 Method of Judicial Determination of Knowingness and Voluntariness of Guilty Pleas

Jurisdiction	Percentage of cases in which judge asked the defendant		
	Judge asked Defendant if he understood charges	Judge asked Defendant if promises other than plea agreement were made	Judge asked defendant if threats or coercion were used to obtain guilty plea
El Paso	87%	17%	21%
New Orleans	74%	21%	96%
King Co.	50%	35%	42%
Pima Co.	84%	96%	97%
Delaware Co.	44%	6%	12%
Norfolk	80%	9%	67%

TABLE 5   Judicial Notification of Rights Waived by Defendant at
            Guilty Plea Hearing

| | Percentage of cases in which judge notified defendant | | |
Right to:	Trial	Remain silent	Confront witnesses
Jurisdiction			
El Paso	100%	59%	50%
New Orleans	100%	52%	60%
King Co.	60%	9%	45%
Pima Co.	100%	94%	97%
Delaware Co.	65%	63%	64%
Norfolk	77%	12%	12%

Another dimension of the defendant's understanding the
nature of his plea is the waiver of certain constitutional
rights. Rights which are specifically waived include the right
to trial, the right to remain silent, and the right to confront
witnesses. Table 5 indicates the frequency with which judges
address the defendant regarding the waiver of these rights.
While the data again indicate a mixed pattern, certain conclusions may be drawn. First, judges are most likely to indicate to the defendant that the plea of guilty involves a waiver
of the right to trial. This was indicated to all defendants in El
Paso, New Orleans, and Pima County. In the three remaining jurisdictions it was noted between 60% and 77% of
the time. In general, the judges in Pima County were consistently thorough in noting the loss of all these rights in the
guilty plea proceeding. The remaining jurisdictions reflect no
particular pattern other than that three of the remaining five
jurisdictions, El Paso, New Orleans, and Delaware County,
note the loss of all the rights at the plea hearing in at least half
the cases.

In terms of the sentencing consequences of the plea, the
four national models cited earlier require the court to personally inform the defendant of any mandatory minimum or

maximum sentence which may be imposed after conviction.[2] Three of the models require the court to note any additional punishments which may be imposed after a guilty plea by reason of any previous conviction.[3] Additionally, in Washington, Virginia, Arizona, and Pennsylvania, criminal rules of procedure require that the defendant be informed by the judge of the minimum and maximum sentences.[4] Case law in Texas provides a similar requirement.[5] Only in Louisiana does there appear to be no requirement that sentencing consequences be explained to the defendant.

Table 6 indicates somewhat of a mixed pattern in the frequency with which sentencing consequences were noted to the defendant. In five of the six jurisdictions these consequences were noted in over half the cases. In Pima County and El Paso it was done with great regularity (90% and 88%, respectively). Only in Delaware County was there a consistent failure on the part of the judiciary to bring this to the attention of the defendant in court.

While the courts explained with some regularity the sentencing consequences of the plea, there was little or no explanation of possible enhanced sentencing which could be imposed because of prior felony convictions. In Delaware County, El Paso, and King County, the issue was never mentioned in court. Only slightly more frequently was the issue mentioned in Pima County and Norfolk at 4% and 3%, respectively. The enhanced sentencing concept was most likely to be noted in New Orleans (15%).

While the above percentages are obviously quite low, it seems to reflect the infrequency with which such sentencing options are invoked in these jurisdictions at guilty please. It occurs less than 1% of the time in King County, Delaware County, and Norfolk; 2% of the time in Pima County; and 4% of the cases in El Paso. New Orleans was far more likely to invoke the process, at 15% of the cases. Finally, regarding collateral consequences of the plea, which include property

TABLE 6 Judicial Notification of the Defendant of the Consequences of Pleading guilty

| | Percentage of cases where | | |
| | Consequences were noted to the defendant by the judge in court | | |
Jurisdiction	Range of Permissible sentence	Enhanced Sentencing Provisions	Collateral Consequences
El Paso	88%	0%	These include property and marital rights, right to vote, and rights involved in obtaining a license to practice certain occupations.
New Orleans	75%	15%	
King Co.	62%	0%	
Pima Co.	98%	4%	
Delaware Co.	6%	0%	
Norfolk	52%	3%	In less than 4% of all cases were *any* of the above consequences mentioned.

TABLE 7   Percentage of Guilty Pleas in Which a Plea Agreement Was
           Noted on the Record in Court

Jurisdiction	
El Paso	4%
New Orleans	48%
King Co.	75%
Pima Co.	100%
Delaware Co.	97%
Norfolk	69%

and marital rights, right to vote, and the rights involved in
obtaining licenses to practice occupations, in less than 4% of
the cases were any such consequences explained to the defendant.

Notation of Plea Agreements on the Record

There has been an increasing trend toward including the
plea agreement as a part of the formal record in court. The
most common procedure is to note only that a plea agreement has been reached between the prosecution and defense.
There are no requirements in any state that the discussions
leading up to an agreement be made part of the record.

Four of the national models and the Federal Rules of
Criminal Procedure require the agreement to be noted in
court and on the record.[6] Washington, Arizona, Virginia, and
Pennsylvania have specific rules which require the plea agreement to be made a part of the record as well.[7] Texas and
Louisiana, however, do not appear to have any requirement
that the plea agreement be placed on the record.

Table 7 indicates the frequency with which plea agreements were made a part of the formal record in court in the
six jurisdictions. In Pima County and Delaware County
proper notation of the plea was made in virtually every case.

It was also done with great regularity in Norfolk and King County. In New Orleans, where there is no state requirement for such a record being made, it was still done in about half the cases. Only in El Paso was it rarely done at all. This, however, accords with all the evidence indicating that plea bargaining was nonexistent in that jurisdiction during the period of this study.

The data in Table 7 suggest two things. First, that most guilty pleas are the result of some form of plea agreement and, second, that there is substantial compliance with state rules requiring that such an agreement be noted on the record. And, while it has been commonly assumed that most guilty pleas are the result of some type of plea agreement, the court record now makes it possible to empirically verify the extent of explicit plea bargaining where data of these kinds exist.

SUMMARY AND CONCLUSIONS

I noted at the outset that a major criticism of plea bargaining was that it is subject to an uneven application of many of the due process procedures that are set forth by the Constitution, case law, and federal and state rules of criminal procedure. And, as a result, it is a system that is basically unfair.

Proponents of plea bargaining, on the other hand, both for ideological and pragmatic reasons, point out that it is possible to insure that due process is carried out in plea bargaining by proper accountability for those involved in the process and through appropriate supervision by the judiciary.

In this article I have briefly examined one component of the oversight process—that of the judicial supervision of the guilty plea hearing. And, while such supervision is only one form of overseeing the guilty plea and plea bargaining system, it is viewed by most legal authorities as being an important one.

The data from our study suggest that there are considerable variations in the comprehensiveness of judges in supervising the guilty plea hearing. In the four areas examined—determination of the factual basis, knowingness and voluntariness, rights waived, and consequences of the plea—judges were more likely to ask a basic question regarding these areas and then move on to another matter. Observations of the plea proceedings suggest that most judges are perfunctory in their examination of the defendants who plea guilty. Indeed, our data showed that in approximately one-half of the cases, the plea hearing took less than three minutes. Only in one jurisdiction, Pima County, were judges comprehensive in their conduct of the plea hearing. In the other five jurisdictions the pattern is too varied to allow any general conclusions other than that they are performing some of their inquiry and oversight functions and not others. Clearly, there is need for improvement in the areas of more comprehensive development of factual basis, notification of the rights being waived, and an explanation of the consequences of pleading guilty. Additionally, the court observers' general notes suggested that a sizable number of judges are very perfunctory in many of the questions they do ask and pose questions in such a way that it would be very difficult for a defendant to give an undesirable response. Overall, there are enough gaps in the procedure so that it is conceivable that a number of defendants are pleading guilty without full knowledge of the consequences of their pleas and the due process rights they have relinquished.

One positive sign which has developed in the last decade is the incorporation of the plea agreement into the formal court record. Our data show that in two jurisdictions it was noted on the court record in virtually every guilty plea case that resulted from plea negotiations. In two other jurisdictions this occurred roughly three-fourths of the time; and in another jurisdiction, approximately half of the time. Only in El Paso, where plea bargaining did not exist, was such a notation virtually unheard of.

Given the amount of judicial discretion that exists and how the court conducts its guilty plea hearings, jurisdictions should give serious consideration to standardizing the plea hearing process. This could be done either through changes in the rules of criminal procedure or by general agreement among the judiciary. In some jurisdictions, the chief judge has certain administrative powers which could facilitate such a change.

Finally, the issue of judicial supervision of the guilty plea hearing must be seen in the context of the general plea process and due process safeguards which are in operation. It is logical and organizationally sound to insist that judicial supervision of the process take place at points well before the guilty plea hearing. In this way, we would be more likely to insure that there be accountability for the process as well as the product of plea bargaining.

NOTES

1. The jurisdictions included: Pima County, Arizona; Delaware County, Pennsylvania; New Orleans, Louisiana; El Paso, Texas; Norfolk, Virginia; and King County, Washington.

2. *ALI Model Code* § 350.4(1)(e) minimum, maximum and parole limitations; *ABA Pleas of Guilty,* § 14-1.4(a) (ii) minimum and maximum, and limitations on parole and probation; *NAC COURTS* § 3.7(6) minimum and maximum; *URCP* 444(b) (1) (iii) minimum and maximum and parole limitations.

3. *ALI Model Code* § 350.4(1) (e) (iii); *ABA Pleas of Guilty,* § 14-1.14(a) (iii); *URCP* § 444(b) (1) (iii).

4. Wash. Cr. Rules, Cr. R. 4.2(g); Ariz. Cr. R. 17.2; Va. Cr. R. 3A:11; Pa. Cr. R. 319.

5. Murry v. State, 561 S.W. 2d 821 (Tex. Cr. App. 1977).

6. *National Prosecution Standards,* § 216.6 (National District Attorneys Association, 1977; ALI Model Code §§ 320.5(4); 350.5(1) and 350.8; ABA *Pleas of Guilt,* § 14-1.7; *NAC*, 3.7; and *FRCP* 11(e) (2).

7. Wash. Cr. R. 42. (g); Ariz. Rules Cr. Proc. Form XIX; VA. Rules of Crim. P., Rule 3A:11; Pa. Rules of Cr. Proc. 319.

REFERENCES

American Bar Association (1979a) Project on Standards for Criminal Justice, Standards Relating to Pleas of Guilty. Chicago: Author.

American Bar Association (1979b) The Prosecution Function and the Defense Function. Chicago: Author.

American Bar Association (1970) Discovery and Procedure Before Trial. Chicago: Author.

American Law Institute (1975) A Model Code of Pre-Arraignment Procedure. Washington, DC: Author.

MILESKI, M. (1971) "Courtroom encounters: An observation study of a lower criminal court." Law and Society Review 5: 473.

MILLER, H. S., W. F. MCDONALD, and J. A. CRAMER (1978) Plea Bargaining in the United States (Phase I report). Washington, DC: Government Printing Office.

National Advisory Commission on Criminal Justice Standards and Goals (1973) Courts and Criminal Justice System. Washington, DC: Government Printing Office.

National Conference of Commissioners on Uniform State Laws (n.d.) Uniform Rules of Criminal Procedure. (unpublished)

ROSETT, A. and D. CRESSEY (1976) Justice by Consent. Philadelphia: J.B. Lippincott.

Chapter 8

FEDERAL SENTENCING GUIDELINES: WILL THEY SHIFT SENTENCING DISCRETION FROM JUDGES TO PROSECUTORS?

WILLIAM M. RHODES
CATHERINE CONLY

In terms of disrupting the lives of private citizens, few federal officials exercise as much authority as does a District Court judge when imposing a criminal sanction. The judge may sentence an offender to a term of incarceration or probation. He may order the offender to pay a fine or to compensate the victim. He may even force the offender to provide a community service.

There is small wonder that critics of the legal system often focus their attention on sentencing. Given the obtrusiveness of the criminal sanction, critics demand that its application be purposeful and equitable. But observers as knowledgeable as Judge Marvin Frankel have concluded that "We have in our country virtually no legislative declarative of the principles justifying the criminal sanction (1973: 106). And researchers have found that in jurisdiction after jurisdiction, sentencing could be described as disparate or, at best, inconsistent (see Rhodes and Conly, 1980; Shane-Dubow et al., 1979).

Sentencing guidelines are often proposed as a method of reforming this morass of sentencing disparity and illogic (see

Wilkin et al., 1978; Calpin et al., 1978; Zalman et al., 1979; Zimmerman and Blumstein, 1979; Minnesota Sentencing Guideline Commission, 1979). Such guidelines are usually predicated on a statistical analysis of past sentencing decisions, the purpose of the analysis being to determine empirically a set of weights that judges seem to associate implicitly with variables describing the offender and his offense. Once determined, the weights can be used to specify mathematically the average sentences that have in the past been imposed on offenders, thus providing a sentencing judge with a future "guide" for imposing comparable sentences on similar offenders convicted under similar circumstances.

Some commentators have argued that guidelines that are based on historical sentencing practices are too static and may perpetuate perverse sentencing decisions from the past (Coffee, 1978; Flaxman, 1979; cf. Zimmerman, 1979; Sparks, 1979). In response, reformers have suggested that historical guideline weights be modified to take into account prevailing opinions about the utilitarian objectives of sentencing and just deserts concerns (Rhodes, 1980). In the federal system, a sentencing commission has been suggested as a vehicle by which those modifications could be made (see Zalman, 1979).[1]

Still other commentators have argued that limiting guidelines to judges may not be adequate to improve sentencing. Sentencing is at least partly a shared responsibility, and disparity and illogic do not arise simply from the exercise of judicial discretion (Alshuler, 1978; Schulhofer, 1979). First, judicial discretion is constrained by federal sentencing statutes that limit sentence severity. Second, U.S. Attorneys are responsible for charging offenders, and because of the prominence of plea bargaining, attorneys also frequently determine the offense with which an offender is convicted. Since the convicting offense constrains the judge in imposing sentence—and moreover since the U.S. Attorney sometimes makes sentence recommendations—the prosecutor may exercise considerable control over the sentence imposed. Third, the imposed sentence does not determine, by itself, the amount of time that a convicted offender serves. The U.S. Parole commission decides when an incarcerated offender is to be freed, provided the offender has been sentenced to more than one year and has served one-third of his sentence.[2] Additionally, the Bureau of Prisons routinely awards incarcerated offenders with "good time," somewhat reducing the amount of time that is to be served (Partridge et al., 1979).

Due to the charging and plea bargaining authority of the U.S. Attorney, some critics contend that implementing sentencing guidelines, which impose no constraints on prosecutor behavior, would shift additional sentencing authority from judges to U.S. Attorneys. Moreover, prosecutors play an adversarial role in the judicial process and, as such, do not necessarily demonstrate the balanced views expected of criminal court judges. Thus, a shift in discretion may have deleterious effects. In the federal system, sentencing guidelines would probably eliminate the federal parole system. It has been argued that parole actually equalizes sentences, thus smoothing out the disparity attributed to U.S. Attorneys and District Court judges (Shin, 1973). If true, then guidelines could further exacerbate sentencing illogic and unfairness by eliminating the moderating influence of the U.S. Parole Commission.

Although the above arguments are credible, we nevertheless believe that sentencing guidelines can have a salutary impact on sentencing. The purpose of this essay is to discuss the roles of District Court judges, U.S. Attorneys, and correctional officials in the federal sentencing process. In part, this discussion draws on surveys with judges, U.S. Attorneys, and defense attorneys.[3] In part, it is based on an extensive analysis of sentencing in the federal criminal courts completed during a recent project (Forst et al., 1979). We believe that the essay makes the point that the most important focus of authority to determine the severity of a sen-

tence resides with the sentencing judge, not with the prosecutor or correctional officials. We do not believe sentencing
guidelines, as they are envisioned for the federal courts, will
shift additional discretion to U.S. Attorneys. Therefore, we
believe that federal sentencing guidelines, although
applicable to federal judges only, can improve the administration of justice in the federal courts.

OFFENSES AND OFFENDERS

To what characteristics of offenders and offenses do judges
typically respond? In assessing this question, we looked at
five federal offenses and corresponding offender types,
selected for reasons explained later. Two of the offenses—
income tax evasion (including nonfiling) and bribery of
public officials—are often considered white collar crimes.
Forgery, another offense studied, is a nonviolent property
offense that frequently is conducted conspiratorially and may
involve the falsification of signatures on stolen U.S. treasury
checks or the counterfeiting of treasury notes. Bank robbery
is a violent property offense; although it rarely results in
death or injury to victims, it typically involves the use, or
threat, of force. Finally, federal drug offenses generally involve the manufacture, distribution, or sale of controlled sub-
stances; less than 2% are cases of simple possession.

In total, we examined approximately 3,000 cases of convicted federal offenders who were the subject of presentence
investigation reports. Data collection consisted of obtaining
information about offenders' childhood backgrounds and
school, work, drug, arrest, and conviction histories, and
recording material about the offenses.

Although the offenders within each offense category were
unique in some ways, they did cluster with respect to certain
characteristics. In general, bank robbers and forgers were
more similar to each other than to the other three offender

types, especially those in the white collar crime group. In turn, income tax offenders and bribers shared more characteristics with each other than with bank robbers, forgers, or drug violators. Finally, drug offenders tended to be dissimilar to the other four offender types. In the following paragraphs, we will briefly outline these similarities and differences.

Males predominated in each offense group, although one-quarter of the forgers were females. Convicted bribers, bank robbers, and forgers were younger than income tax and drug offenders. The mean ages for the former group were between 28 and 31 years; for the latter, convicted offender ages were 49 and 46, respectively. More whites than blacks were involved in committing bribery, income tax, and drug offenses. With reference to bank robbery and forgery, the racial distribution was evenly split. With respect to childhood development, the offenders across the five groups were equally well-situated. Income tax violators were somewhat less likely than the other four offenders to have had parents who were abusive or to have had difficulty obtaining the necessities of life. Forgers and bank robbers were somewhat more likely to have experienced these problems.

Income tax offenders and bribers were likely to have records of steady employment. In contrast, bank robbers and forgers tended toward chronic unemployment. Drug offenders fell between the two extremes but were more likely to be regularly employed than unemployed.

Bank robbers, drug violators, and forgers were considerably more likely to abuse drugs and alcohol than bribers and income tax offenders. Bank robbers had the most serious problems: 33% used opiates and 11% were problem drinkers. In the drug offender sample, 40% smoked marijuana, 26% took stimulants, and 14% used opiates. Most who used opiates were addicts. Forgers fared somewhat better: 23% smoked marijuana or used opiates occasionally, and 11% were problem drinkers.

We observed a mixture of marital stability for the five types of offenders. Bank robbers and forgers were unlikely to be married; and, when married, were apt to have weak marital ties. In contrast, both bribers and income tax violators were likely to have strong marital ties. Drug offenders fell between the two groups but were slightly inclined toward weak instead of strong ties.

Examination of the school and community adjustment of the five offender groups produced the following results. Bank robbers and forgers shared a tendency toward poor social adjustment; bribers and income tax violators were well-adjusted, and drug offenders demonstrated intermediate adjustment.

We also looked at the degree to which offenders interacted with cohabitants, family members, and peers who had criminal records. First, drug offenders, forgers, and income tax violators were most likely to have cohabitants who encouraged crime. Alternatively, bribers were considerably less likely to have criminal cohabitants. And bank robbers fell between the two groups. Second, bank robbers and forgers were most likely to have family members who provided counternormative support. Bribers were least likely to have family members who encouraged crime. Income tax offenders and drug violators were more likely to receive normative support from family members than the first two types, but less likely than bribers. Finally, drug violators were by far more likely to interact with criminal peers than any of the other offenders. Bank robbers followed and forgers and income tax violators were even less likely to associate with criminal peers. Bribers were the least likely to have contacts with criminal friends.

Even better indicators of the criminal involvement of the offenders are included in their histories of arrest and conviction. As might be expected, bribers were least likely to have arrest records. Only 22% of the bribers had been arrested prior to their arrests for bribery, and the majority of those earlier offenses involved nuisance violations, such as disorderly conduct and public drunkenness. Consequently, few bribers had served any previous prison time. Surprisingly, nearly half of the income tax offenders had previously been arrested. Nuisance offenses predominated in these histories, but between 15% and 20% of the income tax offenders had been arrested for commission of white collar offenses, property crimes, or offenses against people. Most had not previously been convicted, and the few who were had received probation sentences.

The arrest histories of drug violators, forgers, and bank robbers were extensive. Drug offenders had a mean of five prior arrests, which most often involved nuisance or drug offenses. The majority of convicted drug offenders had served previous terms of probation. The picture was worse for forgers. Over 80% of the forgers had previously been arrested; the mean number of arrests was seven, with prior property offense arrests predominating. Of those with arrest histories, 35% had served more than one year in prison, and 21% had served less than one year. Finally, 90% of the bank robbers had been arrested prior to their bank robbery arrests. Between 60% and 70% of that sample had at least one arrest for crimes against property, persons, or the public order. Hence, nearly 60% had served previous time in prison; two-thirds of those had served in excess of one year.

The above picture of offenders convicted of five federal offenses generates thought about their treatment after conviction. In the next section, we begin concentrating on the sentences received by these offenders, paying special attention to the role of the prosecutor and judge in the sentencing process.

U.S. ATTORNEY DISCRETION

The answer to the question regarding whether judicial guidelines would reduce sentencing illogic and nonuniformity seems to hinge, in part, on the answer to two questions about the prosecutor's descretion. At present, is the prosecutor's influence at the time of sentencing so great that guidelines imposed on judges would be vacuous? Whether or not the prosecutor's current power is great, would the institution of judicial guidelines enhance the U.S. Attorney's power, thereby thwarting the reform that advocates of guidelines envision?

We can suggest some answers to these questions by investigating plea bargaining as it currently occurs in the federal system. This investigation draws on a random sample of interviews with 103 U.S. Attorneys and Assistant U.S. Attorneys, 264 federal District Court judges, and 111 defense attorneys, including attorneys who represent indigents and retained counsel. We have also drawn on a statistical analysis of sentencing in eight District Courts. Although these findings reveal the current role of prosecutory discretion, they do not demonstrate how this role would change with the institution of guidelines. Thus we must be more speculative in this latter regard.

As noted earlier, the rules of criminal procedure allow various forms of plea bargaining, ranging from charge bargaining to sentence bargaining. In order to determine the predominant form of bargaining, we asked U.S. Attorneys, defense attorneys, and federal judges the question: "Please think of the criminal cases in your recent experience that have reached a disposition in this jurisdiction. Out of every 10 cases, how many times does each of these events occur?" The respondents were provided with a list of possible answers (Table 1).

As Table 1 reveals, most cases in federal courts terminate with a plea of guilty. Attorneys and judges estimated that, out of 10 cases, between 2 and 3 cases are decided by trial. Of the cases ending by a plea of guilty or nolo contendere, a few— less than 15%—involve no explicit bargain although, of course, the defendant who does not receive a bargain might

TABLE 1   Estimates of The Type of Bargaining in the Federal Courts:
Number of Instances Per 10 Terminated Cases

Type of Disposition	U.S. Attorney Estimates	Defense Attorney Estimates	Judge Estimates
Defendant goes to trial	2.6	3.1	1.9
Defendant enters a guilty plea; as a result: The prosecutor *neither* reduces the charges/counts NOR Makes a sentencing recommendation favorable to the defendant	1.3	.8	1.5
Defendant enters a guilty plea; as a result: The prosecutor reduces the charges/counts BUT *Does not* make a sentence recommendation favorable to the defendant	4.7	3.5	4.0
Defendant enters a guilty plea; as a result The prosecutor does *not* reduce the charges/counts BUT *Does* make a sentence recommendation favorable to the defendant	.9	1.3	.9
Defendant enters a guilty plea; as a result: The prosecutor *both* reduces the charges/counts AND Makes a sentence recommendation favorable to the defendant	1.4	2.2	1.2

still anticipate an ultimate sentence concession from the sentencing judge. Most cases involve a guilty plea that arises
from charge bargaining. The surveys indicated that between 4

and 5 of every 10 cases involved either a reduction in the charge or a reduction in the number of counts. About 1 of every 10 cases involved explicit sentence bargaining exclusively, and somewhat more than 1 of every 10 involved a combination of charge and sentence bargaining.

Given that charge bargaining is the dominant mode of negotiation, a question arises concerning the magnitude of the concession that the U.S. Attorney grants in exchange for a guilty plea. Using multivariate statistical analysis, we were able to estimate the magnitude of this concession. However, interpreting the derived figure requires caution. As we have shown, charge bargaining is not the *only* form of bargaining and, therefore, our estimates do not encompass all of the concessions that the prosecutor makes. Also, examining the top charge ignores the reduction in the number of convicting counts resulting from negotiations. Finally, our analysis is based primarily on eight federal districts and those eight districts may not characterize the type of bargaining indicative of the federal system as a whole.

Our analysis proceeded by estimating the probability that a given offender who had committed a given offense would be convicted of a charge calling for an X-year maximum prison sentence. This analysis was conducted for the five offense types discussed earlier. These offenses were part of a larger analysis of 11 offense types and were chosen because for these 5 offenses, but not for the other 6 offenses, the federal statutes provide a sufficient range of "lesser included offenses" to allow for variance in the top charge at conviction.

Findings are presented in Table 2. In columns 1a-1e of Table 2, we have provided the probability that an offender convicted by plea of a given generic offense (bank robbery, bribery, and so on) would be convicted of a subset of that offense that carried a designated X-year maximum. In columns 2a-2e of the table, we provide a corresponding estimate of these probabilities for offenders who were convicted at trial. Since the statistical analysis controlled for both the magni-

TABLE 2   The Probability of Conviction for An Offense With An X-Year Maximum for Persons Convicted By Trial and Persons Convicted by Plea

Maximum Sentence	Drugs		Bank Robbery		Bribery		Forgery		Income Tax	
	Plea (1a)	Trial (2a)	Plea (1b)	Trial (2b)	Plea (1c)	Trial (2c)	Plea (1d)	Trial (2d)	Plea (1e)	Trial (2e)
1 yr	.16	.05			.23	.01			.36	.36
2 yr					.39	.09				
3 yr					.11	.07			.09	.09
4 yr	.11	.07								
5 yr	.23	.19					.34	.14	.55	.55
10 yr			.18	.02			.58	.62		
15 yr	.50	.69			.27	.84	.08	.24		
20 yr			.55	.29						
25 yr			.27	.69						

207

tude of the offense and the offender's background, we submit that these differences can be attributed to plea bargaining.[4]

The impression that Table 1 connotes—at least in our view—is that prosecutory policy, as reflected in plea bargaining, has a sizable impact on the seriousness of the offense with which the offender is convicted. For example, the overall probability that a drug dealer will be convicted by plea of an offense with a 15-year maximum is about .50, but for similar offenders convicted at trial of similar crimes, the probability is closer to .69. For bank robbers the probability of being convicted of a top charge calling for a 25-year maximum is .27 for offenders pleading guilty, but .69 for persons convicted at trial. The offense of bribery of public officials results in a 15-year maximum for about 27% of the offenders who plead guilty, but the probability of a 15-year maximum approaches a near certainty for persons convicted by trial. For forgers, the probability of a 15-year maximum goes from .08 for persons convicted by plea to .24 for persons convicted by trial, and the probability of a 10-year maximum goes from .58 to .62. The only exception to this pattern was for persons convicted of internal revenue code violations. We discerned no charge reductions for tax evaders who entered pleas of guilty.

Although the reader can formulate his own opinion, it seems to us that these bargaining "concessions" are significant, more so because the measure of concession excludes other types of bargains (including sentence recommendations). Given this apparent broad power of the prosecutor and defense to bargain over the charge, it is interesting to ask who is influential in the sentencing decision in the federal courts. Do the prosecutor and defense attorney in fact dominate? Or does the judge retain his dominant role in the sentencing process despite plea bargaining?

We questioned prosecutors and defense attorneys by having them answer the following: "Overall, how much influence does each person/group actually have on the sentence

TABLE 3   Percieved Influence On The Sentence Imposed

Influence on Sentence Imposed	Judge		Defense		Prosecutor	
	By Pros.	By Def.	By Pros.	By Def.	By Pros.	By Def.
Great	.81/.52	.78/.61	.00/.03	.00/.03	.01/.04	.02/.07
Substantial	.10/.18	.10/.23	.01/.12	.03/.10	.03/.18	.23/.19
A lot	.02/.12	.04/.07	.10/.18	.05/.21	.11/.18	.19/.32
Some	.03/.04	.04/.03	.51/.45	.57/.48	.54/.43	.42/.31
Little	.00/.01	.00/.01	.29/.18	.28/.14	.21/.07	.07/.04
None	.01/.03	.02/.00	.10/.03	.05/.01	.10/.09	.05/.04
No answer	.04/.10	.05/.05	.00/.03	.03/.04	.00/.03	.02/.04

that is imposed?" The question was repeated for two situations. In the first situation, "A defendant is found guilty at trial or following a plea and there is no charge, count, or sentence concession whatsoever." In the second situation: "A defendant enters a plea, resulting in either charge/count reduction or a sentence recommendation favorable to the defendant." The allowed responses are listed in Table 3.

In Table 3, the responses are categorized as "great," "substantial," "a lot," "some," "little," "none," and "no answer." Assessments are given for the role of the judge, the defense attorney, and the prosecutor. The responses are differentiated by whether they came from the defense attorney or the prosecutor.[5] The first number in each column pertains to a no plea bargain situation, and the second number pertains to the plea bargain situation.

Table 3 suggests several conclusions about the perceived influence of the judge, prosecutor, and defense attorney on the sentence administered. First, there is agreement that the judge always exercises the most influence over the sentence that is imposed, regardless of the method of disposition. The judge's influence is ranked as at least "a lot" in over 90% of the responses to the first scenario, which is not surprising, but the judge's influence remains quite strong even when a plea bargain is made. Prosecutors see the judge as having at least "a lot" of influence in 8 out of 10 responses to the plea bargaining scenario (1 in 10 was "no answer") and 9 out of 10 defense attorneys perceived the judge as having as much influence. These findings seem to indicate that, according to the perceptions of legal publics, judicial influence remains very strong no matter what the type of disposition.

A second finding is also of interest. Both the prosecutors and defense attorneys agree about the defense attorney's influence on sentencing. When there is no plea agreement, the defense attorney is judged to have "some" or less influence by 9 out of 10 respondents. His influence increases when a plea bargain is entered, but even in this instance he is seen as having at least "a lot" of influence in only 1 of 3 responses.

We conclude that while the defense attorney's influence over the sentence imposed increases as a result of plea bargaining, his influence remains generally limited and never approaches that of the judge.

A third finding relates to the prosecutor's influence over sentencing, as perceived by the prosecutor and defense attorney. Unlike the above responses dealing with the judge and defense attorney's influence, attorneys' perceptions about the prosecutor's role differ. Defense attorneys tend to ascribe greater influence to the prosecutor than does the prosecutor himself. When a case goes to trial, the prosecutor sees himself as exercising "a lot" of influence in about 1 in 10 cases, but he is viewed by the defense attorney as exercising "a lot" in 4 of every 10 cases. Both the prosecutor and the defense attorney agree that the prosecutor's influence increases as a consequence of plea bargaining. Of every 10 presecutors' responses, 4 described prosecutory influence as at least "a lot" for the plea bargaining scenarios. Almost 6 of every 10 defense attorney responses rated the prosecutor's influence as at least "a lot" under the plea bargaining scenarios.

One inference that might be drawn from Table 3 is that plea bargaining shifts sentencing discretion to the prosecutor and, to a lesser extent, to the defense attorney. Nevertheless, perceptions were that the influence of the judge during the sentencing process remains very great. These findings lead us to believe that the judge remains the dominant figure at the time of sentencing even when plea bargaining enters into the disposition process. It would be incorrect to understate the important role of the prosecutor and defense attorney during sentencing, especially when justice is dispensed by negotiated settlements. On the other hand, it would also be misleading to imply that plea bargaining has so eroded the judicial role that the prosecutor and defense counsel actually supplant judicial authority.

The question remains about whether sentencing guidelines would disturb the status quo and shift more discretion to the prosecutor. We asked the opinions of prosecutor and defense counsel on this matter, identifying for them three potential problems or benefits from guidelines and asking them to rank on a scale from 1 to 7 "whether it is a serious problem that should be considered or a possible benefit to strive for." The problems/benefits included: "Some sentencing discretion would be transferred to the prosecutor's office." "Guidelines would increase, for all parties, the certainty of sentences that will be imposed if the defendant is found guilty." "Guidelines would make the prosecutor more open in plea negotiations." Responses 1 and 2 were ranked as extremely negative and responses 6 and 7 were ranked as extremely positive. Unfortunately, because of the wording of these questions, it is impossible to discern whether attorneys were responding to the question "would it occur" or the question "would it be good or bad if it did occur," or both. Therefore, the following conclusions are speculative.

Responses from prosecutor and defenders were not the same. To the possibility that guidelines would increase prosecutor discretion, 48% of the defense attorneys were *extremely positive*, and only 13% of the prosecutors were positive. We also found that 4% of the defenders and 20% of the prosecutors were extremely negative. We might conclude from these numbers that most prosecutors did not foresee a great shift for the better or worse from guidelines, while almost half of the defenders saw a shift to increased prosecutor power.

Prosecutors did frequently perceive guidelines as increasing the certainty of sentences imposed as a result of a guilty plea. Better than half (53%) saw this development as extremely positive compared with about one-third (37%) of the defense attorneys. Only 9% of the prosecutors and 13% of the defenders saw the development as negative.

Very few prosecutors saw the guidelines as making the prosecutor more open in plea bargaining. Only 7% of the U.S. Attorneys judged this eventuality as negative and 12% as positive. Similarly, 10% of the defense counsel saw this development as negative and 31% saw it as positive.

A question posed to judges was more directly to the point and did not suffer from the ambiguity of the above three questions.[6] A total of 128 federal judges were presented with a series of hypothetical guideline schemes and were asked how those schemes would impact on judicial sentencing discretion and prosecutory influence on sentencing. Not surprising was the majority response that judicial discretion would decrease under all but the most vacuous guideline scheme. But more interesting was the finding that, at a maximum, only one in five judges perceived prosecutor influence as increasing. Moreover, a larger number of judges perceived the likely effects of guidelines as *reducing* prosecutor influence. This view is contrary to that held by guideline critics, who contend that the prosecutor's authority would be enhanced by the adoption of federal sentencing guidelines.

In summarizing the above, we did uncover evidence that plea bargaining is an important determinant of the seriousness of the charge with which an offender is convicted. Assuming that this charge is also an important determinant of the sentence that a convicted offender receives, it might be anticipated that the prosecutor dominates the sentencing process. According to the results of surveying prosecutors and defense counsel, however, although the prosecutor's power is not trivial, neither is it so great as guideline critics might assume. This finding implies that the judge remains the dominant figure during sentencing, despite the fact that prosecution and defense have an enhanced influence as a consequence of plea bargaining.

We also uncovered little evidence that prosecutor, defense counsel, and judges anticipate that guidelines would greatly increase the power of the prosecutor and thereby erode judicial responsibility. Even when the perception was that the prosecutor would have more discretion, this increased discretion was viewed positively by the defense counsel.

SENTENCES SERVED BY CONVICTED OFFENDERS

An analysis of sentencing provided further insight into why judges dominate at the time of allocution, regardless of whether a plea bargain was struck. The explanation seems to be that judges take into account many factors in addition to the occurrence of a plea bargain, and these factors are independent of negotiations between the prosecutor and the defense. We present findings supporting this conclusion in this section.

We analyzed the length of time served by convicted offenders, controlling for aspects of their offenses, certain processing variables, their social backgrounds, and their criminal records.[7] Detailed methodology and findings are reported elsewhere (Rhodes and Conly, 1980) and are summarized in Table 4. The table identifies those variables that were statistically significant at a .05 level of confidence in regressions on the sentence received by convicted drug law violators, bank robbers, persons convicted of bribing public officials (or accepting bribes), forgers, and internal revenue code violators. The numbers appearing in the columns can be interpreted as approximations to the incremental prison time associated with each variable for offenders sentenced to prison.[8]

Findings reveal that many factors other than the most severe maximum sentence associated with the top convicting offense influence the average length of time served by convicted offenders. Criminal records are examples. Compared with offenders who had no previous convictions, criminals who served previous sentences in excess of one year (PRIOR LONG TERM) served an extra 11 to 22 months. Criminals who served a previous prison term of less than one year served an extra 8 to 15 months, and offenders who previously served a term of probation received up to 5 extra months. These ranges applied to drug offenders, robbers, and forgers. For bribers and tax law violators—offenders who

TABLE 4   The Relative Impact of Offender Characteristics, Offense Characteristics and Processing Variables On The Length Of A Prison Term

Variables	Drugs	Bank Robbery	Bribery	Forgery	Income Tax
ORGANIZED	14.41				
DISTRIB 1	9.95				
DISTRIB 2	8.04				
DISTRIB 3	6.26				
HEROIN	5.54				
ORGANIZED CON.			1.59		
EQUAL PARTINCIP.			1.62		
PUBLIC OFFICIAL			1.90		
GROUP		8.37			
EXTENUATING		9.77			
B 5 AND 1000		13.12			
GT 1000		13.94			
NO. ROBBERIES		4.87			
MIDDLE AMOUNT				6.49	
LARGE AMOUNT				8.51	
DOLLAR ACTUAL				6.53	0.88
YEARS IN OFFENSE					2.55
ILLEGAL INCOME					2.77
B 32-100,000					2.02
GT 100,000					5.65
MOST SEVERE MAXIMUM	1.20	1.96		0.84	0.74
TRIAL	6.71		1.88	7.39	5.78
SUPPLIED INFORMATION	- 5.78			- 4.25	
COUNTS	4.76				2.02
MALE	16.59			6.34	10.08
EMPLOYMENT	3.99	6.20		4.05	1.26
AGE					- 0.13
DRINK	1.59				
USED DRUGS				1.47	
FAMILY SUPPORT				1.96	
COHABITANT SUPPORT				1.23	
MIXED				- 2.19	
PRIOR LONG TERM	10.88	21.85		12.94	
PRIOR SHORT TERM	9.84	15.09		8.33	
PRIOR PROBATION	2.88			4.68	
PRIOR CONVICTION			9.35		2.28
DETAINERS PENDING		7.51			
ANY REVOCATIONS		6.95		6.84	
SERVE SENT./WARR.				3.96	

Notes: Regression weights derived from using tobit as the estimating technique are reported in the table. These weights can be interpreted as the incremental prison time attributed to a unit change in the independent variables for offenders sentenced to prison.

tend to have minor criminal histories—prior convictions increased the sentences by 2 to 9 months. For robbers and forgers—offenders who characteristically have extensive criminal records—additional time was served by persons who had detainers pending at the time of conviction, by offenders who had probation revoked in the past, and by offenders who were either serving a sentence or who had a warrant outstanding at the time of the instant offense.

The magnitude of the offense also had a strong effect on the average length of time served. For drug offenders, the length of prison increased with the offender's role in the drug's distribution. Persons who organized and managed a drug distribution network fared the worst (ORGANIZED), followed by offenders who sold the drug to buyers who intended to resell to others (DISTRIB 1), offenders who sold to a mixture of final users and lower level distributors (DISTRIB 2), and offenders who sold exclusively to final users (DISTRIB 3). The incremental time indicated in Table 4 is relative to the time served by persons who either were final users or who played only minor supporting roles in the drug's distribution. It also appeared that persons selling heroin, as compared with persons selling other types of contraband, were treated more harshly.

Bank robbers who committed their offenses in groups (GROUP) and offenders who either kidnapped or physically harmed victims (EXTENUATING) were dealt with more harshly than offenders who acted alone and did not physically abuse victims. The sentence increased with the number of robberies (NO. ROBBERIES). Robbers stealing in excess of $500 served about one year more than robbers who stole less than $500.

Looking at bribers, public officials served two months more time than did private citizens. Participants of extensive conspiracies served extra time, although it did not appear to matter whether the offender initiated the crime (ORGAN-

IZED CON.) or simply participated actively in it (EQUAL PART.).

We found that forgers who stole more than $10,000 (LARGE AMOUNT) served about two months more than offenders who stole between $1,000 and $10,000 (MIDDLE AMOUNT). The latter group served about six months more than offenders who stole less than $1,000.

Similarly, the average length of prison time served by convicted income tax violators increased with the amount of tax payment that the offender attempted to avoid. Compared with persons avoiding less than $32,000, persons avoiding more than $100,000 served an extra six months, and persons avoiding between $32,000 and $100,000 served an extra two months. Offenders whose income was derived from an illegal source received an extra three months, and the sentence increased with the number of tax years for which the offender either failed to declare or underreported his income (YEARS IN OFFENSE).

For forgery, income tax, and bank robbery, the dollar amount of the offense pertained to the dollar loss associated with the convicting offense, rather than the dollar loss from the actual offense. The variable DOLLAR ACTUAL indicates that, when the convicting offense understates the dollar loss of the actual offense, the judge increases the sentence and the offender serves more time. Thus these findings seem to show that the judge is not bound by the offense admitted by the offender as a consequence of his guilty plea, but, in addition, looks at the full constellation of elements of the offender's crime.

We have seen that aspects of the offense, as well as the offender's criminal record, are important to the sentencing decision. So also are several variables that relate to the offender's personal background. Males tend to serve more time than do females convicted of similar crimes under similar circumstances. Employment records (EMPLOYMENT) are salient. Indeed, for the three offenses where offenders are frequently either unemployed or underemployed—drugs, robbery, and forgery—offenders with the best employment records serve an average of 16 to 24 months less time than offenders with the worst employment records.[9] For forgers, offenders who have families that are supportive of conventional lifestyles (FAMILY SUPPORT) and offenders who receive such support from cohabitants (COHABITANT SUPPORT) tend to serve less time than do offenders whose social histories do not evidence such support. Drug-using forgers also serve additional time, as do young tax evaders and drug sellers who abuse alcohol.

The reason for detailing these findings is to indicate that, in order to understand sentencing in federal courts, it is necessary to go beyond the offense of which the offender was convicted, as well as the method of conviction, to examine the offender's background and his actual offense. It is insufficient to examine only the type of disposition and the statute applying to the convicting offense. This is not to say, however, that processing variables are irrelevant to the sentencing process. Table 4 indicates the contrary.

The most severe maximum sentence that the judge could impose, given the most serious convicting offense, is strongly correlated with the average length of time that an offender served. Some illustrations make the point. According to our estimates, a forger who had his charge reduced from one with a maximum of 15 years to one with a maximum of 10 years had his sentence correspondingly reduced by about 4 months. A drug dealer who had his charge reduced from one with a 15-year maximum to one with a 10-year maximum would have his sentence reduced by about 6 months. For bank robbers, a reduction from 25 to 20 years accounts for almost 10 months. Income tax violators convicted of an offense with a 1-year maximum rather than a 5-year maximum save about

3 months. For bribers, there is no correlation between the maximum possible sentence and the amount of time served.

With the above estimates, and those estimates provided in Table 2, it is possible to approximate the sentence concessions resulting from plea bargaining. The calculations necessary to make these calculations are complex.[10] The findings reveal that, while drug sellers serve an average of 18 months as a result of charge bargaining, persons pleading guilty serve an average of 3 months less than offenders convicted by trial. Robbers serve an average of 57 months, but those who charge bargain serve about 7 months less than those who do not. Forgers serve an average of 8 months. Forgers who plea bargain serve about 1 month less than offenders who do not.

The consequences of count bargaining are more difficult to estimate. A larger number of counts seems to increase the severity of the sentence for drug law violators and income tax evaders, but not for the other offenders. As illustrated, drug offenders convicted of five separate counts receive an additional eight months compared with offenders convicted of a single count; for income tax evaders the effect is less—about three months. We do not know the extent to which counts are dropped as a consequence of plea bargaining, however, and thus cannot provide estimates of the gain to the offender of count bargaining.

One remaining finding about the implications of a guilty plea is interesting. Holding constant other aspects of the offender's case, including the most severe sentence that could be imposed as well as the number of counts, sentence concessions resulting from pleading guilty rather than going to trial still emerge. Using the formula cited in Note 10, we found that drug sellers serve an average of 18 months, but that offenders convicted by trial serve an average of 7 months more than offenders convicted by plea. Bribers serve an average of 3 months, but bribers convicted by plea serve almost 2 months less than those convicted by trial. Tax evaders serve an average of a little over 2 months, but persons convicted by trial serve about 5 months more than those convicted by guilty plea. Forgers serve an average of 8 months, but if they are convicted by guilty plea, they serve about 7 months less than if they were convicted by trial.

The significance of these findings is that offenders receive sentence concessions for pleading guilty regardless of the charge and count bargaining conducted by the prosecutor and the defense counsel. Although U.S. Attorneys engage in some sentence bargaining, which might explain these findings, the survey results revealed that sentence bargaining is infrequent in federal courts, which leads us to believe that it is primarily judicial initiative that leads to sentence concessions. In support of this conclusion, we note the sentence concession exchanged for a guilty plea per se is considerably greater than the sentence reductions resulting from either charge reductions or count reductions.

CONCLUSIONS

Sentencing guidelines are a potentially important criminal justice innovation for increasing the rationality and uniformity of criminal sanctions. Yet critics of guidelines have contended that these guidelines might shift discretion from the judge to the prosecutor and have warned that, as a consequence, guidelines might reduce rather than increase uniformity and rationality of criminal sanctions. The continuing ubiquitousness of plea bargaining is often cited as the reason for this shift.

These criticisms are well-taken. The prosecutor is an important figure at the time of sentencing, especially if conviction follows a guilty plea. Nevertheless, the picture may be overdrawn, for two reasons.

First, the survey results revealed that judges remain the dominant figure at the time of sentencing even when conviction is the result of a guilty plea. While the prosecutor's influence is not to be discounted, it does not measure up to that of the judge. Critics perceive guidelines as radically changing this relationship, although federal court judges perceived that discretion would be reduced both for judges and for prosecutors.

Second, the empirical findings on actual sentences revealed that many factors were taken into account during sentencing. The fact that conviction was by guilty plea did not dominate all other factors. Also, it appeared that for the most part, sentence concessions were derived from judicial initiative and that charge and count bargaining were less influential in determining the sentence that the offender would receive.

We are led to believe that sentencing guidelines need not shift discretionary authority to U.S. Attorneys. Guidelines that reflect past sentencing practices, including past practices of rewarding guilty pleas with sentence concessions, would not necessarily place the prosecutor in a better bargaining position, thereby providing him with enhanced powers over sentencing.

NOTES

1. A sentencing commission has been proposed by both houses of Congress as part of the revision of the federal criminal codes.

2. For an excellent description of the federal sentencing process, see *Partridge* et al. (1979).

3. The survey instruments were developed jointly by the staffs of Yankelovich, Skelly and White, Inc. and the Institute for Law and Social Research; the former conducted the surveys and was responsible for data processing.

4. The dependent variable was measured on an ordinal scale determined by the maximum sentence that could be imposed given the top convicting offense. Probit was used to estimate the equation.

B_T is the parameter associated with the variable trial (T), and the X's indicate variables that represent aspects of the offense and the offender's background. Let Pj be the probability that an "average" offender would be convicted of a charge with a maximum sentence falling into category j, such that Pj = $\theta(Z)$, where θ represents the standard normal probability distribution and Z is the standard normal deviate. Let Pj be the observed frequency of category j in the sample, then, it is possible to solve for Z. To determine the effect of a trial on this probability, solve the simultaneous equations:

(1) $Pj^T = \theta(Z+\alpha)$
(2) $Pj^P = \theta(Z-\delta)$
(3) $\alpha + \delta = B_T$

where α and δ are numbers and Pj^T is the probability of being convicted of an offense with a sentence in category j following conviction by trial, and Pj^P is the corresponding probability following conviction by plea.

5. These questions were not asked of judges due to resource limitations and a need to ask judges about other matters.

6. These findings were reported in a companion project report (Yankelovich, Skelly and White, Inc., n. d.).

7. Time served rather than sentence imposed was the dependent variable. Thus these findings are influenced by the policy of the U.S. Parole Board and the Bureau of Prisons.

8. Tobit was the estimating technique. As the text indicates, the numbers in Table 4 are only approximations to the incremental time served because these variables also influence the probability of a prison term. Later calculations take this latter fact into account.

9. The variable EMPLOYMENT is a factor score derived in the original study. The statement in the text was determined from a calculation in which the regression parameter associated with employment was multiplied by four standard deviations of the employment variable, which is standardized.

10. Let E(SVT) and E(SVP) equal the expected value of the most severe maximum sentence associated with the cases of persons convicted by trial and persons convicted by guilty plea, respectively. These numbers were calculated from Table 2.

Let y(i) equal the average time served, where:

i = 1 for all offenders
i = 2 for offenders convicted by trial
i = 3 for offenders convicted by guilty plea.

Let

S = the standard error of the tobit regression
T = the percent of offenders convicted by trial
P = the percent of offenders convicted by guilty plea
PR(z) = the standard normal distribution function
D(z) = the standard normal density function.

Then the difference in the amount of time served by persons convicted by trial and persons convicted by guilty plea, attributed exclusively to the charge reduction typically received by the latter, can be approximated as the solution to the following set of simultaneous equations.

Let DIFF equal this difference. Then:

(1) $DIFF = Y(2) - Y(3)$
(2) $Y(2) = L(2)*PR[L(2)/S + S*D[L(2)/S]$
(3) $Y(3) = [L(3) = B]*PR[L(3) - B/S] + S*D[L(3) = B/S]$
(4) $Y(1) = T*Y(2) + P*Y(3)$
(5) $B = E(SVT) - E(SVP)$

For an explanation of these formulas, see Tobin (1958).

REFERENCES

ALSHULER, A. W. (1978) "Sentencing reform and prosecutorial power: A critique of recent proposals for 'fixed and presumptive' sentencing." University of Pennsylvania Law Review 126: 550-577

CALPIN, J. C. et al. (1978) Analytical Basis for the Formulation of Sentencing Policy. Albany, NY: Criminal Justice Research Center.

COFFEE, J., JR. (1978) "The repressed issue of sentencing: Accountability, predictability, and equality in the era of the sentencing commission." Georgetown Law Journal 66: 1035.

FLAXMAN, K. (1979) "The hidden dangers of sentencing guidelines." Hofstra Law Review 7: 259-280.

FORST, B., W. RHODES, and C. WELLFORD (1979) "Sentencing and social science: Research for the formulation of federal sentencing guidelines." Hofstra Law Review 7.

FRANKEL, M. (1973) Criminal Sentences: Law Without Order. New York: Hill and Wang.

Minnesota Sentencing Guidelines Commission (1979) Summary Report: Preliminary Analysis of Sentencing and Releasing Data. St. Paul: State of Minnesota.

PARTRIDGE, A. et al. (1979) The Sentencing Options of Federal District Judges. Washington, DC: Federal Judicial Center.

RHODES, W. M. (1980) "Alternative logics for the structuring of federal sentencing guidelines." (unpublished)

RHODES, W. M. and C. CONLY (1980) "Toward sentencing guidelines: An analysis of sentencing in federal courts." (unpublished)

SCHULHOFER, S. J. (1979) "Prosecutorial discretion and federal sentencing reform." (unpublished)

SHANE-DUBOW, S. et al. (1979) Felony Sentencing in Wisconsin. Madison, WI: Public Policy Press.

SHIN, H. J. (1973) "Do lesser pleas pay—accommodations in sentencing and parole practices." Journal of Criminal Justice 1: 27-42.

SPARKS, R. (1979) "Prediction and guidelines." Presented to the Academy of Criminal Justice Sciences, Cincinnati, March 14-16.

TOBIN, J. (1958) "Estimation of relationships for limited dependent variables." Econometrica 26 (January).

WILKINS, L. T. et al. (1978) Sentencing Guidelines: Structuring Judicial Discretion. Washington, DC: Government Printing Office.

YANKELOVICH, Skelly and White, Inc. (n.d.) "Judicial reaction to sentencing guidelines." (unpublished)

ZALMAN, M. (1979) "Making sentencing guidelines work: A response to Professor Coffee." Georgetown Law Journal 67.

ZALMAN, M. et al. (1979) Sentencing in Michigan: Report of the Michigan Felony Sentencing Project. Lansing: State of Michigan.

ZIMMERMAN, S. (1979) "Problems of design in sentencing guideline instruments." Presented to the Academy of Criminal Justice Sciences, Cincinnati, March 14-16.

ZIMMERMAN, S. and A. BLUMSTEIN (1979) A Strategy for the Empirical Analysis of Sentencing Behavior in Sentencing Guideline Development. Presented at the meeting of the American Society of Criminology, Philadelphia, November 9.

Chapter 9

JUDICIAL RESPONSES TO TECHNOCRATIC REFORM

ARLENE SHESKIN
CHARLES W. GRAU

An emerging consensus of divergent disciplines and political perspectives depicts the American judicial system as in crisis (Unger, 1976; Kamenka and Tay, 1975; Balbus, 1977; Jenkins, 1980; Trubek and Galanter, 1974; Heydebrand, 1979). The main symptom of this crisis is the inability of judicial resources and organizational capacity to keep pace with the rising demand for its services (Heydebrand, 1979: 29). Underlying these symptoms are broader social dynamics: the growing need for the state to intervene in the private economy (Heydebrand, 1979: 23; Heydebrand, 1977; Baran and Sweezy, 1964; O'Connor, 1973; Wolfe, 1977; Kidron, 1972); an evolving "structural gap" between state revenues and necessary expenditures—a "fiscal crisis" (O'Connor, 1973); and expanded use of the courts by a "myriad of supplicants" (Jenkins, 1980; Handler, 1978). Heydebrand suggests that the response to these growing demands and declining resources has been to "rationalize" judicial structures and

Authors' Note: *The views expressed are solely those of the authors. This project was supported by LEAA Grant 79-NI-AX-0064. Authors' names are listed randomly. Our thanks to John Paul Ryan, Susan Mauer, Judy Byers, Judy Glennon, and Louise Cainkar.*

procedures by adopting "technocratic" modes of administration long-characteristic of private industry (Galbraith,
1967), but largely absent from the public sector (Heydebrand,
1979: 33-35).

The technocratic form of administration is best understood when compared with two other strategies which have
been adopted to deal with the courts' crisis. The "professional strategy" assumes that, given an adequate flow of
resources, the system is capable of operating adequately
without structural modification (Heydebrand, 1979: 35;
Halliday, 1979: 246f, 262). Its answer to the problems of
demand, backlog, and delay is a greater allocation of external
resources—more judges, more support staff, more facilities.
A second strategy, the "bureaucratic-administrative"
strategy, aims to make better use of existing resources—to be
more "efficient" by extending the division of labor, subordi-
nating routine work functions to centralized administrative
control, and delegating particular work functions to nonjudicial personnel.

Technocratic administration synthesizes, yet transcends
both its predecessors. It seeks to expand the resources available to courts and to make more efficient use of all resources.
Unlike the professional strategy, which calls for the *quantitative* expansion of judicial resources, the technocratic
strategy seeks the *qualitative* expansion of resources utilized
by the courts. Unlike the bureaucratic strategy, which
fashions hierarchical administrative structures, the technocratic strategy decentralizes some aspects of administration
while centralizing others. Technical and managerial innovations characterize this approach, including data processing (Adams, 1972; White, 1971) and video technologies
(Coleman, 1977; McCrystal, 1978; Murray, 1978), elaborate
forecasting models (Goldman et al., 1976; Heydebrand,
1979), professional court administrators, utilization of social
science research (Wheeler and Whitcomb, 1976; Sarat, 1978;

Gallas, 1979), and the redefinition and expansion of judicial boundaries (Skoler, 1977; Hofrichter, 1978; Harrington, 1979, 1980).

Central to the technocratic strategy is the integration of administrative tasks with traditional professional roles, an integration which routinizes and trivializes professional work. While routinization of the work process is common to a number of occupational groups, it is relatively new to professionals, although it is even apparent in such a rarefied profession as medicine, which has long been thought a model in writings on professions (see McKinlay, 1977; Alford, 1975). Given that the *sine qua non* of a profession has been the ability of its members to be autonomous and self-regulating (see Friedson, 1970), the emergence of technocratic modes of administration may be taken as a direct assault upon the judicial prerogative of independence, contributing to what has been termed the deprofessionalization, or proletarianization, of professionals (Haug, 1973; McKinlay, 1977; Oppenheimer, 1973). Therefore, the trend toward technocratic administration is neither so far advanced nor as easily implemented as Heydebrand implies. Moreover, the deprofessionalization which technocracy portends for judges identifies them as a likely source of resistance to the rationalization of the judiciary. One critical limitation to both bureaucratic and technocratic rationalization is the professional status of judges, a status anchored in norms of autonomy and discretion and buttressed by the state as a sanctioned monopoly. Although judges' professional status is undercut by their fiscal dependence upon the state (Heydebrand, 1979: 43), it is strongly reinforced by the ideology of the rule of law and the centrality of that ideology to the cohesion of the social order (Weber, 1954; Trubek, 1972; Balbus, 1973; Balbus, 1977; Horwitz, 1977; Tushnet, 1978). Because both technical and bureaucratic modes of organization can be subordinated to the professional interests of bench and bar, the "transformation" of the judicial system (Harrington, 1980) cannot be understood as a simple, structural reflex, but rather as a process strewn with contradictions and conflict over the substance of changes and ultimate control over them.

An administrative reform illustrating these contradictions was adopted by the Ohio Supreme Court in 1971. This reform—the Ohio Rules of Superintendence—embodies significant aspects of the technocratic strategy. The rules qualitatively expand judicial resources by introducing new video technologies. More important, they establish a centralized administrative structure which, although hierarchical, decentralizes a number of administrative tasks. Directed toward the judiciary, the rules mandate an individual calendar and set time frames within which cases are to be disposed. Monthly reports must be filed with the state Supreme Court, allowing that Court to monitor judges' dockets and embarass or reward them on the basis of it.

When these rules are coupled with the authority given the Chief Justice to take any action necessary to cause delinquent criminal cases to be tried (*R. Sup.* 8), and that given the Administrative Director of the State Courts to publish annual reports and develop methods to insure the accuracy of judicial statistics (*R. Sup.* 5), they create a definite administrative hierarchy with the Chief Justice of the Supreme Court at its pinnacle. But while the rules' central theme is one of administrative hierarchy, they stop short of total centralization. Significant authority to deal with delay is delegated to local judges. Although they are urged to adopt strict continuance policies, a uniform procedure is not mandated (*R. Sup.* 14). The local administrative and presiding judges, who are selected by their colleagues rather than the Supreme Court (*R. Sup.* 2,3), are also given major responsibility to ensure compliance with the rules. Local courts also are authorized to adopt rules which facilitate the early disposition of cases, including the restriction of attorney caseloads (*R. Sup.* 9).

While this delegation further emphasizes the expansion and importance of judges' administrative roles, and the necessity for them to be answerable to a higher authority, the dependence upon the local judges' discretion for its effectiveness affords them the opportunity to subvert the technical and bureaucratic rationality of the rules. By making judges responsible and accountable for the eradication of these problems, the Supreme Court established its authority over the work environment of judges. By emphasizing fiscal responsibility and efficiency, the court attempted to alter the content of judges' jobs. But rather than eliminating judicial autonomy and discretion, the Court sought to use them in "solving" the "problem" of delay. The Rules of Superintendence thus promoted two contradictory processes: By emphasizing centralized procedures, they eroded professional autonomy; but because they respected and depended upon that autonomy, they opened the possibility for the subversion of their administrative goals.

To analyze the interplay of these contradictory tendencies, this article will examine the politics surrounding the promulgation of the rules. We will consider the extent to which local judges participated in their promulgation, taking this as an indicator of their ability to define the conditions of their work and maintain their autonomy. Whether it is they or a centralized authority who determined the need for, and content of, the rules will be a central concern. Given the implementation of the rules, however, we will also gauge the extent to which compliance has been achieved and work habits affected by them. Finally, we will comment upon new procedures which may allow judges to modify changes in their work routine, thus maintaining some professional prerogatives.

METHODS

Data were collected in 20 open-ended, intensive interviews with judges, prosecutors, and defense attorneys in a large Ohio city. All but two members of its Court of Common Pleas were interviewed, and the remaining attorneys and prosecutors were contacted through a snowball sampling procedure which emphasized experience in criminal work. Ten state officials with special knowledge of the development, promulgation, and monitoring of the rules were interviewed, as were 22 courtroom actors in four other Ohio cities. These latter data serve as a comparative base for the analysis of our site. In addition, courtroom proceedings were observed, laying the grounds for hypotheses and allowing us to validate remarks made during interviews.

SITE DESCRIPTION

The site of our study is a Court of Common Pleas, a court of general jurisdiction. The court is composed of 11 Republicans and 1 Democrat, reflecting the political make-up of the community. Their range of service on the bench extends from 1 to 25 years, with most having served at least 6 years. Of the 12 judges, elected to six-year terms, 4 are former prosecutors, and all but 1 had formerly served on the municipal court. Party affiliation is the key to election and once a judgeship is secured, its holder can be assured of reelection.

In 1979, the court was faced with a pending criminal caseload of 697. With 3,300 arraignments, and 3,483 terminations, they were left with 514 cases pending at the end of the year (*Ohio Courts Summary, 1979*). Examining both criminal and civil filings, a total of 7,878 cases were filed in 1979, with an average of 656 cases filed per judge. There was a modest increase in criminal filings between 1967 and 1979 and a steady increase in civil filings during that same period. Only 2 new judges have been added to the court since 1926, and for the past 10 years, the court has been battling with the legislature for additional judgeships. The common complaint of the judges on this bench is that they carry too heavy caseloads and that this problem can only be solved by adding additional judgeships, a view not shared by the state legislature.

JUDGES AS PROFESSIONALS

Professional work is marked by a number of characteristics which distinguish it from other occupations. Foremost among these is the autonomy of professionals to define the parameters and conditions of their work. Friedson (1970) suggests that autonomy is the prize sought by virtually all occupational groups, for it represents freedom from the direction of others and freedom to perform one's work the way one desires. This claim to autonomy is, in turn, based upon a professional ideology which stresses the specialized knowledge of the group, their ability to work without supervision, and the necessity for them to be self-regulating (Friedson, 1970: 137). Because they have convinced those who have granted them this license that their altruism and disinterest in abusing these privileges can be assumed, they are largely left to control the universe of their work.

Judges can easily be seen as professionals. As members of a legal society, they lay their claim to expertise on a body of knowledge which is in part created, but certainly disseminated, by members of the group. These members, in turn, determine the content of knowledge to be taught and the standards by which individuals will be admitted to practice. In keeping with notions of professionalism, they are their own gatekeepers, claiming a license to carry out certain activities and a mandate to define the conditions under which they are done (Hughes, 1971). While members of the legal profession, judges are apart from it in that other members must defer to them, accepting their interpretation of law and their predilections in the courtroom. In the profession of law, judges may then be seen as prestigious members, although their status will be affected by the type of court in which they are seated (Blumberg, 1967; Auerbach, 1976; Wice, 1978).

As members of this order, they share the same professional claims as attorneys, but as judges new dimensions are added. While attorneys may claim autonomy and freedom from supervision on the basis of specialized skills, in most cases an attorney is working alone on particular cases. Dissatisfied clients can always go elsewhere. But because judges are involved in larger networks, when they define the parameters of their work, they do so for other actors as well. Just as physicians' claims to autonomy and expertise allow them to shape the organization of hospitals and tasks of other workers (see Friedson, 1970), so are judges able to influence the organization of courts and the work of those who must operate within them. The professional privilege of working without supervision, when accorded to judges, has greater impact than it does for attorneys. The claim to disinterested service is another important component in the autonomy professionals claim. Judges claim neutrality, for example, and expect to be believed because they are professionals and better able to resist temptations than other workers. Finally, in keeping with notions of expertise and autonomy, judges are self-regulating with regard to disciplinary matters. Judicial discipline commissions are orchestrated by other professionals, because it is assumed that laypeople alone do not possess the expertise to evaluate their conduct.

Since judges are deferred to in ways associated with professionals, one might conclude that their professional status is assured. However, the professional status of a group rests upon the recognition of its claims by others; there is little inherent in the work which guarantees autonomy and self-regulation. Thus, when the organizational context of work is changed, the claims upon which professional status rests are challenged. Those who have experienced this status, however, do not readily relinquish it.

MANDATING CHANGE: THE JUDGES' ROLE

The process by which the courts' problems were defined and solutions to them fashioned posed a critical challenge to judges' professional status. In developing the Rules of Superintendence, the Chief Justice attempted to secure input from at least some judges, hand-picking 12 of "the best" judges from the courts "where the real problems were." Each of these judges was granted one-half day before the Supreme Court to discuss what was "wrong" with their courts and how rules could be used to eliminate the problems. According to the late Chief Justice, the 12 judges reached an amazing consensus in identifying 10 sources of delay. In addition, the state bar association was asked to recommend solutions to lawyer-induced delay and the state medical association was asked to recommend a solution to delay caused by the difficulties in securing testimony and depositions from expert-witness doctors. After consulting with these groups, the Supreme Court staff drafted and circulated a set of 17 proposed rules. Written comments were solicited, though few were received; hearings were held in different areas of the state, though few attended.

Officials at the state level share the view that, from the start, the rules incorporated the views of judges and were addressed to their concerns. They stress judicial participation in the process, although they are sometimes unable to recall the particulars. An official at the state level summarizes this view:

The methodology employed by the court in developing the rules was rather than superimposing them from the top, the

court sought the advice of those to be affected by the rules—
that is, the trial court judges. In line with that, we had a series
of conferences where various judges from different jurisdictions over the state were invited into the court and simply
asked, what are your problems? After these meetings, it was
apparent that there were a number of problems and that
everybody had the same problems and so the rules were really
drafted to address each one of the problems. They were generated, really, in response to what those people believed their
problems were and I suppose there were some additions as to
what our court thought the problems were as maybe a little
different viewpoint from what they thought.

This latter point, emphasizing the possible variation between
the Supreme Court's interpretation of problems and that of
the judges, reflects the differential power of the two groups to
define problems and create solutions that serve their different interests. For example, when judges unanimously
urged increasing judicial personnel as the solution to courts'
problems, the Supreme Court adamantly refused. Emphasizing the fiscal constraints facing the judiciary, the Chief
Justice responded, "Forget it, we'll first see what we can do
with what we've got." These differences become further apparent when judges comment upon their own perceptions of
the promulgation of the Rules and their solution to courtroom problems.

   While some judges may have been consulted about the
rules, these judges were few in number. Of the judges interviewed, only one had attended a meeting about the rules with
the Chief Justice, but he perceived participation somewhat
differently than did state officails:

The fact is that the rules of superintendence were issued like a
judicial fiat from on high, but there was no imput. It wasn't
like the legislature where you go up and argue against them. I

mean the Supreme Court, I think, published the proposed rules and then said anybody that has any complaints, suggestions, etc., file it in writing—otherwise they'll be made the rules in thirty days. And, in effect, nobody was really involved except the Supreme Court of Ohio which was dominated by the Chief Justice.

The other judges assumed the rules were created to address backlog problems, but they were neither consulted about them nor know of anyone who was. For them, too, the rules were an edict from on high, attributed to the forceful personality of a state Supreme Court Justice who was called "the Great Hammurabi" by one observer. As another judge explained:

> I don't think the Chief Justice did that too much—going around consulting with people. He would get an idea and it would become one of the rules. Oh, I guess there were committees, the judicial association and everything like that, that gave some input on their viewpoints, but I don't think that either one of the Rules would have stopped just because 95% of the judges were against it, if in fact they happened to be. The Chief Justice was a forceful enough man that that's the way things happened.

That state-level officials are more likely than judges to depict the rules as products of judicial participation and embodiments of judicial interest is no surprise. While few judges believed judicial participation had been meaningful, participation itself was an important symbolic gesture on the part of the Supreme Court, a defense against the expected complaints of malcontents. Reflecting on this strategy, the Chief Justice said:

> When somebody griped about the first rules of superintendence, I'd say "who told us about this? The trial judges

told us what the problems were. They recommended solutions, your colleagues." When somebody griped about the
power to remove a lawyer from a case, we said, "the lawyers
proposed this. They know the problem; they proposed it."
And when somebody got out of line and blasted the Court, we
depended on the newspaper editors to blast them back the
next day in the editorial columns.

Although this symbolic gesture did not convince judges that
the rules embodied their interests, they did not directly
challenge the authority of the state Supreme Court to impose
rules upon them. Thus, the legitimating strategy fashioned at
the state level never needed to be activated.

SANCTIONS

Although the Rules of Superintendence specified mandatory procedures and time frames for processing cases, they
did not provide formal sanctions or incentives for compliance. The individual calendar and reporting system, however, did provide a ready foundation upon which a structure
of informal sanctions and incentives could be raised. The
informal sanctions ranged from personal reprimands to
awards issued for maintaining "clean" dockets to the "moral
authority" of the Supreme Court.

Among the higher circles of the Ohio courts, the former
Chief Justice's personal efforts to enforce the rules were
legendary. For example, he threatened to publicize the docket
statistics of dilatory judges. He was also said to have
personally reprimanded judges. One state official reported
that he

had a real bug-a-boo about delay in justice and had been
known to take a look at a particularly bad record of a judge

and get in his car and arrive at that judge's chambers and ask
him point blank, face-to-face, "Why are you late?" You could
imagine the moral effect that would have. Word got around
pretty damn quick—he was no respecter of persons.

The higher circles believed that press reports on dockets and
unexpected personal visits worried judges, inducing them to
move their cases more quickly.

> Over cocktails, after the meeting, why I've heard them
> (judges) say, "I really don't want the Chief Justice knocking
> on my door."

But just what the sound and fury surrounding the Chief
Justice's flamboyant style actually signified is problematic.
Few judges knew of the personal reprimands supposedly
delivered. The administrative judge in a large city observed
that he could not have delivered too many, for he knew of
judges with severe backlogs within several blocks of the
Supreme Court who were never reprimanded. Nor could
anyone at the state level recall even a single instance where
backlog statistics were reported by the press. That the Chief
Justice made such visits is not to be doubted, but the judges
interviewed knew of no such visits, nor did they fear them.
Thus, whatever enforcement efforts were made must be seen
as cases of specific rather than general deterrence.

The flamboyant administration of the rules died with the
Chief Justice in 1978. Whereas tales of his surprise appear-
ances and telephone tirades were repeated admiringly by state
level officials, none was to be told of his successor. One
Supreme Court Justice summarized the Court's current attitude toward the administration of the rules:

> As far as the reports go, we're not policemen and it doesn't
> mean a thing to me whether a judge falsifies his report or not.

That's between him and his God ... the purpose of those
reports is for the judge to know how he stands on his own
docket, not for me to be a policeman and call him up and say,
"Hey, you only got rid of 30 files and picked up 50 last month
and you're falling behind."

Nevertheless, state court administrative officials reiterated
that judicial self-policing had characterized the administrations of both Chief Justices, despite the differences in
rhetoric. While docket reports are checked for statistical
accuracy, they are not audited. Some efforts are made to
ensure consistent interpretation of the reports' statistical
categories, but, as judges are well aware, this is not a high
priority. Nor does the Court use these statistics as a management tool. As state administrative officials explained:

In other words, the underpinning of this is really based on the
idea that the people in the field are following the rules appropriately and doing what they should do and it's dependent
upon their integrity. These forms and these numbers aren't for
us—they don't mean anything to us, which is true. They
don't. They are meant for the judges. They are management
tools for the judges.

Judges, then, were not to be sanctioned for failing to clear
their dockets.

CHANGES IN JUDGING

Despite the lack of sanctions, judges did establish a reporting system, keep track of their dockets, and play a more
active role in processing cases, even though they were not
always successful in meeting the specified time limits. No
longer merely judges, removed from the minutia of record-

keeping to concentrate on weighty legal matters, they were now administrators. A state administrator explained how the nature of judging changed with the advent of the rules:

> There has been a theory and I suppose it still abounds whereby the court is simply there and the court does the business that the lawyers want the court to do instead of vice-versa. Under our rules, the opposite of that is true. The cases are supposed to be managed from the time they're filed until the time they are terminated by the court itself. I think our courts generally have sort of gone along with the idea now that courts should be managed in a business-like fashion, whereas before, it wasn't true.

These changes signified a redefinition of judges' work and augured the possibility of judges' having to work harder. To meet the time constraints, they began scheduling more cases. For the first time, too, they were to be accountable for the number of cases disposed. Thus, their autonomy to run the courts in the way they wished was challenged. As one judge put it, the rules made him an "expeditor and administrator," a change he did not relish.

It is important to stress, however, the speedy disposition of cases is not solely within the judges' control. Efforts to control the speed at which cases are disposed, for example, mean that judges must exert control over actors whose concerns and goals are different. As previously noted, the traditional model of courtroom activity is one where court officials wait for lawyers to be ready to try cases. By making judges responsible for the disposition of cases, they were also made responsible for the actions of attorneys, a reorientation which many found beyond their competence and desire to effect. As one particularly discontented judge described it:

> The stress on judges, under these rules, is that you're a kindergarten teacher. And I resent that. I'm not so sure I resent the

Supreme Court imposing these rules, but I resent the reason
for them, and the reason is that lawyers, who are being paid
well by their clients, really don't want to do much to move
their litigation along in the civil arena. I am a kindergarten
teacher, because I am now making these people do what they
are paid and supposed to do. I make them come to a pretrial
or a report. I have to set it; they don't request setting, or come
in and set it themselves; I have to make them come in. Or, i.e.,
hang up your coat in the coatroom. I make them accomplish
their discovery within a certain period of time, i.e., you will
now go to lunch. I make them come in for subsequent reports,
pretrials, forced settings. Let's see, you will now take a nap.
So I resent the bar, and the litigation culture, that has precipi-
tated these rules which, in turn, make me into a kindergarten
teacher with a sort of a whip and a gun.

Other judges complained that if it were not for lawyers,
they could easily meet the required time frames. One wanted
to send letters to clients whose cases had been frequently
reset, absolving himself for the delay and blaming it on the
attorney. Although the rules allow judges to replace attorneys
unable to dispose cases expeditiously, no attorneys have been
replaced, or even threatened. Nor have the judges adopted
local rules limiting the number of cases attorneys may handle,
despite their authority to do so under the rules (*R. Sup.* 7,9).
Although judges maintain they make continuances more
difficult to obtain, they often see little choice but to grant
them. The problem, according to most judges, is not that
attorneys have too many cases, but whether judges should
move attorneys toward settlement. Regarding civil cases, one
judge explained:

If a case is important, lawyers and their clients will pursue it.
If it's not important or settling, they will not pursue it and
why the court should force lawyers to pursue a case that they
aren't interested in pursuing, I really don't know. In other

words, just to be able to say, we have no pending cases or there are very few, doesn't mean much because pushing a case to completion often causes injustice, and in my opinion, it interferes with settlement of the case. Some take a long time to right and the backlog, alleged backlog, in many simply involved cases that no one was interested in pursuing. I haven't found any backlog of any case anybody really wanted to try.

It is clear from their comments, however, that the judges perceived few defenses against this ordered job enlargement. Because their job description had changed, they had to change as well.

Our superintendent is the Chief Justice and the Supreme Court. If they instruct us, we have an obligation to comply. It's a practical requirement. If you're attempting to do the job, you should be following them.

While some judges resented being made accountable, this new work-style offered some benefits. As the Supreme Court thought it would, case reporting alerted some judges to the actual composition of their dockets and allowed them to exert some control over it. As they described it:

I think the rules have value. I think they're valuable and that they have given the judge personal responsibility for cases, triggering a sense of responsibility and pride in disposing of it. It also helps by keeping a judge familiar with a particular case—that he doesn't come into a case about which he knows nothing in mid-stream.

I think it's a matter of personal satisfaction, personal pride. I think that judges generally have a feeling that they want to do a good job. Part of their job is what the Rules of Superintendence say.

Gaining control of their dockets gave some judges a quantitative measure of achievement about which they could feel good. Since judges believe that the court is not salient to the public, and since other aspects of judicial performance may be more difficult to measure, docket control served as a benchmark of judicial achievement, even when it was not perfect. Judges feel some satisfaction by just complying and doing well vis-à-vis their colleagues. While all the judges denied that their relative standing affected them, they did check their disposition statistics against those of the others. Such incentives are apparent in the following remarks:

> Just having the reporting system gives me certain goals. My constable will come up to me from time to time during the month and say, well, judge, you're even for the month, or you're 20 behind, or you're 30 ahead, or whatever, and we had a situation recently where—I forget what it was exactly—but we had come out ahead by one month and we had some other entries that we could have rushed through on the report for the 30th of June, for instance, and he said, well, we might as well save them for July 1st because it would look better.

Each year, judges who cleared their dockets received "Superior Judicial Service" awards from the Supreme Court. This practice not only encouraged greater attention to administration but also transformed what it meant to be a "good judge." One judge described the standards inherent in being a good judge:

> Good judges know how to run a trial. They know how to write opinions. Their integrity is not in question. They are workers, and are not lazy. Now when it comes to administration, there are a lot of things they don't think are their problems. They don't think, for example, if the jail is overcrowded, that it's their problem. They don't think that if

something is wrong with the assignment system, that it's their problem. It is somebody else's. They don't think that the idea of controlling their docket is their problem.

The conflicts created by new administrative standards are apparent in the following remarks:

> Let's say that I'm on a court with six other judges. And they may be great judges. And to tell you the truth, out of the seven, we had five very good judges. And they were conscientious. Now they weren't good administrators, and they had been on the court a long time, and they had strong convictions, like you didn't have trials in the summertime. And that the single assignment system wouldn't work. So, administratively they weren't strong. But trial judges—it was a great court.

One can be a "good judge" according to the standards of colleagues, yet fail to be recognized for "Superior Judicial Service" by the state Supreme Court. For the Court now defines the "good judge" solely in terms of clear dockets. To be recognized as "good judges" by the Court, they feel they must spend more time on administration. Resenting this trivialization of their work, they fear the substantive components of judging will be sacrificed.

> It has created obligations and duties about filing which don't seem compatible with doing your job. If you're going to do a conscientious job, you shouldn't have to fill out a form. I don't know if justice is served by the Rules of Superintendence.

> Well, I think it's unfair to recognize jucicial service solely on the basis of statistical reports because it doesn't give any relationship to the quality of the service and it certainly hasn't any relationship to the ability of a particular judge to service

his particular responsibility. And it does pit judges against each other on a very arbitrary and rather, I think, unprofessional basis. One of the proofs of the pudding is a judge who received the largest number of awards and probably had the lowest esteem.

Judges particularly fear that "justice" will be compromised. Under the rules, one judge explained:

The prosecutor would come in and say, "we've agreed to reduce this to so-and-so." I might not really approve of that, but I say, "well if both sides agree to it, okay." If we didn't have this system, I think that some of those cases I might be more tempted to say, "well, I just can't go along with reducing this." Let me give you a ridiculous example—reducing a rape to assault and battery—and therefore I just won't play ball with you. Now, there are cases where I do have to say I just can't in my own conscience approve of that, but I would frankly think they are less frequent under superintendence, under the pressure.

Whether judges would actually spend more time deliberating about cases if they did not feel pressure to move them along is questionable. What is not, however, is that they believe they need more time "to think" and that the present system does not allow it. They fear deliberation is being replaced with what they claim is a "numbers game" which induces too many judges to "cook" their required reports:

You can't avoid the quantity over quality that is created by the presence of those rules. You know, the golden gavels are not given for how good a judge you are from a qualitative standpoint; you are judged on a numerical standard. How your report card looks.

Some judges complain that the "numbers game" has led colleagues to deliberately misstate their docket status.

Some judges cook their numbers. Now you take that other county. They say they have twice as many trials as we do. That's B.S. You know they have to be cooking that up, and I'm told, on good authority, that some of the probate judges cook these numbers up, too.

I suppose, too, there's a final question about how accurate they are. Even before those rules, cases were kept track of, and there was an internal court reporting that went on. One judge was notorious for simply taking a bunch of cards out of his file and throwing them in the wastebasket. And, you know, the judge's name was used—it wasn't Gibson, but say it was Gibson, that was called, "Gibsonizing" the cases. And even now, if you threw away 30 civil cases, the chances are you would never hear about them again. Nobody would ever raise them and if they did, you would simply resurrect the cases, but you just dismiss 30, and write them off.

Yet the "numbers game" can be allowed to continue because administrative officials refuse to push the issue by auditing judges' reports. To do so would challenge judges' personal and professional integrity. Administrative officials also are hesitant to police their colleagues because all the judges in this state are elected. Explaining why the Chief Justice does not play a more active role in auditing these reports, one judge said:

I'd have the Chief do it. Why doesn't he? Politics. He has to get re-elected, just like anybody else, and it doesn't make any-one happy if he goes around doing that.

That there was some glorious past during which judges, freed of administrative matters, could really be judges, and that they would do so again if freed from managing heavy case-loads, is problematic. With less emphasis on speed, and a lighter caseload, criticisms similar to the ones today were lodged against courts in the 1920s and 1930s (Feeley, 1979). The glorious days when judges became personally involved in each case are perhaps more a figment of imagination than they ever were a reality. Feeley's observation that there will always be too many cases because most participants have an interest in being someplace else is particularly apt. Despite the emphasis upon dispositions, some judges still have time to consider legal arguments, conduct research, write opinions, and take additional cases from other judges. The rules of superintendence, and their supposed pressure to move cases more quickly, may allow some judges to avoid, and rationalize, not doing work they would have preferred not to do anyway.

JUDGES' DEFENSE

Although the rules eroded judges' autonomy, they did not decimate it. One of the options available to professionals— that of redefining their own work and delegating "dirty work" to subordinates—has been retained. The judges in our site have, in part, dealt with demands for efficiency by redefining many of their tasks and delegating them to others. Just as physicians redefined inoculation as a nursing task, so have judges redefined several of their tasks, delegating them to others and acquiring additional resources to perform them.

With the advent of the rules, for example, the Court of Common Pleas established a referee system and an arbitration board for "minor" cases, allowing judges to divert nearly 6,000 cases a year from their dockets. Judges argue that by diverting such cases, they have more time to devote to weightier matters.

They also requested the state to assign visiting judges to help them handle their caseloads. The visiting judge system has greatly aided the judges, who quadrupled their use from 1972 to 1979. Visiting judges are called upon the request of sitting judges, who decide the number and type of cases assigned to them. As one judge described it:

> We now use visiting judges on a regular basis and don't know how we got along without them. It's been a tremendous help. They are the escape valve for the steam that builds up in a system, because we have no limit upon the number we can call as long as they are available. If we have a lengthy trial we know we are going to ask a v.j. to handle, we can assign it in advance. If we have just a tremendous amount of cases set, we can request v.j.s on a case-by-case basis for a month or two and we can notify our court administrator and he'll do his very best to bring down whatever number is needed from whatever part of the state he can find them.

Since the visiting judge system was used heavily only after the adoption of the rules, it also may be seen as a judicial attempt to retain professional prerogatives. By using these mechanisms, judges maintain some control over the size and nature of their dockets. Although judges lost some autonomy because of the rules, all was not lost to them. Despite their inability to wage a battle against the imposition of external authority, they were able to circumvent the process by establishing auxiliary services and ridding themselves of excess tasks.

While judges grumbled about the imposition of the rules, their responses were individual rather than collective. When their autonomy was threatened, they sought to deflect their loss rather than pursue other strategies; they did not formally protest the rules or seek to amend them. One impediment to such protest was the recognition that the Supreme Court had the legal authority to impose rules. Their knowledge of this authority and their belief in its legitimacy militated against collective action. Moreover, judges are poor lobbyists and, while it may now be important for them to lobby, they are hindered by their perceptions of professional conduct. Their allegiance to traditional notions of professionalism constrain their actions at the very time that these notions are being challenged by others.

CONCLUSIONS

Faced with burgeoning dockets and declining state revenues, the Ohio Supreme Court instituted major administrative reforms designed to qualitatively expand the resources used to process cases and to enhance case-processing efficiency. By making judges responsible for the status of their dockets, the Supreme Court induced judges to move their cases more quickly. In rewarding this behavior, the Supreme Court emphasized the significance of administrative prowess; in establishing uniform standards throughout the state, it ensured the dominance of centralized procedures over the predilections of local judges, thereby undermining judges' ability to run their courtrooms as they saw fit. Judges feared that traditionally valued aspects of their work, such as concern with individual justice and substantive legal issues, would be sacrificed for administrative expedience.

But although their professional norms precluded collective actions to oppose or change the rules, they were not without defenses. The rules undermined their professional status, but this very status was a weapon against those who sought to rationalize their work. Respect for judges' professional status prevented the Supreme Court from publicly embarrassing or punishing those who failed to meet the established guidelines. Nor did administrative officials challenge the judges' professional integrity by auditing their statistical reports. Beyond the impediment judges' professional status posed over administrative manipulation, it provided them with avenues for deflecting, or avoiding, some of their new administrative responsibilities and the increased work they augured. Their use of referee and arbitration systems and visiting judges are examples of their still-remaining professional prerogatives.

Faced with exploding demands for their services and dwindling budgets to provide them, the courts confront a dilemma to which there is no simple solution. No longer free to expand the quantity of services, they must develop new, less costly resources as well as make more "efficient" use of old ones, thereby effecting a qualitative transformation of their structure and functions. But this transformation is not a simple structural reflex to changed circumstances. Rather it is a process impeded by the interests and power of those upon whose work administrative reforms impinge.

REFERENCES

ADAMS, E. (1972) *Courts and Computers.* Chicago: American Judicature Society.

ALFORD, R. (1975) *Health Care Politics.* Chicago: University of Chicago Press.

AUERBACH, J. (1977) *Unequal Justice.* New York: Oxford University Press.

BALBUS, I. (1977) "Commodity form and legal form: An essay on the relative autonomy of the law." Law and Society Review 11: 571.

BALBUS, I. (1973) The Dialectics of Legal Repression. New York: Russell Sage.

BARON, P. and P. SWEEZY (1964) Monopoly Capital. New York: Monthly Review Press.

BLUMBERG, A. (1967) Criminal Justice. Chicago: Quadrangle.

COLEMAN, G. V. (1977) Video Technology in the Courts. Washington, D.C.: National Institute of Law Enforcement and Criminal Justice.

FEELEY, M. (1979) The Process is the Punishment. New York: Russell Sage.

FRIEDSON, E. (1970) The Profession of Medicine. New York: Dodd Mead.

GALBRAITH, J. K. (1967) The New Industrial State. New York: Signet.

GALLAS, G. (1979) "Court reform: Has it been built on an adequate foundation?" *Judicature* 63: 28.

GOLDMAN, J., R. HOOPER, and J. MAHOFFEY (1976) "Caseload forecasting models for federal district courts." Journal of Legal Studies 5: 201.

HALLIDAY, T. (1979) "Parameters of professional influence: Policies and politics of the Chicago Bar Association, 1945-70." Ph.D. disssertation, University of Chicago.

HANDLER, J. (1978) Social Movements and the Legal System. New York: Academic Press.

HARRINGTON, C. (1980) "Historical analysis of delegalization reform movements." (unpublished)

HARRINGTON, C. (1979) "Voluntariness, consent and coercion in adjudicating minor disputes." Presented at the meeting of the Western Political Science Association.

HAUG, M. (1973) "Deprofessionalization: An alternate hypothesis for the future," in P. Halmos (ed.) Professionalization and Social Change. *Sociological Review* 20: 195.

HEYDEBRAND, W. (1979) "The technocratic administration of justice," in S. Spitzer (ed.) *Research in Law and Sociology*. Greenwich, CT: Jai Press.

HEYDEBRAND, W. (1977) "The context of public bureaucracies: An organizational analysis of federal district courts." Law and Society Review 11: 759.

HOFRICHTER, R. (1978) "Neighborhood justice and the social control problems of American capitalism: A perspective." Presented to the Conference on Critical Legal Studies, Madison, Wisconsin.

HORWITZ, M. (1977) *The Transformation of American Law*. Cambridge, MA: Harvard University Press.

HUGHES, E. (1971) The Sociological Eye—Book 2. Chicago: Aldine.

JENKINS, I. (1980) Social Order and the Limits of Law. Princeton, NJ: Princeton University Press.

KAMENKA, E. and A. TAY (1975) "Beyond bourgeois individualism: The contemporary crisis in law and legal ideology," in E. Kamenka and E. Neal (eds.) Feudalism, Capitalism and Beyond. New York: Arnold.

KIDRON, M. (1972) Western Capitalism Since the War. Baltimore: Penguin.

McCRYSTAL, J. (1978) "Videotaped trials: A primer." *Judicature* 61: 250.

McKINLAY, J. (1977) "Towards the proletarianization of physicians." (unpublished)

MURRAY, T. (1978) "Videotaped depositions: The Ohio experience." *Judicature* 61: 258.

O'CONNOR, J. (1973) The Fiscal Crisis of the State. New York: St. Martin's.

Ohio Courts Summary. (1979) Columbus: Office of the Administrative Assistant, the Supreme Court of Ohio.

OPPENHEIMER, M. (1973) "The proletarianization of the professional." in P. Halmos (ed.) *Professionalization and Social Change. Sociological Review* 20: 213.

SARAT, A. (1978) "Understanding trial courts: A critique of social science approaches." *Judicature* 61: 318.

SKOLER, D. (1977) Organizing the Non-System: Government Structuring of Criminal Justice Systems. Lexington, MA: D.C. Heath.

TRUBEK, D. (1972) "Max Weber on law and the rise of capitalism." *Wisconsin Law Review* 720.

TRUBEK, D. and M. GALANTER (1974) "Scholars in self-estrangement: Source reflections on the crisis of law and development studies in the United States." Wisconsin Law Review 1062

TUSHNET, M. (1978) "A Marxist interpretation of American law." *Marxist Perspectives* 1: 96.

UNGER, R. (1977) Law in Modern Society. New York: Free Press.

WEBER, M. (1954) Max Weber on Law in Economy and Society. New York: Touchstone.

WHEELER, R. and H. WHITCOMB [eds.] (1976) Judicial Administration: Text and Readings. Englewood Cliffs, NJ: Prentice-Hall.

WHITE, S. (1971) The Use of Electronic Data Processing in Court Administration. Chicago: American Judicature Society.

WICE, P. (1978) Criminal Lawyers. Beverly Hills, CA: Sage.

WOLFE, A. (1977) The Limits of Legitimacy. New York: Free Press.

Chapter 10

MISSISSIPPI JUDICIAL SELECTION:
Election, Appointment, and Bar Anointment

JAMES J. ALFINI

How should judges be selected? At present, five formal methods are used for selecting judges in the United States: popular election by partisan ballot, popular election by non-partisan ballot, gubernatorial appointment, legislative election, and the merit (or Missouri) plan. Although the merit plan has been most widely adopted in the past 25 years (Ashman and Alfini, 1974; Alfini, 1977) and has been identified as the preferable selection method by various national commissions (American Bar Association, 1974; National Advisory Commission on Criminal Justice Standards and Goals, 1973), scant empirical evidence has been produced to support the position that any one of the five basic selection methods is inherently superior to the other four. Thus, there continues to be widespread disagreement over the efficacy of each of the selection methods (see, e.g., the writings in Winters, 1973).

A principal cause for this disagreement over judicial selection methods is an inability to agree on purpose. Those

Author's Note: *The research for this article was performed in partial fulfillment of a subcontract between the American Judicature Society and Resource Planning Corporation. Under contract with the Governor's Criminal Justice Planning Division, Resource Planning Corporation had undertaken the development of a* preferring the merit plan or gubernatorial appointment take the position that the selection method should have as its primary purpose the placement of the best judicial talent available on the bench and that this can best be achieved by taking politics out of the selection process (Nelson, 1962; Hunter, 1964; Niles, 1967; Utter, 1973). On the other hand, those supporting the elective selection methods argue that in a democracy the people have the right to select their judges and thus the primary purpose of the selection method should be the attainment of the democratic ideal, regardless of outcome (Beattie, 1953; Burnett, 1966; Harding, 1969; Crockett, 1975).

Despite this normative debate, there have been relatively few studies that systematically analyze how selection methods operate in practice. Those few studies that have been conducted suggest that particular selection methods do not operate as their proponents have claimed. In the most ambitious study to date, Watson and Downing (1969) found that Missouri's merit plan had not eliminated politics from judicial selection. Others have indicated that *nonpartisan* elections offer the voter little guidance and thus tend to reduce judicial accountability (Adamany and DuBois, 1976). Finally, some studies have suggested that judicial elections in states using *partisan* elections are much less competitive than their proponents would have us believe (Melone, 1977; Hannah, 1978).

This article seeks to add to this emerging body of empirical studies by examining the partisan elective method of selecting trial judges presently in operation in Mississippi. Toward this end, election data and field interviews with Mississippi judges

courts master plan for the state of Mississippi in 1975. The author accepts sole responsibility for any errors of fact which may be contained herein. Similarly, points of view or opinions stated in this article are those of the author and do not represent the official position or policies of the American Judicature Society, Resource Planning Corporation, or the state of Mississippi.

and lawyers are analyzed to assess the openness of the judicial recruitment process and the competitiveness of judicial elections. In addition, mail questionnaire survey data are presented to assess the attitudes of Mississippi judges and lawyers toward various aspects of the selection process. What emerges from this inquiry is a judicial selection process in which the influence of the local bar is preeminent.

JUDICIAL SELECTION IN MISSISSIPPI

The Mississippi Constitutional Convention of 1832 produced the first wholly popularly elected judiciary in America. The Constitution of 1832 also limited judicial tenure to a term of years. Prior to that time, the prevailing methods of selecting state judges in the United States were election by the legislature or appointment by the governor, with most judges serving during good behavior (Haynes, 1944).

The method of selecting Mississippi judges was changed at two later dates in the history of the state. The Mississippi Constitution of 1869 changed the method of judicial selection to gubernatorial appointment for a fixed term and the Constitution of 1890 reverted back to a system of popular elections (Coyle, 1972). Today Mississippi is one of 21 states that still elects all or some of its judges by partisan ballot (Berkson, 1980).

At present, the Constitution of Mississippi requires that judges of the circuit and chancery courts be popularly elected. The Mississippi legislature has provided that county court judges be elected in the same manner as circuit judges and they hold office for the same term as circuit judges (Miss. Code. Ann., Sec. 9-9-5). All chancellors, circuit court judges, and county court judges are elected every four years at the same general election in which representatives to Congress are chosen (Miss. Code Ann., Sec. 9-5-235). However, vacancies occurring between these elections are filled at the next regular election for state officers or for representatives in Congress, occurring more than nine months after the existence of the vacancies to be filled (Id. Sec. 23-5-247). The governor has the power to appoint persons to fill these vacancies until such an election is held (Miss. Const. art. VI, Sec. 177; Miss. Code Ann., Sec. 23-5-247).

Generally, the Mississippi laws governing the general elections also apply to the election of Mississippi judges (Id. Sec. 23-5-235 and 23-5-243). Upon entering a primary race for party nomination, candidates for judicial office are required to file affidavits promising compliance with all relevant provisions of the Corrupt Practices Act (Id. Secs. 23-3-3). Judicial candidates must also pay an assessment to the secretary of the state election commission if they are not affiliated with a political party.[1]

A few of the provisions of the Mississippi election laws apply specifically to judicial candidacies. Of particular importance is Sec. 23-3-63:

> It shall be the duty of the judges of the circuit court to give a reasonable time and opportunity to the candidates for the office of judge of the supreme court, circuit judge and chancellor to address the people during court terms. And in order to give further and every possible emphasis to the fact that the said judicial offices are not political but are to be held without favor and with absolute impartiality as to all persons, and because . . . the judges thereof should be as far removed as possible from any political affiliations or obligations within their party, it shall be unlawful for any candidate for any other office nominated or to be nominated at any primary election, wherein any candidate for any of the judicial offices in this section mentioned, is or are to be nominated, to align himself with any one or more of the candidates for said offices or to take any part whatsoever in any nomination for any one of the judicial offices herein mentioned.

In addition to this apparent attempt to "depoliticize" judicial election campaigns, another provision places limitations on judical campaign financing. Under this provision, judicial candidates are strictly forbidden from accepting contributions for anyone but members of the state bar who are not themselves candidates for any office in the same primary. In addition, the candidate may not accept more than $50 from any one member of the bar (Id. Sec. 23-3-65).

In sum, the Mississippi judicial selection process, as established by various constitutional and statutory provisions, contemplates selection through regular partisan elections with gubernatorial appointments to interim vacancies. In addition, at least two statutory provisions represent an apparent attempt to "depoliticize" the process by placing certain limitations on campaign financing and discouraging candidates from involvement in the broader political arena.

THE ELECTIVE PROCESS

Field interviews with judges and members of the Mississippi bar were conducted[2] and state election records examined to determine the extent to which the partisan elective process contemplated by the foregoing constitutional and statutory provisions has been borne out in practice. The specific objectives were to assess the competitiveness of the elective process and the openness of the recruitment process.

It should come as no surprise to any student of American politics (given the dominance of the Democratic Party in Mississippi) that Democratic candidates rarely are faced in a judicial election by a candidate of an opposition party. Of the 27 chancery court judgeships up for election in 1970, only 1 of the judgeships was contested in the general election. Similarly, only 1 of the 25 circuit court judgeships and only 1 of the 18 county court judgeships were contested. All of the successful chancery court judges ran as Democrats (the lone Republican challenger was defeated), while all but one of the successful circuit court judges had the Democratic Party designation (the single exception was designated an "Independent").[3]Although the selection process clearly is not "partisan," it could be said to have a competitive character if the people were regularly presented with a choice of candidates in the primary. Indeed, it has been suggested that the judicial selection process in some partisan election states (particularly in the South) resembles the process in nonpartisan states (Canon, 1972: 589). However, primary contests were held for only 17 trial court judgeships (24% of the total number of trial court judgeships) in 1970.[4] Thus, in fewer than one out of four of the judgeships up for election in 1970 were the people presented with a "choice" in either the primary or the general election. That is, the process could not be described as competitive for over 75% of the judgeships.

"Bar anointment"[5] is a more accurate label than "partisan election" for the judicial selection process that occurs in Mississippi every four years. Most of the judges and lawyers interviewed identified the local bar as the single most important influence in securing judicial candidates. Upon the occurrence of a judicial vacancy in most Mississippi judicial districts, the local bar leaders generally get together informally to decide who among them would make the best judge. In some cases, they send letters to the chosen individual encouraging him to run for office (and discourage others from seeking the office). One of the judges interviewed had been on the bench for over 20 years. He related a story to dramatize how well-recognized the "bar anointment" process is. In one instance, a judicial vacancy had occurred between elections. Under these circumstances, the governor is empowered to appoint someone to fill this vacancy until the next election. However, recognizing the influence of the local bar, the governor refused to appoint anyone until the bar had "elected" the individual. So, the members of the local bar got together one evening at the courthouse and "anointed" a local lawyer. That individual was promptly appointed by the governor to fill the vacancy.

One of the judges whose description of his elevation to the bench fits the "bar anointment" scenario stated that he has stood for election on three separate occasions. In each of these three election years, he had been unopposed in both the primary and general elections and stated that if he ever faces opposition for his judicial position, he would drop out of the race. He explained that he had once run for a nonjudicial elective office and had been defeated and he thus felt that the people would not elect him over an opposition candidate.

Although the local bar generally exercises considerable influence in the initial selection of judicial candidates, they exercise little influence over those few primary or general judicial elections that ultimately are contested. There are more than 70 local bar associations in Mississippi and only 1 of these bar associations has ever conducted a poll of its members to determine the qualifications of opposing judicial candidates and subsequently to advise the electorate of the poll results. There are a number of possible explanations for this, including the belief of some lawyers and judges that the electorate would not be influenced by what the lawyers thought of judicial candidates. However, the most plausible explanation, and the explanation offered by most of the interviewees, is that the lawyers fear reprisals if the non-endorsed candidate ultimately is elected.

Not surprisingly, the one county in which the local bar association conducts a poll is the most populous county in the state—Hinds County (Jackson). Because there are so many lawyers in Hinds County, the informal ("bar anointment") selection scenario is least appropriate for judicial candidates in Hinds County, and judicial reprisals less likely.

THE APPOINTIVE PROCESS

Thus, with some notable exceptions—namely, the more populous counties—the "partisan elective" process for Mississippi judges might be more appropriately labeled "bar anointment with confirmation by the electorate." There is, however, a second judicial selection process in operation in Mississippi. As noted, the governor is empowered to appoint judges to vacancies occurring between elections. As the Mississippi Judiciary Commission noted in 1970, this selection process is of great significance. In their 1970 report, the commission stated:

> Although Mississippi does not have the problem of parti-sanism, as far as political parties are concerned, in its elections, there are still some shortcomings to the method of selecting the judiciary. . . In Mississippi the judicial elections are on off years and in many instance, there are not contests in judicial elections. However, we do not in truth have a wholly elected judiciary but substantially an appointive one by the governor, a political figure who has no assistance from the bar association or any other professional group nor any control by lawyer-oriented groups for these appointments.

To support this statement, the commission indicated the number of judicial appointments made by the governor during each four-year period beginning in 1948. Updated statistics[6] indicate that the governor made a total of 69 appointments to circuit, changery, and county court positions between 1948 and 1975.[7]

It should be noted here that, in conjunction with the creation of *new* judicial positions, the legislature may determine the mode of filling this new vacancy (Miss. Const., art. IV. Sec. 103). Recently, the legislature has tended to favor the calling of a special election rather than providing for gubernatorial appointment. In 1975, special elections were held in connection with the filling of three new chancery court positions, two new circuit court positions, and one new county court position.

Although it is impossible to forecast whether this trend (i.e., holding special elections rather than providing for gubernatorial appointments to new judicial positions) will continue, it would be safe to assume that as long as the governor retains the power to appoint judges to fill interim vacancies, a substantial portion of the Mississippi judges will continue to attain the bench initially by gubernatorial appointment. Of the current judges who came to the bench within the past 12 years, 8 (30%) of the chancery judges, 11 (44%) of the circuit judges, and 8 (50%) of the county judges were appointed initially.[8] Thus, 40% of the trial judges who came to the bench during the last 12 years were appointed initially. Because judicial election contests in Mississippi are seldom contested, the governor's interim appointments normally are considered to be permanent.

As previously suggested, however, Mississippi governors generally defer to the local bar in making appointments to judicial vacancies occuring between elections. Most of the lawyers and judges interviewed indicated a belief that a governor is able to make "better" appointments by relying on the local bar's ability to encourage lawyers who otherwise might be uninterested to accept an appointment to the bench. Some pointed out that it is flattering for a lawyer to be "elected" by his peers, while others suggested that prominent members of the local bar may pressure a lawyer into accepting a judicial appointment by appealing to his sense of responsibility to the legal fraternity. Regardless of the procedures or tactics that may be employed in a particular locale, Mississippi lawyers and judges generally believe that selection by the local bar tends to enhance the prestige of a judgeship.

The present Mississippi governor has adopted a more formalized procedure for involving the bar in the judicial appointive process. By an Executive Order issued on August 27, 1980, Governor Winter voluntarily committed himself to make appointments from a list of nominees submitted to him by a Judicial Nominating Committee, all of whose members are appointed by the governor.[9] Six committee members are to be chosen from each of the three supreme court districts within the state and each of these three "subcommittees" is required to "seek, receive, and review applications" to fill all vacancies within the district. Three of their number must be practicing attorneys recommended by the President of the Mississippi State Bar, while the remaining three members may also be practicing attorneys. The chairman of the 19-member committee must be a lawyer and is responsible for appointing the subcommittee chairmen (who must also be lawyers) for each of the three districts.

Because the "merit plan" contemplated by this executive order clearly anticipates a lawyer-dominated committee, it is unlikely that the bar's influence in the judicial selection process will be diluted. In fact, individual lawyer members of the committee probably will be in a better position than the governor to enlist the aid of local lawyers in the recruitment process.

Although the local bar generally exercises considerable influence over gubernatorial appointments to the Mississippi trial bench, at least one former governor attempted to negate this influence. In an interview conducted with former Governor Waller, on June 29, 1976, the governor stated that he knows most of the outstanding lawyers in the state. He said that Mississippi is a small state and since he had gone to law school in Mississippi he generally knew whom he wanted to appoint when a judicial vacancy arose. Governor Waller cited one case in which he was made aware of the local bar's "anointment" of a particular attorney, but he appointed another attorney, whom he believed would make a better judge. He also made it clear that if an attorney had supported him in his quest for the state house and that attorney was interested in judicial office, he would have the upper hand over other candidates.

Governor Waller also explained that some of the lawyers he had solicited for judicial appointments had turned down the position. He stated that there is "no onslaught of top lawyers" for judicial positions in Mississippi and offered the opinion that, "less than 10% of the best qualified lawyers seek judgeships." Given this perception concerning the (un)desirability of Mississippi judgeships, it must be asked why Governor Waller refused to accede to the "bar anointment" process, or at lease enlist the aid of local bar leaders in encouraging qualified candidates to accept offers of judicial positions. Perhaps he believed that the need to pay off, or create, political debts through judicial appointments outweighed any political rewards that could be realized by involving the bar in the selection process.

Governor Waller offered certain reasons for this general disinterest in judgeships. He stated that there is not much prestige in becoming a judge in Mississippi. He said that the younger lawyers will not take the pay cut because they do not get the money back in prestige. He placed compensation at the top of the list of discouraging factors in this regard. Next he indicated that tenure in office was a problem. Attorneys do not want to give up a law practice for a four-year position. Third on his list of discouraging factors was an inadequate retirement plan for Mississippi judges. Finally, he indicated that the staffing situation in the local trial courts tended to discourage qualified attorneys for seeking the bench. He indicated that judges do not have administrative control over their courts. He said that the lawyers are well aware of this and that if the judges did have administrative control over the local court system, more attorneys might be willing to accept a judgeship.

LAWYER ATTITUDES TOWARD JUDICIAL OFFICE

Mississippi lawyers responding to a questionnaire survey[10] tended to support former Governor Waller's contention that most Mississippi lawyers are not interested in judicial service. Of those lawyers responding to the questionnaire, only 23% indicated that they had ever considered seeking a circuit court judgeship. Fewer yet stated that they had considered seeking a chancery court judgeship (21%) or a county court judgeship (8%). Even these figures may be somewhat inflated since only one-third (33%) of those who responded that they had considered seeking a judgeship indicated that they had been serious enough to take even the preliminary step of seeking the endorsement of influential groups, individuals, or the media.

The lawyers were then asked to rank order the following factors, indicating which were most important potentially in *discouraging* them from seeking circuit, chancery, and county court judgeships:

(1) (short) term of office
(2) (low) judicial salary/fringe benefits
(3) (inadequate) judicial retirement plan
(4) (uninteresting) nature of judicial work
(5) (high) judicial workload
(6) (high) degree of involvement in partisan politics.

For each of the three types of trial court judgeships, "degree of involvement in partisan politics" was rated the single most discouraging factor by more lawyers than was any of the other factors. Of the lawyers, 38% ranked this the

TABLE 1   Factors Discouraging Mississippi Lawyers from
Seeking Judgeships

| | *(N= 153)* | | |
| | % *of Lawers Listing Factor as Either* *First or Second Most Discouraging* | | |
Factor	*Circuit*	*Chancery*	*County*
Politics	59%	57%	61%
Salary	50	48	51
Term of Office	29	25	29
Retirement Plan	21	21	15
Nature of Work	17	21	23
Workload	12	13	11

single most discouraging factor in seeking a position on the
circuit court, 37% for a position on chancery court, and 39%
for a position on the county court. If the lawyers who ranked
this as the *second* most discouraging factor are added to those
ranking this as the first most discouraging factor, the percentages exceed 50% for all three types of judgeships: 50% for
circuit court, 57% for chancery court, and 61% for county
court. Thus, more than half of the lawyers considered
"degree of involvement in partisan politics" to be either the
first or second most discouraging factor in seeking each of the
three types of trial court judgeships.

Table 1 contains the results of the survey with respect to
the percentage of lawyers who ranked each of the factors as
being either the first or second most discouraging. The
factors are listed from the most discouraging to least discouraging.

Interestingly enough, two of the factors that former
Governor Waller identified as among the most discouraging—salary and term of office—emerged as the
second and third most discouraging factors in this survey.
Perhaps more interesting, however, is the fact that politics,

not even mentioned by Governor Waller as a discouraging factor, emerged as the single most discouraging factor among the lawyers responding to the survey. This suggests that, although those who are closest to the judicial selection process may view the process as nonpolitical, members of the bar tend to have the opposite view.

Although these findings relating to the factors that Mississippi lawyers find most discouraging help to explain the dynamics of the judicial recruitment process in that state, it could be argued that they are unique to Mississippi. Would lawyers in states with a merit plan or an appointive process for electing judges consider the need to become involved in "politics" a discouraging factor? Would lawyers in states that paid judges significantly higher salaries rank the salary factor so high? In fact, at the time of this study Mississippi was ranked 30th in the nation in salaries paid to general trial court judges (National Center for State Courts, January, 1976).[11]

The judicial recruitment literature suggests, however, that such factors are, in varying degrees, applicable in other jurisdictions. In examining Missouri's merit plan—the selection method that ostensibly is most removed from the political process—Watson and Downing conclude that "it is naive to suggest . . . that the Plan takes 'politics' out of judicial selection" (1969: 331). They found that some attorneys are discouraged from seeking judicial office "because they feel that political considerations (their minor party affiliation or lack of political involvement) will eliminate them from serious consideration as candidates for the bench (1969: 332). They also emphasize the important role of "bar politics" in the selection process, particularly with regard to the competition among attorneys for seats on the nominating commissions (1969: 19-42). Indeed, extrapolating from the Watson and Downing (1969) and Skogan (1971) studies, Jacob concludes that while the bar's influence over judicial selection plays a dominant role in merit plan states, the bar's influence over judicial selection in elective or appointive states is nominal, with political party officials playing the dominant role (1973: 72-73). Because these Mississippi data indicate otherwise, it may be difficult to generalize the role of "politics" in the selection process along the lines that Jacob suggests. What the judicial selection and recruitment studies do suggest is that some brand of "politics" is inevitable and that, regardless of the form it takes, some lawyers will be deterred from seeking judicial office because of a perceived necessity to become involved in some political arena.

Similarly, it would appear that, in varying degrees, salary will discourage some segment of the bar in all jurisdictions from seeking judicial office. Although Mississippi ranked 30th in salaries paid to general trial court judges ($30,000), the national average for general trial court judges at the time of our study was not significantly higher ($32,527) than that of the Mississippi judges (National Center for State Courts, 1976).

Beyond these specific concerns, the judicial selection and recruitment literature suggests that some attorneys are deterred from seeking judicial office simply because of the nature of the position. Watson and Downing explain that not all lawyers feel the "pull of the robe," preferring the role of the "advocate" to that of "referee" (1969: 332). Jacob's comments along these lines are even more pointed. He characterizes a trial court judgeship as "a mind-deadening, stupefying post" (1973: 67) and suggests, therefore, that lawyers with more modest credentials may not only be those who are generally recruited for judgeships but may actually be "better suited to the actual functions that trial judges perform" (1973: 69). These notions find some support in the responses of the Mississippi lawyers to the questionnaire survey. As indicated in Table 1, approximately 20% of the lawyers ranked "nature of work" as either the first or second most discouraging factor.

A final factor that must be considered is whether some lawyers might be more or less inclined to seek or accept a judgeship at different stages of their legal careers. Of the lawyers responding to the questionnaire survey, almost one-half (47%) stated that they would be most receptive to holding judicial office at a "late" stage of their legal career (over age 55). Only 14% indicated that they would be most receptive at an "early" stage (ages 24-40), while 39% said they would be most receptive at a "middle" stage (ages 40-55).

JUDICIAL ATTITUDES TOWARD JUDICIAL OFFICE

To develop an understanding of the backgrounds and attitudes of the lawyers who had acceded to trail court judgeships in Mississippi, a questionnaire was mailed to Mississippi trial court judges.[12] For the most part, the judges' responses—particularly to the background questions—were not unexpected. The mean age of the responding judges was 52. (The national mean of the trial judges responding to the survey of Ryan et al., 1980, was 53.) Not surprisingly, 94% of the judges stated that they had sought the Democratic Party nomination in obtaining their judgeship (4% indicated Republican and 2% "Other").

Less expected, however, was the fact that 71% of the judges stated that they had been in private practice immediately prior to going on the bench. Of the remaining judges, 13% indicated that they had been prosecuting attorneys and 16% stated that they had been elected officials (principally state legislators and judges). Because most of the judges came from private practice as opposed to generally less lucrative public service positions, it would not be surprising to find that many had taken a cut in pay in accepting a judgeship. Indeed, fully

70% of the judges stated that, on assuming their present judgeship, their judicial salary represented a *decrease* from their previous salary. Only 19% claimed a salary *increase*, while 11% indicated no difference in salary.

To assess the general attitudes of the judges toward positions on the bench, the judges were asked to rank order the same factors presented in the lawyer survey, indicating which factors were most important potentially in *discouraging* them from seeking (re)election to their present office. Table 2 contains the results with respect to the percentage of judges who ranked each of the factors as being either the first or second most discouraging. Approximately half of the judges ranked term of office, salary, or retirement plan as either the first or second most discouraging factor. It is not surprising that the judges ranked these "bread-and-butter" factors higher than the lawyers did. It is also not surprising that a much smaller percentage of judges (3%) found the nature of the work discouraging than did the lawyers (20%). What is somewhat surprising is the fact that a much smaller percentage of judges (22%) than lawyers (59%) ranked politics high on the list of discouraging factors. This suggests that there is a significant segment of the bar whose aversion to "politics" would preclude their seeking a judgeship.

Although most of the lawyers and judges interviewed acknowledged that the partisan elective system did not truly operate as such for the selection of judges in Mississippi, they generally expressed satisfaction with this initial selection system. They stated that any other form of judicial selection would be unacceptable to the Mississippi electorate. In addition, many expressed the belief that the local bar's involvement in the selection process tended to create a "merit plan" for the selection of Mississippi judges in that it had the effect of putting the best local legal talent available on the bench.

The questionnaire mailed to Mississippi trial court judges sought to determine the selection methods favored by the

TABLE 2   Factors Discouraging Mississippi Judges from Seeking
           (Re)Election

	(N = 62)
	% of Judges Listing Factor as Either First or Second Most Discouraging
Term of Office	53%
Salary	52
Retirement Plan	49
Workload	22
Politics	22
Nature of work	3

Mississippi judiciary for (1) the initial selection of Mississippi trial judges and (2) the filling of interim vacancies in the office of trial judge. With regard to initial selection, the judges were asked whether they favored (1) partisan election, (2) nonpartisan election, (3) gubernatorial appointment, (4) gubernatorial appointment with bar screening, (5) gubernatorial appointment from a list supplied by a nominating commission, or (6) some other method. Table 3 contains the judges' responses to this question.

As indicated, 49 (80% of those responding) of the Mississippi trial judges favor some type of elective system for the selection of Mississippi judges. Interestingly, most of these judges (52.5% of the respondents) prefer a nonpartisan elective system. This probably reflects the fact that most of these judges either believe that Mississippi has a nonpartisan elective system (although a nonpartisan system contemplates the judges' running without party designation) or feel that the nonpartisan character of the present system should be institutionalized. The single judge who responded "other" indicated that he favors selection by the local bar. Again, this probably reflected a desire to institutionalize the local bar's influence over the present system.

TABLE 3   Judicial Selection Methods Favored by Mississippi Trial
Judges—Initial Selection

Method	*(N=61)* Number of Judges Favoring Method	Percent of Total
Partisan Election	17	27.9%
Non-Partisan Election	32	52.5
Gubernatorial Appointment	–	–
Gubernatorial Appointment with Bar Screening	6	9.7
Gubernatorial Appointment from List Supplied by Nominating Commission	5	8.2
Other	1	1.6

When questioned on the selection method they favored for
the filling of interim vacancies, the judges tended to be more
receptive to the alternatives of gubernatorial appointment
with bar screening or from a nominating commission. Table 4
contains the judges' responses with regard to the filling of
interim vacancies.

Of interest is the fact that less than one-third of the judges
favor the present system for filling interim vacancies (gubernatorial appointment). There were no significant variations
on this point when the responses were broken down according to the means by which the judge obtained his judgeship
initially. That is, only one-third of the judges who were
appointed initially to the bench by the governor favored this
method of selection. Predictably (in light of the present influence of the bar), 39% favored gubernatorial appointment
with bar screening. Again, this probably reflects a desire to
institutionalize the role of the bar.

CONCLUSION

The judicial selection system officially mandated by
Mississippi—partisan elections with gubernatorial appoint-

TABLE 4   Judicial Selection Methods Favored by Mississippi Trial Judges-Interim Vacancies *(N=62)*

	Number of Judges Favoring Method	Percent of Total
Gubernatorial Appointment	20	32.3%
Gubernatorial Appointment With Bar Screening	24	38.7
Gubernatorial Appointment from List Supplied by Nominating Commission	13	21.0
Other	5	8.1

ments to interim vacancies—is not borne out in practice. Because very few judgeships are contested in both primary and general elections, the "election" process has neither a partisan nor a competitive character. Similarly, characterizing the system for filling interim vacancies as "gubernatorial appointment" is misleading. With one recent exception, Mississippi governors have traditionally deferred to others in making judicial appointments.

Because the local bar exercises the most pervasive influence over the judicial selection process, the system is perhaps best characterized as "bar anointment." The local bar generally anoints one of its number to stand (generally uncontested) in judicial elections. Similarly, Mississippi governors normally accede to the wishes of the local bar in making interim appointments. Although the present governor has initiated a nominating commission plan for filling judicial vacancies, the predominance of lawyers on these commissions suggests that the bar's influence over the judicial selection process will continue.

Such a result may be inevitable in light of the unattractiveness of Mississippi judgeships. The survey of Mississippi lawyers indicates that most are discouraged from seeking judgeships because of the relatively low salary and short term of office, combined with a perceived need to become involved in partisan politics. However, the closed recruitment process predicated by the "bar anointment" scenario may add enough additional prestige to the judicial office to encourage lawyers who would not otherwise be inclined to seek judgeships to leave private practice for a position on the bench.

Because judicial salaries in Mississippi were among the lowest in the nation when this study was conducted, it could be argued that this bar anointment selection process is probably unique to Mississippi. However, the salary differential between Mississippi judges and those in most other states is not that great. In all American jurisdictions, judicial salaries are well below those of the more successful members of the practicing bar.

Thus, it would appear that a society that recruits its judges from the ranks of the practicing bar inevitably must rely on a *prestige* factor to heighten the attractiveness of the judicial office. Permitting the bar to exercise a significant (formal or informal) influence over the judicial recruitment process would appear to be the most logical means of establishing or maintaining the prestige of the judicial office. However, it could be argued that the prestige factor is influential with a relatively small segment of the bar. That is, judges will inevitably be recruited from a relatively small segment of the bar. For many lawyers, the low salary, necessity for involvement in "politics," and the uninteresting nature of the work tend to overcome the "pull of the robe."

NOTES

1. The assessments for the various judicial offices are as follows: supreme court judge—$500; circuit judge—$200; chancellor—$200; and county judge—$30 (Id. Secs. 23-1-33 and 23-1-35).

2. During the first six months of 1976, interviews were conducted with 16 trial judges and 24 lawyers in urban and rural areas throughout Mississippi.

3. This information was obtained from "The Blue Book," *Mississippi Official and Statistical Register 1972-1976*.

4. This was also taken from "The Blue Book." The breakdown by judicial office was as follows: three chancery judgeships, nine circuit judgeships, and five county judgeships.

5. This term was suggested by former Mississippi Governor William Waller in an interview conducted on June 29, 1976.

6. The updated information was secured from the Register of Commissions, Office of the Secretary of State, state of Mississippi.

7. The breakdown of judicial appointments by the governor during this period is as follows:

YEAR	Circuit Court	Chancery Court	County Court
1948-1951	1	5	0
1952-1955	1	8	5
1956-1959	1	2	4
1960-1963	4	5	0
1964-1967	2	6	4
1968-1971	5	3	5
1972-1975	4	2	1

As the Judiciary Commission pointed out, these statistics do not include judges who were appointed to the bench initially to fill in for judges who were temporarily unable to serve.

8. This information was secured from the Register of Commissions.

9. Voluntary nominating commission plans previously have been adopted by governors in at least six other states (see Ashman and Alfini, 1974).

10. Questionnaires were sent to a random sample of 500 members of the Mississippi bar. Of the lawyers, 153 (31%) completed and returned the questionnaire.

11. In January of 1976, the annual salary of circuit and chancery judges was $30,000. Their salaries are presently $45,000, ranking them 15th in the nation (National Center for State Courts, July, 1980).

12. Questionnaires were sent to all of the 85 trial court judges in Mississippi. Of the judges, 62 (73%) completed and returned this question-

naire. The response rate by court was as follows: Circuit Court, 22 (73%); Chancery Court, 29 (83%); and County Court, 11 (55%).

REFERENCES

ADAMANY, D. and P. DuBOIS (1976) "Electing state judges." Wisconsin Law Review 731.

ALFINI, J. J. (1977) "The trend toward judicial merit selection." Trial 13: 40.

American Bar Association (1974) Standards Relating to Court Organization. Chicago: American Bar Association.

ASHMAN, A. and J. J. ALFINI (1974) The Key to Judicial Merit Selection: The Nominating Process. Chicago: American Judicature Society.

BEATTIE, S. E. (1953) "A new method of judicial selection—the negative argument." Michigan State Bar Journal 32: 30.

BERKSON, L. (1980) "Judicial selection in the United States: A special report." Judicature 64: 176.

BURNETT, W. (1966) "Observations on the direct election method of judicial selection." Texas Law Review 44: 1098.

CANON, B. C. (1972) "The impact of formal selection processes on the characteristics of judges—reconsidered." Law and Society Review 6: 579.

COYLE, A. B. (1972) "Judicial selection and tenure in Mississippi." Mississippi Law Journal 43: 90.

CROCKETT, G. W., Jr. (1975) "Judicial selection and the black experience." Judicature 58: 438.

GARWOOD, W. St. J. (1973) "Judicial revision—an argument for the merit plan for judicial selection and tenure." Texas Tech Law Review 5: 1.

HANNAH, S. B. (1978) "Competition in Michigan's judicial elections: Democratic ideals vs. judicial realities." Wayne Law Review 24: 1267.

HARDING, R. M. (1969) "The case for partisan election of judges." American Bar Association Journal 55: 1162.

HAYNES, E. (1944) Selection and Tenure of Judges. Washington, D.C.: National Conference of Judicial Councils.

HENDERSON, B. C. and T. C. SINCLAIR (1968) "The selection of judges in Texas." Houston Law Review 5: 430.

HUNTER, E. B. (1964) "A Missouri judge views judicial selection and tenure." Judicature 48: 126.

JACOB, H. (1973) Urban Justice. Englewood Cliffs, NJ: Prentice-Hall.

MELONE, A. P. (1977) "Political realities and democratic ideals: Accession and competition in a state judicial system." North Dakota Law Review 54: 187.

National Advisory Commission on Criminal Justice Standards and Goals (1973) Courts. Washington, DC: Government Printing Office.

National Center for State Courts (1976-1980) Survey of Judicial Salaries. Williamsburg, VA: Author.

NELSON, D. (1962) "Variations on a theme—selection and tenure of judges." Southern California Law Review 36: 4.

NILES, R. D. (1967) "The changing politics of judicial selection: A merit plan for New York." Record of the Association of the Bar of the City of New York 22: 242.

Report of the Mississippi Judiciary Commission (1970) Jackson: State of Mississippi.

RYAN, J.P., A. ASHMAN, B. SALES, and S. SHANE DuBOW (1980) American Trial Judges: Their Work Styles and Performance. New York: Free Press.

SKOGAN, W. G. (1971) "Party and constituency in judicial recruitment: The case of the judiciary in Cook County, Illinois." Ph.D. dissertation, Northwestern University.

UTTER, R. F. (1973) "Selection and retention: A judge's perspective." Washington Law Review 48: 839.

WATSON, R. A. and R. DOWNING (1969) The Politics of the Bench and Bar. New York: Wiley.

WINTERS, G. R. (1973) Selected Readings on Judicial Selection and Tenure. Chicago: American Judicature Society.

ABOUT THE AUTHORS

JAMES J. ALFINI is Assistant Executive Director of the American Judicature Society. He is a member of the New York and Illinois Bar Associations. He received his A.B. in 1965 from Columbia and J.D. in 1972 from Northwestern. Mr. Alfini has published numerous articles and papers on matters pertaining to the judiciary.

LENORE ALPERT is currently Assistant Professor of Political Science at the University of Georgia. She received her B.S. and M.S. from Florida State University and Ph.D. from Northwestern University. She has published several articles relating to the judiciary, particularly in the areas of personality and socialization.

CARL BAAR is Associate Professor of Politics and Director of the judicial administration program at Brock University, St. Catherines, Ontario, Canada. He is author of *Separate but Subservient: Court Budgeting in the American States* and has written and lectured on many aspects of court administration.

DEAN J. CHAMPION is currently Professor of Sociology, University of Tennessee, Knoxville. He received his B.S. and M.A. from Brigham Young University and Ph.D. from Purdue. Dr. Champion has authored several books including *Basic Statistics for Social Research,* (2nd ed., Macmillan); *The Sociology of Organizations,* (McGraw Hill, 1975); *Methods and issues in Social Research* (Wiley, 1976) and has had articles appear in numerous professional journals. He is currently completing an Introductory Sociology text with James A. Cramer and others.

CATHERINE CONLY is a Research Analyst at the Institute for Law and Social Research. In 1975, she received a B.A. in criminal justice from the University of Delaware and in 1978, an M.A. in criminology from the University of Maryland. Prior to joining the institute, Ms. Conly worked as a counselor in a juvenile correctional facility and later as a research assistant examining health care in jails. Her areas of expertise include criminology theory, legal and judicial decision making, and evaluation research.

JAMES A. CRAMER is Lecturer with the Far East Division, University of Maryland. He earned his B.S. in criminology and corrections from Florida State University and Ph.D. in sociology from the University of Tennessee, Knoxville. He was a senior research sociologist with the Institute of Criminal Law and Procedure, Georgetown University Law Center, from 1975 to 1980 where he conducted national research in plea bargaining and police-prosecutor relations. He has edited two books including *Preventing Crime,* and *Plea Bargaining.* He has published articles in several journals. He is currently completing an Introductory Sociology text with Dean Champion and others.

CHARLES W. GRAU is a senior research attorney with the American Judicature Society. He received his B.A. in Political Science and Economics from the University of Wisconsin—Madison and J.D. from the University of Wisconsin Law School—Madison. His publications have appeared in *Judicature* and the *Wisconsin Law Review.* He has most recently served as project director for a study of court practices in Ohio.

RANDALL GUYNES is a senior researcher, Institute for Economic and Policy Studies, Inc. He received his A.B. in

Government and Economics from East Texas State University and Ph.D. in Political Science from the University of Kansas. He has conducted numerous research projects in political research and has published articles in *Public Opinion Quarterly* and *Publius.*

THOMAS A. HENDERSON is Vice President of the Institute for Economic and Policy Studies, Inc. He is currently Project Director of a comparative study of the effect of court unification in six states, which builds on the theoretical framework presented in his essay here. He received the A.B. from Haverford College and Ph.D. from Columbia University. His previous work includes several publications and reports on administrative reorganization issues, the budget process, criminal justice, and urban government. His books include *The Urban Policy Game* (w. J. Foster, Wiley, 1978), and *National Policy Game: A Simulation of the American Political Process,* (W. J. Foster and D. Barbee, Wiley, 1978). His research has appeared in several journals.

WILLIAM M. RHODES is Senior Economist at the Institute for Law and Social Research. He received a B.A. from Bowdoin College and a Ph.D. in economics from the University of Minnesota. Before joining the institute Dr. Rhodes taught on the faculty of the School of Criminology at Florida State University. He has conducted extensive research on sentencing in the criminal courts. He has also published work on the mathematical modeling of criminal courts and criminal behavior. His work has appeared in several journals.

ARLENE SHESKIN is a research associate with the American Judicature Society. She received a B.A. from Queens College, M.A. from Boston University, and Ph.D. from the University of Tennessee. She most recently served as co-principal investigator on a study of court practices in Ohio. She has also served on the faculties of Central

Michigan University and the University of Tennessee. Her publications include numerous articles and a book, entitled *Cryonics: The Sociology of Death and Bereavement* (Irvington, 1979).

PAUL B. WICE is Associate Professor, Department of Political Science, Drew University. He received his Ph.D. in political science from the University of Illinois in 1972. He has been a Visiting Fellow at the Justice Department's National Institute of Law Enforcement and Criminal Justice. He is a consultant to the Institute for Law and Social Research and the Bureau of Social Science Research in Washington, D.C., and is a member of the A.B.A's committee on the Economics of the Practice of Criminal Law. He has published numerous articles and monographs in criminal justice. His books include *Criminal Lawyers* (Sage, 1978) *Freedom for Sale* (Lexington, 1974) and *Actors of Justice* (Prentice-Hall, 1980).